Essential Grammar

What is grammar? Why is it so central to the teaching of English? How can we teach it with confidence in secondary schools?

Essential Grammar will provide clarity, meaning, and teacher expertise to this much-debated area of the English curriculum. By exploring grammar as applied to literary analysis and using a range of examples from commonly taught and popular texts, this highly accessible book provides an extensive overview of how to use grammar to enhance the teaching of academic and creative writing. Drawing on a range of resources, best-selling authors Webb and Giovanelli:

- discuss the context of grammar teaching in schools
- provide a clear overview of concepts and terminology for the teacher
- offer a wide range of examples of how grammar can be applied to the analysis of texts and the development of students' writing
- debunk the unhelpful view of grammar as a list of prescriptive rules and limits
- outline grammatical concepts in a way which is clear and simple to understand
- provide a huge range of practical ways to ensure that teaching of grammatical concepts can be rigorous and successful for all.

This resource, with its grounded and straightforward approach to grammar, will be immediately useable in the classroom with strategies that can be utilised by teachers in their classroom today. For any training and practicing secondary English teachers, **Essential Grammar** will be a compulsory classroom companion.

Jennifer Webb is an English teacher, school leader, educational author, and speaker. She tweets as @funkypedagogy and runs the popular blog www.funkypedagogy.com.

Marcello Giovanelli is Reader in Literary Linguistics at Aston University. He has previously authored *Teaching Grammar, Structure and Meaning* (2014), *Knowing About Language* (2016), and *Teaching English Language and Literature 16–19* (2021), all for Routledge.

Essential Grammar

The Resource Book Every
Secondary English Teacher
Will Need

**Jennifer Webb and
Marcello Giovanelli**

Routledge
Taylor & Francis Group

LONDON AND NEW YORK

Designed cover image: Jennifer Webb

First published 2023
by Routledge
4 Park Square, Milton Park, Abingdon, Oxon OX14 4RN

and by Routledge
605 Third Avenue, New York, NY 10158

Routledge is an imprint of the Taylor & Francis Group, an informa business

British Library Cataloguing-in-Publication Data
A catalogue record for this book is available from the British Library

Library of Congress Cataloging-in-Publication Data
Names: Webb, Jennifer (English teacher), author. | Giovanelli, Marcello, author.
Title: Essential grammar : the resource book every secondary English
   teacher will need / Jennifer Webb and Marcello Giovanelli.
Description: Abingdon, Oxon ; New York, NY : Routledge, 2023. |
   Includes bibliographical references and index.
Identifiers: LCCN 2022058311 (print) | LCCN 2022058312 (ebook) |
   ISBN 9781032007113 (hardback) | ISBN 9781032007137 (paperback) |
   ISBN 9781003175261 (ebook)
Subjects: LCSH: English language—Grammar—Study and teaching
   (Secondary)
Classification: LCC LB1631 .W3478 2023 (print) | LCC LB1631 (ebook) |
   DDC 428.0071/2—dc23/eng/20230215
LC record available at https://lccn.loc.gov/2022058311
LC ebook record available at https://lccn.loc.gov/2022058312

ISBN: 978-1-032-00711-3 (hbk)
ISBN: 978-1-032-00713-7 (pbk)
ISBN: 978-1-003-17526-1 (ebk)

DOI: 10.4324/9781003175261

Typeset in Univers
by Apex CoVantage, LLC

Printed and bound in Great Britain by Bell and Bain Ltd, Glasgow

Contents

■ Contents

Figures

Tables

About the authors

Jennifer Webb is a mum, wife, English teacher, and Assistant Principal. She is a best-selling author of several books for teachers and provides a popular online continuing professional development program. Jennifer has been shaped by her dual British-Caribbean heritage and a family of dynamic women. Coming from a low-income, single-parent household, Jennifer achieved a place to read English at Merton College, Oxford and has since taught in a number of schools in West Yorkshire. Jennifer is a teacher 'tweeter' @funkypedagogy and is interested in curriculum, literacy, cognitive science, and teacher development.

Marcello Giovanelli is Reader in Literary Linguistics and Head of English, Languages and Applied Linguistics at Aston University. He was a teacher of English, has been a middle and senior leader in secondary education, and has always believed passionately in the value of language education in schools. He tweets @mmgiovanelli.

Acknowledgements

JW – I'd like to thank my lovely, clever little boys. The poetry of your fledgling speech – the boundless choice and creation – is the greatest joy of my life.

Also, the English team at Trinity Academy Cathedral in Wakefield. Warmth and joy mingled with academic enquiry and aspiration. Thanks for putting up with all my grammar chat.

MG – As always, thanks to Jennie, Anna, Zara, and Sophia.

The authors would like to thank; Efrat Furst for generously granting permission to use her original visuals for the Memory Model and Jeffrey Boakye for a conversation about grammar and identity which shaped the direction of some of this work.

Preface

THE PURPOSE OF THIS BOOK

We want people to see grammar differently.

> Grammar isn't something you should be scared to get 'wrong.' It's not a person you can offend or a faux pas waiting to trip you up.
>
> Grammar is a system for describing language. It is not grammar which judges you; snobs judge you.

We hope that this is a practical, informative, and enjoyable read for teachers. Our book will not (and should not) plan your grammar curriculum for you. It will not plan your lessons for you. But it will give you the knowledge, tools, and questions you need to do these things in your own unique context.

> *Give* a person a fish and they will eat for a day. *Teach* an English teacher about subordination and they will delight their classes **for life**.

(That was an example of isocolon – you can read more about it on page 192.)

One of us once observed an experienced teacher with a group of Y13 students.

> She was teaching *Richard II* and came across the line: *With eager feeding food doth choke the feeder*.
> This is a great line.
> She began to unpick it with the class, starting with the word 'eager' and then moving on to 'choke.'
> She then paused, a little unsure, and started to move on to the next line when a student put a hand up.
> 'What is that called, though? There are three versions of "food" but they are different. Is it repetition? Is it a triplet?'
> (. . .)

What she would have *liked* to do was look at the shifting word classes in the line and then explore the subtly different power of each: *feeding* (noun, gerund), *food* (noun, subject), *feeder* (noun, object). She might have liked to know that this is called *polyptoton* – using the same word repeatedly but in different forms – and that it is used a lot in Shakespeare. She might also have liked to talk about the use of 'food' as the agent in this sentence, which is the thing doing the 'chok(ing)' – the use of the active voice lends a sinister air to the 'eager(ness)' being described here. These grammatical features are absolutely central to the meaning of this line, which sets us up for John of Gaunt's great, patriotic death-bed speech.

(NOTE: she might also have pointed out the fact that the 'with' prepositional phrase is unusually fronted – an example of the dreaded fronted adverbial!)

This was a brilliant teacher, but on this occasion she was held back by her lack of knowledge and confidence in grammar.

Possession of an English degree does not a grammar expert make. Most English teachers are literature specialists and, though we can *use* language features accurately as writers and speakers in our own right, the explicit knowledge of *why* things work and *what* they are called often eludes us.

> Why can 'crashing' be a *verb* in some situations, a *noun* in others and then function *adjectivally* when it fancies it? What is a *subordinating conjunction*? How might the use of the *simple past tense* support English language acquisition? What is the difference between the *agent* and the *patient* when we are describing grammatical *voice*? How can grammar concepts support the teaching of rhetoric? What is a *modal adverb* and how might it support my students to write speculatively? How do Blake and Owen use positioning to create meaning?

This book is going to help with all of that.

We will start by providing some context and answering some key questions: why so many people struggle with grammar; how grammar education has shifted and evolved over time; and what that might mean for us now. Then, we will outline the foundations of grammar knowledge and move through to more complex concepts to explore the craft of the writer. We aim to present that body of knowledge with clarity by providing highly practical classroom strategies and modelling ways to build grammar into the curriculum.

While this book is going to explore grammar in the secondary English classroom, we hope that it will also offer insights and strategies which will be useful to colleagues in other subjects, and to people leading elements of language work across schools.

HOW TO USE THIS BOOK

There is a lot of terminology in the world of English grammar. One language feature can often be described in dozens of different ways, and even some of the most common terms have slightly different definitions depending on whom you ask.

Our goal is to simplify things as far as possible without losing any of the brilliant richness which some of that complexity brings with it. The purpose of this book is to support English teachers and their students, so we have selected devices which we deem useful for that purpose. There might be terms or concepts which you feel we have missed, or some which you have seen used in different ways before, and for that we can only apologise. We just hope that the choices we have made will help to create a coherent body of knowledge to support an ambitious curriculum. You will find most of the explanations in Section 2, and practical applications of many of these are directly explored in Sections 3 and 4. Look in the margin to find helpful notes and page references.

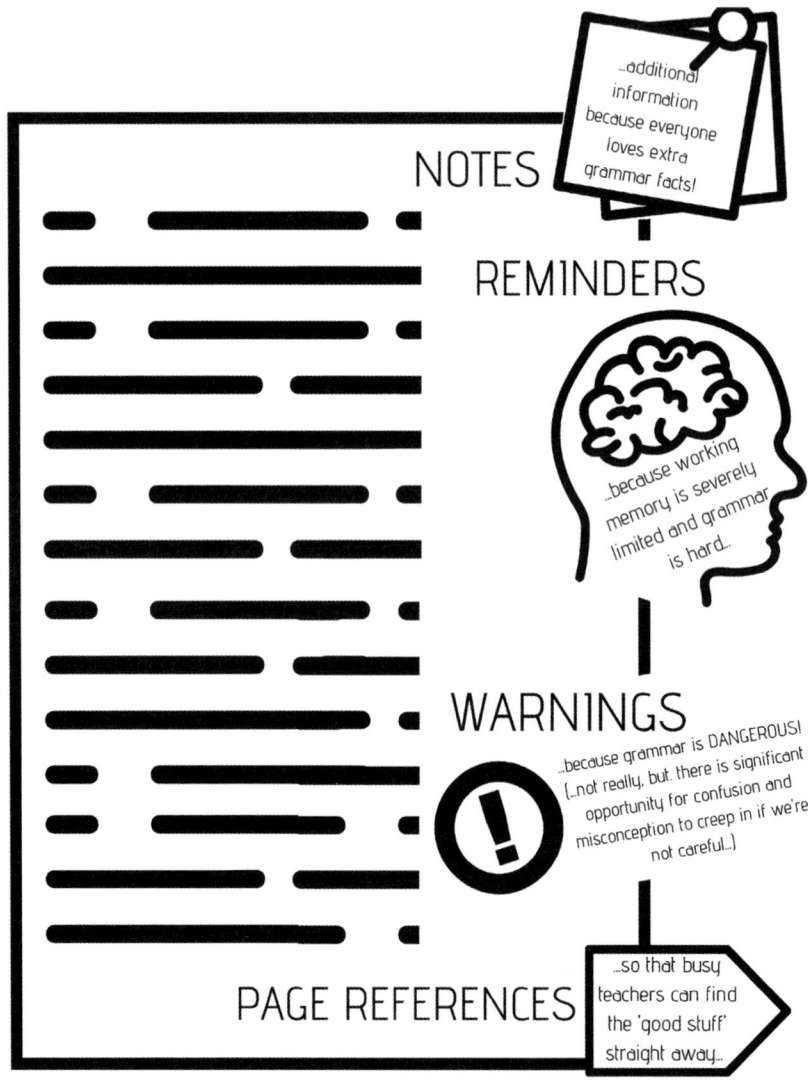

NOTES

...additional information because everyone loves extra grammar facts!

REMINDERS

...because working memory is severely limited and grammar is hard...

WARNINGS

...because grammar is DANGEROUS! (...not really, but there is significant opportunity for confusion and misconception to creep in if we're not careful...)

PAGE REFERENCES

...so that busy teachers can find the 'good stuff' straight away...

0i.1

You will see a comprehensive alphabetised list of all terms at the back of this book, but you will also see margin references to help you to connect definitions to practical strategies.

Each chapter ends with a visual summary of the key ideas and strategies we have outlined therein.

CONTENTS:

SECTION 1

The grammar debate

1 What is grammar and why is it important?

GRAMMAR AS LANGUAGE AWARENESS

Grammar is a loaded term. From the Classics lessons of private schools to the highest levels of government; from artists testing their limits to winners of the Man Booker Prize; from the rapid evolution of online language to the changing discourse of power dynamics, grammar reaches every corner of our social, political and artistic life.

But what *is* grammar? This book doesn't take a narrow view: grammar is not a list of rules and fixed ideas. Put simply, grammar describes how language conveys meaning at every level – from the smallest detail to whole text structure and, ultimately, the context in which communication takes place. And because 'communication' means every instance of expression in the English language, knowledge of grammar is actually a path to understanding and engaging with the world around us. If people are to fully understand the letter they receive from their local MP, and the contract they must sign when opening a bank account, and the advertising slogan they encounter on the side of a bus, they need knowledge of grammar. More than this though, if they are to advocate for themselves, or compel others into action, or ask for the things they need, then explicit grammatical knowledge is a resource that can help them make speaking and writing choices. People need to be able to write accurately, yes, but they might also need to be convincing, stylish, entertaining and charming. Knowledge about language empowers all of this, and everyone deserves to acquire it.

The teaching of grammar has been conspicuously absent from the core business of teaching English in the secondary classroom for around 60 years. In the few places where it has been explicitly taught, it has often been done badly or unsystematically. How did *we* find grammar?

> Jenny was never taught grammar explicitly at her northern inner-city state school. She arrived at university unable to use a possessive apostrophe, and had to rely on a fellow undergraduate (with a private school background) to fill in the blanks when she was thrown headfirst into an Anglo-Saxon confusion of nominatives, genitives and present indicatives.

DOI: 10.4324/9781003175261-2

Marcello went to a grammar school but was never taught anything about language in English lessons (beyond the obligatory lit-crit terminology). He came to grammar through studying Latin and French at GCSE and A-level although he was told that this knowledge would be of no use when it came to studying texts in English.

Grammar has been branded as elitist, dry, oppressive and pedantic. People have come to think of it as a long, complex set of rules, and this has tinged grammar with an aftertaste of judgement and shame which is closer to class differences than linguistic reality.

(We explore the history of grammar teaching in the UK in more detail on pages 11–13.)

If there is a 'correct' way of doing something, the implication is that some people are right and some are wrong. Some people are enlightened, and some are in the dark. This gives rise to many unhelpful and often ridiculous ideas at the extremes such as 'poor' grammar being a kind of crime. A prominent popular book on grammar in recent years went so far as to provide stickers and encourage people to police the grammar and punctuation transgressions they came across in everyday life. On the opposite side of the scale are those who claim that grammar is completely useless: 'a package of outdated, rigid, misleading, prescriptive, disputed terms' (Michael Rosen writing in *The Guardian*, 23 January 2021, www.theguardian.com/education/2021/jan/23/dear-gavin-williamson-could-you-tell-parents-what-a-fronted-adverbial-is). Those on this side of the debate have tended to claim that teaching grammar is boring and crushes children's creativity. Both these approaches to grammar are cartoonish and absurd, and they have reduced the level of discourse around grammar teaching to superficial bearbaiting on social media. What we really need is reasoned, intelligent exploration of disciplinary knowledge which doesn't shy away from nuance.

Our point in this book is simple: knowledge of grammar is empowering, and language awareness more generally is empowering. Students with strong language awareness are best placed to become confident and critical users of language in a range of different contexts.

Beyond students' writing, the ability to *read* critically can be hampered by a lack of grammar knowledge. A person's ability to read is not just dependent on decoding phonics – it also requires comprehension. When we read something, we create a mental model of what the text describes by integrating the words and sentences into a meaningful whole. Knowledge about language can help us to see how meaning may change. For example the famous grandma sentence which is on the wall in almost every British school:

Let's eat Grandma.
vs
Let's eat, Grandma.

This example is rather tired, but the point is clear – you have to know that the comma after 'eat' means that 'Grandma' is not the direct object of 'eat' and so

Grandma is going to live. When there is no comma, we read 'Grandma' as the direct object of 'eat', which makes us all cannibals.

A better example might be the use of language in this rental agreement:

> The tenant shall not keep any pets or any other animals **on or in the property** without the prior written consent of the landlord (such consent not to be unreasonably withheld or delayed). The landlord should accept such requests where they are satisfied that the tenant is a responsible pet owner and that the pet is of a kind that is suitable to be kept at the property, in relation to the nature of the property.

For a person to read and understand this text, they have to see the link between clauses – they have to see that the suitability of the pet will be judged in connection with the nature of the property. They might conclude from that final clause that it would be judged to be inappropriate to have a very large dog in a small flat with no garden, but that a landlord might allow a hamster in a property of that size. This might seem like a frivolous example, but consider the myriad situations in which the young people we teach will go on to read formal legal language: employment contracts, insurance documents, rental agreements, warranties for large purchases, communications from HMRC about income tax – the list goes on. People *must* understand words and phrases in the context of the wider text or situation, and this means reading the grammatical structures of the text. The ability to read and recognise grammatical choices made by writers and speakers is a key aspect of critical literacy.

Another very important consideration for teachers is that grammar is not simply drawn along class lines but is also inextricably linked to the linguistic identity of many cultural groups. For example the word 'man' in Standard English is a concrete noun, meaning a single male person. In youth slang, however, the word 'man,' 'mans' or 'manz' (derived from Jamaican Patois and the evolving language of the black British diaspora) can be used as a personal pronoun by the subject – see these lines from *Human Yet* by Saju Ahmed:

> You try to keep an eye on man
> But you end up putting an iron on man

There are many different English grammars in existence – many varied systems of rules and norms which are understood within communities and differ from the 'standard.' If Ahmed was writing in Standard English, he might have said 'putting an iron on me' or 'on us,' but the power of using the non-standard version in a poem about the oppression of minority culture is undeniable. All varieties of English have their own grammar. Recognising how speakers or writers use language conventionally or not can be incredibly empowering.

Jenny's grandfather came to the UK from St Kitts in the Caribbean. His Kittitian patois, characterised by a fundamental difference in markers for tense and use of pronouns, is an English with clear rules and principles which are understood by speakers within that community.

> For example he might have said: **mi a go walk** (I am going to walk/I will go on a walk)
>
> Or: **I see she** (I saw her)

The way we speak is inextricably linked to our identity, how we frame our beliefs, communicate with our loved ones, and frame the world around us.

Bernardine Evaristo, speaking of her superb novel Girl, Woman, Other said, 'it was creatively liberating to get rid of the full stops . . . the sentences, paragraphs and clauses merge into each other' (Evaristo quoted in Saha 2020). Those normal features of written English, being absent, are powerful. Evaristo's isn't a novel without grammar – it is one which makes a profound choice about language. Grammar isn't wrong, absent or broken here, this is simply a deviation from convention.

(NOTE: grammar of the various types of Caribbean patois is utterly fascinating, and something worth reading up on if you like to geek out.)

Essential Grammar does not make any claims about Standard English being superior to any other. Nor do we believe that everyone should speak and write in Standard English all the time. Grammar isn't about rules: it is about possibilities. As teachers, it is our moral duty to uphold and respect the grammars which students will inevitably carry with them. But it is also our job to ensure that, where it is appropriate and necessary, students are able to recognise when they need to use Standard English and can do so with confidence and precision.

(NOTE: we talk about Standard English and attitudes in more detail in Chapter 7.)

GRAMMAR IS POWER

The structures of language in the media, in politics, in the world of work, all affect meaning in a powerful way. Knowledge about grammar can help us be critically aware. Grammar is essentially about how meaning is created using structures at a micro- and a macro-level. The challenge is that this meaning is subtle: secret. Grammatical features such as positioning, order, and tense easily slip under our radar; obvious things like word choice and huge sweeping images are noisy in comparison.

For example let's look at some political rhetoric:

On 13 November 1913, Emmeline Pankhurst made a speech in Hartford, Connecticut. She repeatedly referred to herself as a soldier, and to the wider cause as a militant one, "I am here as a soldier who has temporarily left the field of battle." Any student in the secondary classroom would likely identify the metaphor and make some attempt to talk about its implications here. The device is obvious and powerful in its simplicity. It does what it says on the tin.

Compare this 'noisy' language device with something quieter. In March 2020, spokespeople for the British government began to use the phrase 'the science' to refer to advice which it received from experts as the global pandemic raged. In terms of the grammar, 'science' by itself is a non-specific noun – a word

(See more about nouns on page 23.)

which can refer to a wide range of ideas and disciplines. If someone says they are 'following science,' there is a clear indication that they are doing something in line with an academic discipline, but there remains a lack of clarity about *which* science, or which specific theory or interpretation is being 'followed' among many possible choices. If the government was 'following science,' we might reasonably ask: *which* science?

The use of the definite article 'the' implies that there is *one* science – the science being followed is the only one, and there has been no choice to make. The definite article makes it seem as though nobody in government has made a choice, because they were compelled to follow *the* science: the *only* science.

(The relative *quietness* of grammar is one of the reasons why it is so difficult to teach, and something we tackle in Chapter 4.)

This is subtle. There wasn't an obvious slogan or loud piece of rhetoric pronouncing "it's not our fault – it's the scientists," but the grammar in this phrase – one which was repeated ad nauseam by politicians – was a clear choice which created meaning for political reasons.

People's ability to identify grammatical choices in what they read and hear is about more than basic understanding – it is a defence against gullibility.

(GRAMMAR) KNOWLEDGE IS POWER

Everything we know about cognitive science tells us that knowledge is power. The more we know, the easier it is to encounter new things and embed them into long-term memory, because the brain seeks to make connections with prior knowledge in order to build understanding. People with less prior knowledge find it harder to learn new things. Educators have begun to understand the way schemata are formed in the learning process; cognitive frameworks which help to organise and embed information. In general, teachers have come to accept that a powerful curriculum is one where we sequence core knowledge to ensure that students have all the foundational schema in place to enable them to learn new things more easily and move on to new skills with increasing complexity and challenge.

(see a more detailed explanation of how this works in Chapter 4.)

So, to teach anything well, we must build very strong foundations, ensuring that there is a mastery of core knowledge and then build this up. If we will accept that our subject is English, and that knowledge about language is the foundation upon which that English is built, we must agree that grammar is central to how writers create meaning and how readers receive it. We must allow grammar to be more than just a set of rules or restrictions on language and, instead, recognise it as an enabling and fundamentally *creative* toolkit.

Feature spotting or reeling off grammatical definitions by rote are pointless goals in the English classroom. Feature spotting is unhelpful in grammar just as it is when students simply say 'this is a metaphor' and stop there. However, when used well, that initial knowledge is absolutely critical. Students cannot exhibit skill in literary analysis or creative writing (or anything else, for that matter!) unless they are coming from a place of *knowledge*. When a student writes a story, they draw on their knowledge of words, phrases, ideas, genre, character tropes, metaphor etc. For someone to write really stylishly, shaping sentences and phrases with absolute precision, they must also write from their knowledge of grammar – be that conscious, explicitly taught knowledge, or unconscious application of things they have absorbed from what they have heard and read. When teachers invest time in explicitly teaching a range of challenging tier 2 vocabulary, this can help students write with greater precision and sophistication. This is the same when students are explicitly taught grammatical features – their knowledge enriches both their writing and their appreciation of structures in the texts they read.

GRAMMAR: THE (SEEMINGLY ETERNAL) INTERNAL CONFLICT OF LANGUAGE VS LITERATURE

The division of 'language' and 'literature' is a strange academic amputation. We have attempted to rend apart 'words and stuff' from the very foundations upon which those words are built. We put imagery in one pile and positioning in the other. Repetition goes in one pile and word classes go in the other. When all these features of language have equal power to create meaning, and all of them are used by writers in combination towards the greater whole, it is nonsensical to separate them so crudely.

Part of this is certainly linked to the division of language and literature at General Certificate of Secondary Education (GCSE) – we make literature all about poetry, feelings, and surface literary devices; language becomes the boring, functional twin. There is a reason why students struggle with structure questions in English Language GCSE: 'structure' refers largely to grammar, and most students don't understand it. There are many GCSE units of work which get to the Language papers in Y10 or 11 and suddenly provide lists for students of what constitutes 'structure,' because until this point it hasn't been explicitly taught as part of the English curriculum.

This is a travesty – not only because we need to get students through GCSE qualifications without resorting to last-minute feature spotting checklists – but because it means that we miss out on a huge part of the artistry of our subject. Let's look at a commonly studied moment from *Macbeth* as an example:

ACT 5, SCENE 1

LADY MACBETH

Out, damned spot! out, I say! – One: two: why, then, 'tis time to do't. – Hell is murky! – Fie, my lord, fie! a soldier, and afeard? What need we fear who knows it, when none can call our power to account? – Yet who would have thought the old man to have had so much blood in him.

. . .

LADY MACBETH

To bed, to bed! there's knocking at the gate:
come, come, come, come, give me your hand.
What's done cannot be undone.
– – **To bed, to bed, to bed!**

Parenthesis and sequence of clauses:

Frequent switching between the present 'out, I say!,' reliving the past: 'then, 'tis time to do't,' exclamative: 'hell is murky!' and direct conversation with an imaginary Macbeth: 'fie, my lord.'

Use of a rapid sequence of clauses creates potential for an erratic and unpredictable performance and demonstrates the character's fragmented thought patterns.

Imperatives:

'Out' – Lady Macbeth is giving orders to imaginary blood on her own hands. This is the image of someone who has no grasp of reality. The use of imperative here also appears to lend some agency to the blood itself, as though it is sentient and can be compelled to leave her.

'To bed, to bed,' 'come, come' etc. – Lady Macbeth is giving orders to Macbeth and reliving the night of Duncan's death.

'Come' links directly to her Act 1 Scene 5 soliloquy where she commands the 'thick night' and demands that the 'spirits' also 'come' to her. These earlier uses of the imperative 'come' demonstrate a power and strength which is in stark contrast with the confusion and vulnerability of this character in Act 5. The asyndetic listing – 'come' used four times, 'to bed' five times – seems to imply that her speech is an uncontrolled stream of consciousness, and that her experience following the death of Duncan has somehow imprinted itself on her mind.

Wider Discourse

This scene is unusual because rather than verse, it is written in choppy, abrupt prose. The character perhaps doesn't have the mental composure to speak in considered, structured verse.

This mixture of very short prose statements, questions, and commands is a clear shift in tone from previous scenes.

Immediately prior to this scene, Macduff reacts to the tragic death of his entire family, and even this catastrophe is not enough to make him break out of verse. The audience recognises the shift in tone prompted by the switch to prose and short, disconnected clauses.

It is clear that grammatical knowledge enables insight and meaningful analysis of this scene. A focus on sentence crafting and punctuation choice also supports interpretation for performance – an actor might take these structural features as an indication of the character's mental state, pacing, and delivery. At first, grammatical analysis might seem technical and concrete, but it has considerable power to unearth the intangibles in literature.

When we teach students to interrogate and analyse texts, we should treat grammatical features as equal to those things we would traditionally call 'literary' devices. In many cases, we would argue that analysis at a language level, rooted in the language choices the writer has clearly made, is often better than what passes as 'literary' analysis.

We believe that grammar teaching is essential to the teaching of English. We can't claim to teach this subject without engaging fully with the components which make up its foundations.

1.1

Grammar describes how language creates meaning. It is not about rules.

Grammar wasn't taught in the majority of British state schools for the second half of the 20th Century...

'Language awareness' is a broader and more inclusive way of describing grammar knowledge.

There are many varieties of English. Standard English is just one of them, and there is no hierarchy...

Subtle grammar choices can be powerful. Grammar can be political.

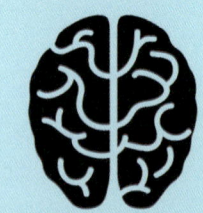

The more we know, the more easily we learn new things. Knowledge of grammar is powerful.

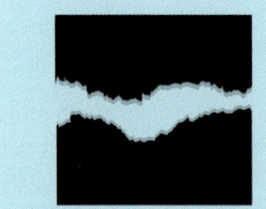

English shouldn't be split according to Language or Literature...

Grammatical features ARE literary devices...

Grammar can often provide a more <u>fruitful</u> base for literary analysis than talking about metaphors...

2 Which grammar?

MANY GRAMMARS

What do we mean by grammar? This is both an easy and a difficult question. Easy because technically 'grammar' relates to the ways in which we can describe the structure of a language (English grammar, French grammar, Spanish grammar, and so on) and so is concerned with how words are formed (morphology) and how those words form larger structures that we use for speaking and writing (syntax). More difficult because as we will discuss in this section, there are multiple and often competing theories of language which, in turn, form different models of grammar. Furthermore, the purpose of learning about and using grammar in schools has been heavily disputed.

The grammar that was taught in English schools until the 1960s – and still persists in some cases today – is what we might call *traditional grammar*, which summed up the structures of English as a system of rules drawing on ideas that had been used to describe classical languages such as Latin and Greek. The emphasis on rules often ended up promoting Standard English as 'correct' and other varieties as 'incorrect' as well as generating dubious rules about style such as avoiding splitting infinitives (wrongly based on the fact that Latin cannot split its infinitives as they exist as one single word as opposed to the to+verb form in English) and ending sentences with prepositions. The kinds of classroom activities that traditional grammar led to usually involved naming parts of made-up sentences which tested the ability to remember word classes but asked little else of students. Unsurprisingly, research showed that this kind of language work had little if any effect on students' ability to read or write well. More generally, together with the relative lack of interest shown by university academics in developing the subject within schools and the rise of English literature as an academic discipline, grammar teaching became less and less popular and, unfortunately, ultimately devalued by the teaching profession.

An alternative to traditional grammar is offered by more functional approaches, which place an emphasis on the contextual and interactional aspects of language as well as the more formal textual features and rules. Michael Halliday's *systemic functional linguistics*, including his model of *functional grammar*, is built on broader discourse phenomena such as the social context, the topic

DOI: 10.4324/9781003175261-3

of communication, the relationship between writer/speaker and reader/listener, and the mode of expression. Functional linguistics treats language as a resource that is used by people in social contexts to get things done (whether that be to put together ideas in a meaningful and coherent way, to provide an opinion on or view of the world, or to interact with others). Grammar then is a way of making meaning rather than simply a set of prescriptive rules. We'll return to this important point later in the chapter.

Another alternative can be found in cognitive linguistics, a broad set of ideas about language which nonetheless share some important common ground. Like functional linguistics, cognitive linguistics stresses the social and contextual aspect of language but also draws on knowledge from cognitive science and cognitive psychology to highlight the psychological dimensions of language. Some key principles include the following:

(See Chapter 7 for linguistic investigations you might be able to do with students.)

- the idea that our experience is always mediated by our physical existence in the world and this influences how we think and use language
- the idea that we draw on concrete objects to help us explain more abstract concepts, for example through the use of metaphors to explain concepts and emotions
- the idea that we can evoke mental representations of future and imagined events and situations by using language.

Given that functional and cognitive linguistics are still fairly recent fields, it is unsurprising that traditional grammar has dominated and still tends to dominate school curricula, for example in the Key Stage 2 grammar, punctuation, and spelling (GPS) tests. At secondary level, in England at least, there is somewhat of a curious vacuum in terms of grammar teaching; there is hardly any guidance in the National Curriculum, and (at the time of writing this book – although we hope this may change) the absence of any opportunity for students to do meaningful language at Key Stage 4 means that there is little need for a theory of language and a grammar that is coherent and pedagogically enabling.

Of course, the question of 'which grammar?' is also linked to the question of 'what for?' In fact, this question is also inherently related to the very question of what 'English' as an academic subject is conceived. Over 50 years ago, Michael Halliday (1967: 83) outlined what he saw as the three different types or aims of grammar/language work:

- prescriptive, focused on learning rules or 'linguistic table-manners'
- productive, focused on developing skills such as speaking, reading, and writing
- descriptive, focused on developing students' ability to learn about and describe language at various levels to aid interpretation (including of literary texts) and generally increase knowledge about language.

Halliday was writing in the 1960s and so the first aim was largely still very common whereas the second and third were emerging as more valuable ways of doing language work in schools. Over time, as the growth of A-level English Language over the last 30 years has demonstrated, secondary teachers have probably considered the remit of language work as more descriptive. As we suggest in Chapter 1, language work can also have a productive effect in that a genuinely enabling language pedagogy can help students to become more confident and better users of language as well as more critical and reflective ones.

GRAMMAR AND MEANING

With so many different models of language to choose from, it's easy to get confused over which is best from a pedagogical perspective. In the UK, which has generally served its teachers less well in terms of providing a coherent pedagogical theory of language, one of the main barriers to language and grammar work being effectively undertaken in the classroom is that often the models that underpin such work have not been meaning-centred.

By meaning-centred, we refer to theories and models of, but above all approaches to language study that give prominence to meaning rather than seeing grammar as a system of rules that need to be learnt, or an exercise in labelling word classes in made-up sentences. Functional linguistics and cognitive linguistics, which connect language structures to particular meanings, are naturally meaning-centred theories of language and so emphasise that when we describe something, we are necessarily making choices about the way we describe it. Language – and grammar – then is seen as a set of resources from which we choose one particular word or group of words at the expense of others which might carry and convey different meanings.

As an example, look at this next sentence which appeared as part of a news report of a then major story during the first COVID-19 lockdown when the Prime Minister's aide, Dominic Cummings, was found to not have followed the government's guidelines on staying at home.

2.1

Cummings broke stay home rule
AGENT   VERB   PATIENT

This is a straightforward example of the use of the active voice in which the entity responsible for the action (we can call this the agent) is at the beginning of the sentence and therefore given prominence. We can say this drawing on an analogy from the physical world that things that are nearer to us or appear in the front tend to attract our attention more. In contrast, the entity that is broken (we can call this the patient) appears after the verb in the active voice, further down the sentence chain, and so is less prominent.

(We explain all about voice on page 40.)

The passive voice, of course, reverses this order.

2.2

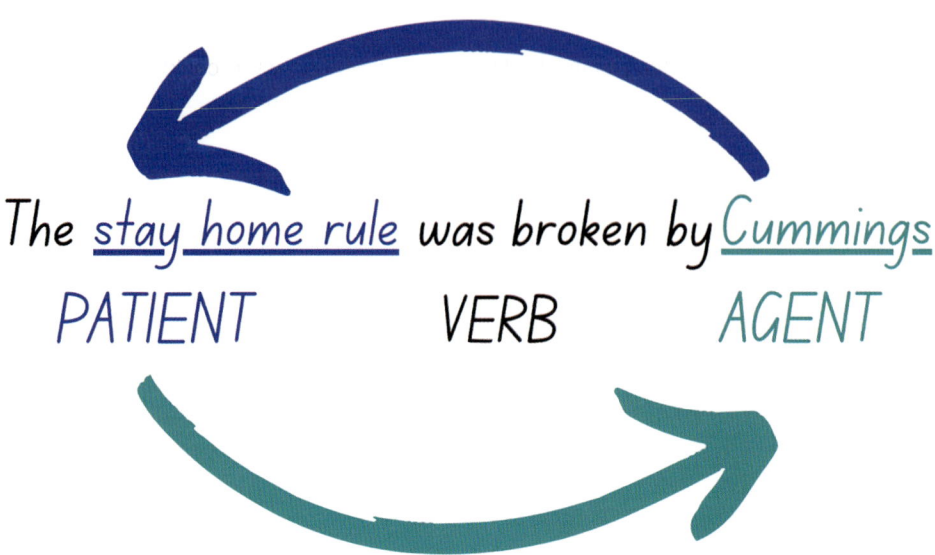

The <u>stay home rule</u> was broken by <u>Cummings</u>

PATIENT   VERB   AGENT

Now, the patient appears at the beginning of the sentence and so is marked as prominent and the agent appears further down the line, signifying that the fact that Cummings did this is less significant or, at least, responsibility is being downplayed.

These examples show, at a very basic level, that the difference between the active and passive voice is more than simply moving things around in a sentence. Both forms are structures that carry particular meanings: the active voice highlights the agent and responsibility; the passive voice does the opposite by shifting responsibility to the end. This difference can account for why a writer might want to choose one over another and what the effect of that choice might be.

There are also other ways of presenting the previously mentioned information which show how grammar is connected to meaning. For example the passive voice could be used but with no indication of the agent, who is omitted entirely.

2.3

The <u>stay home rule</u> was broken by Cummings

PATIENT   VERB

In this instance, the responsibility for the action is completely obscured and so the emphasis is simply on the action itself.

Omitting the *by-agent* part of the passive voice is not the only way that a degree of agency can be presented. In the next two examples, the passive voice is used and an agent is presented but under-specified; in the first, the agent is named by role instead of personal name; in the second, the use of 'someone' means that we have as little information about who was responsible as in the passive form that omits the by-agent entirely. In fact, it could be argued that the use of 'someone' more strategically denies agency by obscuring the entity responsible.

2.4

The <u>stay home rule</u> was broken by <u>the PM's aide</u>
PATIENT   VERB   AGENT

2.5

The <u>stay home rule</u> was broken by <u>someone</u>
PATIENT   VERB   AGENT

The beauty of looking at grammar as meaning-oriented is that further ways of presenting the same scene reveal inherent meaning capacity. All the examples so far have involved a verb either as part of the active or passive voice, but equally the scene could be presented differently. Look at the following example:

2.6

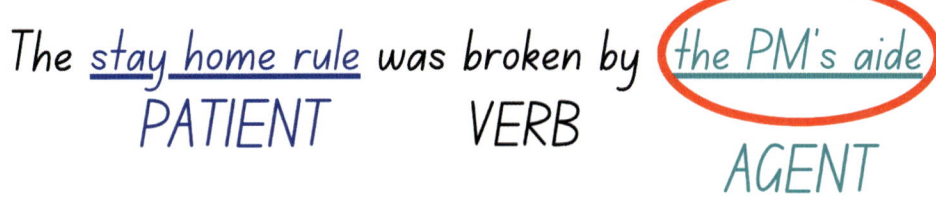

<u>Broken</u> stay home rule
ADJECTIVE
(MODIFIER)

In this example, 'broken' is used as an adjective to modify 'stay home rule.' So now, as there is technically no verb, there's neither an agent nor a patient. So in this alternative, responsibility for an action is not even hinted at.

(We explain adjectives and modification on page 25.)

There are other ways in which the event could be presented; each way or grammatical structure brings with it a certain way of highlighting the action and the entities involved in it. This really means that grammar is central to representation and that particular structures offer certain ways of presenting the world and drawing attention to some aspects of it over others. In the examples that we have looked at, we would probably say (in keeping with English as a language more generally) that the active voice is probably the default choice but no choice is ever neutral, and examining the various alternatives and what they highlight, downplay, or omit provides a neat way of aligning grammar with motivation and ideology: we present the world as we want others to see it.

The idea of grammar as a resource is powerful not only because it is aligned with modern theories of linguistics but also, from a pedagogical perspective, because it opens up interesting and enabling ways of thinking about language descriptively rather than in a prescriptive or proscriptive way. So we can think about how grammar is related to aspects of audience, purpose, context, and register and think about how language choices reflect individual and shared ways of thinking and speaking. The emphasis then is less on how language *should* be used and more on how it *is* and *can* be used.

This emphasis was at the heart of initiatives such as Halliday's Schools Council Project (a project set up in London schools that ran from 1964–1971)

Myhill: 'Grammar as Choice' Pedagogy   2.7

Links a link is immediately made between whatever grammar is introduced and the type of writing being taught so that the grammar is contextualised and students have a clear motivation for learning about grammar.

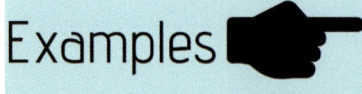

Examples teaching is led by examples of grammar in action (as in the active and passive distinction discussed in this chapter) rather than through dry definitions and lists of rules.

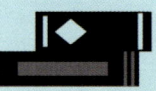

Authentic texts real-world texts rather than made up artificial sentences are used to show how grammar works and to connect grammatical forms to meanings, purpose, audience and context.

Discussion students are encouraged to explore the interpretative effects of particular grammatical structures and choices in texts and through their own writing and to consider the effects of various alternatives by comparing them.

and the Language in the National Curriculum (LINC) Project run by Ronald Carter at the University of Nottingham from 1989–1992. It's probably an emphasis that is shared by teachers who have worked on A-level English Language courses over the last 25 or so years, particularly those run by AQA. And it's certainly formed the basis of language work in some parts of Australia, for example in literacy/writing programmes based on genre-based pedagogies (effectively a teaching strategy that explicitly focuses on the grammar of particular genres to teach writing) as well as in the United States in the form of *meaning-centred grammar* (Hancock 2005) and *rhetorical grammar* (Kolln and Gray 2016). In the UK, the most notable influence, aside from the National Strategies in the 2000s, which drew on some ideas from genre-based pedagogies, has been the work of Debra Myhill and her team at the University of Exeter. Over many years, Myhill has worked with teachers and students exploring the ways in which grammar can be taught most effectively to improve students' writing. Drawing on a broadly functional approach, Myhill's research has demonstrated that the explicit teaching of grammar in a contextualised way (for real purposes, using real texts as models and drawing the idea of grammar as a set of resources) can have positive effects on students' ability to craft their own writing and see the connection between grammatical forms and possible interpretative effects. In her most recent work related to the project, Myhill and her team have developed a *Grammar as Choice* pedagogy based around LEAD principles.

Myhill's work provides a clear and enabling model that highlights the connection between language awareness broadly and writing outcomes. In particular she is keen to emphasise that good grammar teaching should allow students to be attentive to language in a way that is focused on meaning rather than memorising lists of definitions, provides plenty of opportunities for students to explore language and its possible effects in a variety of texts and in their own writing, and allows students time to discuss language choices explicitly and view them as a resource which writers draw on to position readers in particular ways.

We share this sentiment and approach in this book. As we argue in Chapter 1, we believe that grammar teaching should be explicit and that language awareness is at the heart of good English teaching, whatever the content. But we also take a meaning-centred approach and believe that as Carter (1990: 120) suggests:

> Knowing more about how grammar *works* is to understand more about how grammar is used and misused. Knowing more about grammar can impart better choice and control over grammar, as an expressive and interpretive medium. Knowing more about grammar, as part of KAL [Knowledge About Language], is to be empowered to respond to and to use grammar as central to the creation of textual meanings.

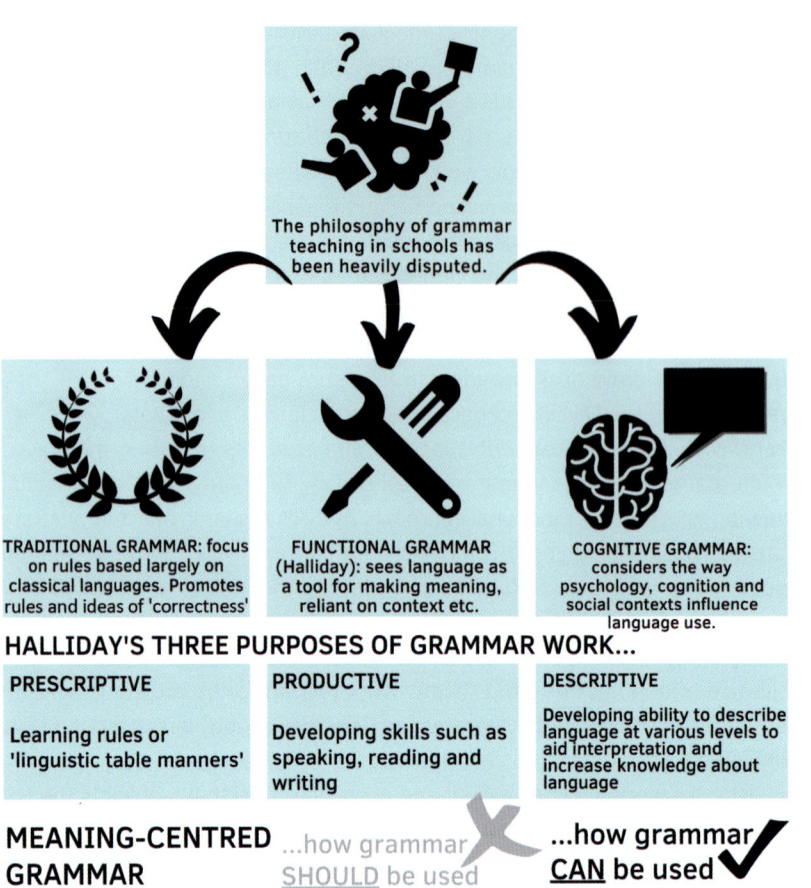

2.8

HALLIDAY'S THREE PURPOSES OF GRAMMAR WORK...

PRESCRIPTIVE	PRODUCTIVE	DESCRIPTIVE
Learning rules or 'linguistic table manners'	Developing skills such as speaking, reading and writing	Developing ability to describe language at various levels to aid interpretation and increase knowledge about language

MEANING-CENTRED GRAMMAR

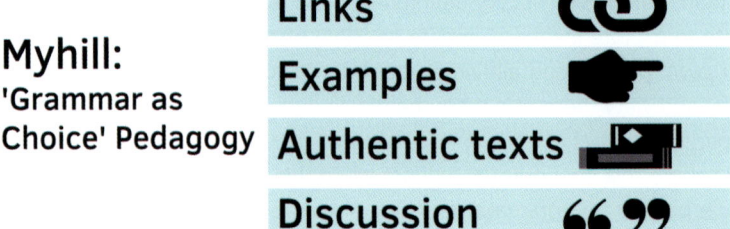

Myhill:
'Grammar as Choice' Pedagogy

Definitions and principles of teaching

WE ARE NOW ENTERING THE MURKY WORLD OF LANGUAGE AWARENESS AND TERMINOLOGY

Note on 'language awareness' vs 'grammar knowledge'

We generally use the term 'language awareness' instead of 'grammar knowledge' because it more accurately describes the broad, inclusive way we see language.

Note on content

Throughout this book, we provide clear outlines and definitions of language concepts which we think are useful to teach in the classroom. This includes some content from the National Curriculum and things drawn from more traditional descriptive grammars as well as functional and cognitive ones. We have also drawn on our own experience in the classroom and selected a range of concepts from the field of rhetoric which we have seen to have significant impact on student writing. Although this creates a hybrid set of ideas, we feel that this is useful in explaining how more traditional ideas (e.g. on word classes) can connect with more recent ideas which teachers might not have encountered (e.g. on discourse grammar).

For ease of use, we have separated this body of concepts into the foundational knowledge which forms the basis of how language works (words, clauses, sentences, etc.), and some of the more specialised knowledge applicable to certain types of reading and writing. In this chapter, we outline those foundations, and then the other concepts are threaded in to the relevant chapters alongside practical classroom strategies.

(An index of concepts and exactly where they appear in the book can be found at the end of the book.)

WARNING #1: the 'knowledge' we cover in this book isn't a definitive outline of *all* the possible grammar knowledge that exists – this is just OUR selection. Take it, leave it, adapt it, but whatever you do, make it work in your context.

WARNING #2: many grammar terms have definitions which are disputed by academics. We are going with our own definitions, but it's not the terms and definitions which are important. Ultimately, the act of interrogating and describing language will develop greater language awareness in students.

WARNING #3: many language 'things' can be described in multiple ways at once and all these labels can be simultaneously correct. This can be very confusing, but we are used to this in the more 'traditional' literary devices, too. For example:

'Look the innocent flower, but be the serpent under it'

This line from *Macbeth* could be labelled and analysed in multiple ways using a range of different (or subtly different) terms:

Imagery
Religious imagery
Metaphor
Personification
Zoomorphism
Foreshadowing
Symbolism
Paradox
Contrast
Juxtaposition
Close vocabulary work: innocent, flower
You could even do some cheeky grammar work on the following:
Look, be: imperatives
But: conjunction
Under: preposition – connotations of acting in an underhand or untrustworthy manner

As you can see, there are many, many options for the literary scholar. This is the same with grammar terminology. Try not to fixate on labels and rules. Focus instead on what *job* something is doing and what meaning is being created.

3 Definitions

This section will provide an overview of the key foundational concepts which make up English grammar.

LINGUISTIC RANK SCALE: DESCRIPTIVE, NOT PRESCRIPTIVE

Our first set of key concepts and terms is structured in a way that reflects what is known as the linguistic rank scale, which shows the connection between different levels of analysis. As we move along the scale from left to right, each consecutive unit consists of all those units in the rank before it: for example phrases contain words which are made up of morphemes and so on.

3.1

morpheme < word < phrase < clause < sentence < text

SMALLER UNITS   **LARGER UNITS**

As the rank scale demonstrates, the smallest unit of analysis is the morpheme. Free morphemes generally can stand alone as words on their own, for example 'house.' Bound morphemes, however, do not exist as words on their own but rather 'bind' onto free morphemes to form new words. For example 'houses' consists of the free morpheme 'house' and the bound morpheme 's' which pluralises the singular noun 'house.'

DOI: 10.4324/9781003175261-5

The '-s' in 'houses' is an example of how bound morphemes may have an inflectional function in pluralising a noun, or else changing the tense of a verb: for example '-s' also turns the base verb 'run' into the present tense 'runs.' As the inflectional morpheme, in these instances, appears after the free morpheme, it is known as a suffix.

Alternatively, a bound morpheme may have a derivational function in that it attaches to a free morpheme to make a completely new word (rather than simply altering the tense or number of an existing one). Derivational morphemes may also appear as suffixes, as in '-ly' which attaches to 'accurate' to transform the original word from an adjective to an adverb. But they may also appear as prefixes, attached the front of the word whose meaning it alters. Common prefixes include '-dis,' '-un,' '-de,' and 're,' all of which alter the meaning of the original words:

appear	>	disappear
lucky	>	unlucky
value	>	devalue
view	>	review

Together prefixes and suffixes are known as affixes, and a free morpheme to which an affix attaches is known as the base.

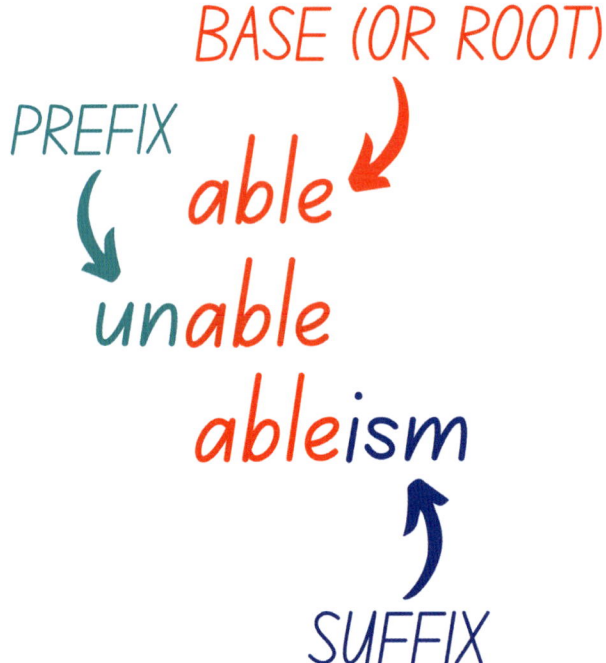

3.2

Words

A word's class refers to its general characteristics and its functions in speech and writing. The main word classes are:

Noun: identifies a thing or a concept, e.g. 'John,' 'carpet,' 'love'

Verb: identifies a process (an action, a state of being, thinking, or saying) that takes place through time, e.g. 'make,' 'be,' 'think,' 'talk'

Adjective: modifies a noun, e.g. '<u>large</u> shed,' 'the teacher is <u>tired</u>'

Adverb: modifies a verb, adjective, or another adverb, e.g. 'talk <u>quickly</u>,' '<u>extremely</u> hungry,' '<u>very</u> suddenly'

Pronoun: replaces a noun, e.g. 'he,' 'she,' 'they,' 'it'

Determiner: specifies some aspect of the noun, for example definiteness, number, or possession, e.g. 'the,' 'a,' 'some,' 'her'

Preposition: shows relationships between other words in terms of space or time, e.g. 'in,' 'under,' 'around,' 'during'

Conjunction: connects other words and help to form larger structures such as phrases and clauses, e.g. 'and,' 'but,' 'or,' 'because.' Sometimes known as 'connectives,' although the latter is more of a less specific umbrella term for any word that has a connecting function.

Generally, word classes also have several sub-types which can help us to describe their form in texts more specifically.

Nouns

3.3

NOUNS identify a thing or a concept, *e.g. John, carpet, love*

PROPER
refer to names of people, organisations and brands, events or places
Joanna, World Cup, London, Pepsi

CONCRETE
refer to objects that generally can be perceived by the senses

ABSTRACT
refer to states, feelings and concepts that cannot generally be perceived by the senses
love, hate, Socialism, honesty

COUNTABLE
<u>can</u> be pluralised
cars, children, hospitals, countries

MASS
do <u>not</u> take plural form
water, sugar, air, spaghetti

Verbs

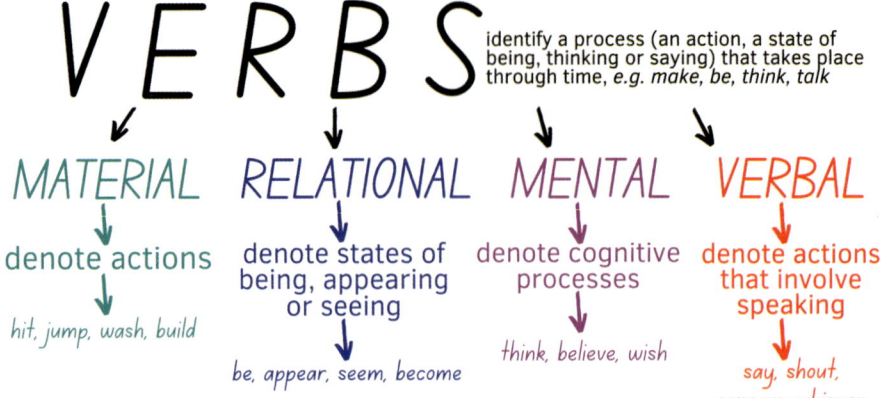

V E R B S

identify a process (an action, a state of being, thinking or saying) that takes place through time, *e.g. make, be, think, talk*

MATERIAL

denote actions

hit, jump, wash, build

RELATIONAL

denote states of being, appearing or seeing

be, appear, seem, become

MENTAL

denote cognitive processes

think, believe, wish

VERBAL

denote actions that involve speaking

say, shout, scream, whisper

PARTICIPLES

A verb form which can be used:

1) as an adjective
2. to create tense
3) to create the passive voice

BASE VERB	PRESENT PARTICIPLE	PAST PARTICIPLE
hide	*hiding*	*hidden*
break	*breaking*	*broken*

Present participles end in -ing
Past participles usually end in -ed, -d, -t, -en, or -n

PHRASAL VERBS

A special kind of verb with a two-part structure. These are generally either:

verb + preposition
He takes after his parents
Can you look after my dog?

verb + participle
Don't bring up the past
Get over it

Phrasal verbs are two words which, together, create a completely new verb. They are often not related to the original meaning of the words, or are metaphorical tin some way. For example, 'takes after' isn't related meaning-wise to 'takes' and 'bring up' draws on a physical analogy to express its meaning. In these cases, the two-part structure acts as a single unit of meaning.

AUXILIARY VERBS

Sometimes called a 'helping word', an auxilliary verb is an element which adds meaning to the clause, indicating: *tense, aspect, modality, voice, emphasis,* etc.

We will be at the church. ← 'Will' is a modal auxiliary verb, It indicates how likely it is that they will be at the church.

Do you like it? ← 'Do' is an auxilliary verb which indicates that this is a question.

Modal words indicate the level of certainty, ability, obligation or intent.

MODAL VERBS

0%   could   will   must 100%
    might

TRANSITIVE VERBS

A transitive verb is one which needs an object to complete it. e.g.

She brought ← 'brought' doesn't make sense by itself - we need an object which is *being* brought

She brought the tea ← 'the tea' is the object which completes the action

An INTRANSITIVE verb can make sense without an object. Some verbs can be both.

LEXICAL VERBS

Any verbs which describe actions or processes, rather than auxiliary verbs which just 'help' other verbs.

walk, think (lexical)
might, can (auxiliary)

3.4

Adjectives and adverbs

3.5

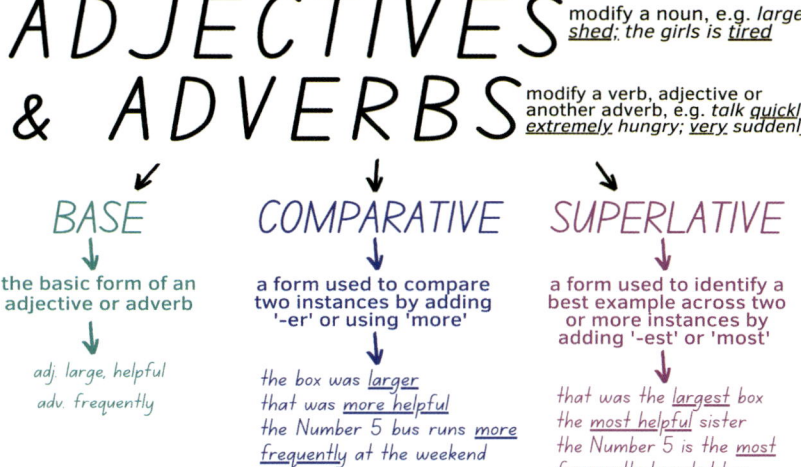

ADJECTIVES
modify a noun, e.g. *large shed*; *the girls is tired*

& ADVERBS
modify a verb, adjective or another adverb, e.g. *talk quickly*; *extremely hungry*; *very suddenly*

BASE
the basic form of an adjective or adverb

adj. large, helpful

adv. frequently

COMPARATIVE
a form used to compare two instances by adding '-er' or using 'more'

the box was *larger*

that was *more helpful*

the Number 5 bus runs *more frequently* at the weekend

SUPERLATIVE
a form used to identify a best example across two or more instances by adding '-est' or 'most'

that was the *largest* box

the *most helpful* sister

the Number 5 is the *most frequently* boarded bus

NOTE: WHAT IS MODIFICATION?

We have used the word 'modify' to explain what adjectives do to nouns, and adverbs to verbs. Modification is a concept we need to have a firm understanding of because when students appreciate modification in full, they make better choices in their writing but also have a better appreciation of the language choices of writers they encounter in literature.

A modifier is a word or phrase within a phrase or clause structure which modifies (changes) the meaning of another element within that same structure. A simple example of modification is an adjective ('big') modifying a noun ('tree') – 'the big tree.' There are many types of modifiers and contexts in which they are used.

3.6

PRE-MODIFICATION
(the modifier is BEFORE the noun)

The old car was parked.

MODIFIER
(ADJECTIVE)

POST-MODIFICATION
(the modifier is AFTER the noun)

The car, old and rusting, was parked.

MODIFIER
(ADJECTIVAL
PHRASE)

Pronouns

(We have written about this in more detail, along with ways to explore this in student writing, in Chapter 6.)

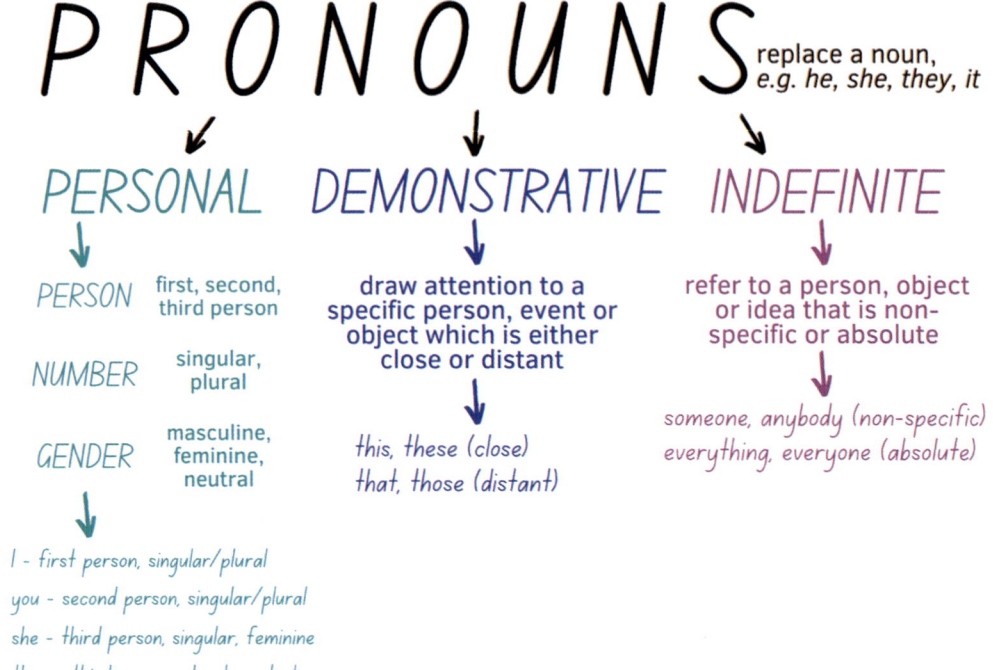

P R O N O U N S
replace a noun,
e.g. he, she, they, it

PERSONAL

PERSON — first, second, third person

NUMBER — singular, plural

GENDER — masculine, feminine, neutral

I - first person, singular/plural
you - second person, singular/plural
she - third person, singular, feminine
they - third person, plural, neutral

DEMONSTRATIVE

draw attention to a specific person, event or object which is either close or distant

this, these (close)
that, those (distant)

INDEFINITE

refer to a person, object or idea that is non-specific or absolute

someone, anybody (non-specific)
everything, everyone (absolute)

3.7

Determiners

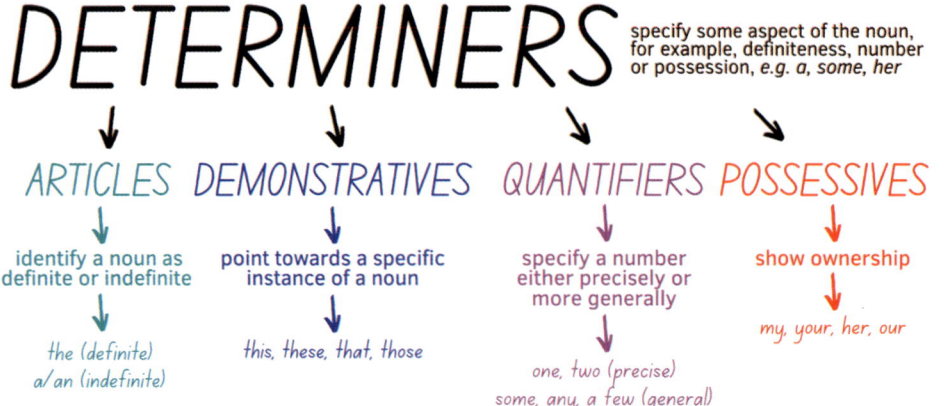

DETERMINERS
specify some aspect of the noun, for example, definiteness, number or possession, *e.g. a, some, her*

ARTICLES
identify a noun as definite or indefinite

the (definite)
a/an (indefinite)

DEMONSTRATIVES
point towards a specific instance of a noun

this, these, that, those

QUANTIFIERS
specify a number either precisely or more generally

one, two (precise)
some, any, a few (general)

POSSESSIVES
show ownership

my, your, her, our

3.8

Prepositions

3.9

PREPOSITIONS
show relationships between words in terms of space or time, *e.g. in, under, around, during*

↓   ↓

SINGLE   ## COMPLEX

↓   ↓

consist of one word   consist of two or more words

↓   ↓

in, on, under, across   *on top of, next to*

Conjunctions

3.1.1

CONJUNCTIONS
connect words and help to form larger structures such as phrases and clauses, *e.g. and, but, or, because*

↓   ↓

CO-ORDINATING   ## SUB-ORDINATING

↓   ↓

link words or larger structures such as phrases and independent clauses together

link clauses together where one or moreis dependent on another

(NOTE: to see more about coordinating and subordinating conjunctions, see the explanation in the section on clauses on page 34.)

↓   ↓

and, but, or, yet   *because, although, while, for*

Note: conjunctions are sometimes known as 'connectives', although the latter is more of an umbrella term for any word or phrase that performs a connecting function.

(WARNING: conjunctions are sometimes known as 'connectives,' although the latter is more of an umbrella term for any word or phrase that performs a connecting function. Another linked term is 'discourse marker.' See more about conjunctions, connectives, and discourse markers for writing in Chapter 6)

Phrases

Following the linguistic rank scale, we can describe and analyse language at the level of the phrase, here defined as a group of words built around a headword. Phrases may be built around the major word classes: noun phrases, prepositional phrases, verb phrases, adjectival phrases, adverbial phrases.

WARNING: the same phrase can be described in multiple ways at once – it is possible for phrases to be embedded within each other (e.g. the noun phrase 'the house by the sea' also contains an embedded prepositional phrase 'by the sea' which also has a further noun phrase 'the sea' embedded')! We explain this more below.

We have just looked at words. Let's take a noun.

3.1.2

NOUN
house

This noun can be the headword for a noun phrase:

3.1.3

DETERMINER   *HEAD NOUN*

The old house

ADJECTIVE, PRE-MODIFIER

This example contains a pre-modifying adjective 'old.' Adjectives are one of the most common ways in which noun phrases are expanded although there are other ways such as through possessive forms:

3.1.4

DETERMINER
PRE-MODIFIER

My house
HEAD NOUN

3.1.5

POSSESSIVE NOUN
PRE-MODIFIER

John's house
HEAD NOUN

Alternatively, noun phrases may be post-modified in that the additional content comes after the head noun. This is often through a prepositional phrase. In the next example, there is a wider noun phrase with 'house' as the head noun:

3.1.6

NOUN PHRASE

The house by the post office

But within that noun phrase is an embedded prepositional phrase which post-modifies the 'house' (i.e. adding information about *where* the house is):

3.1.7

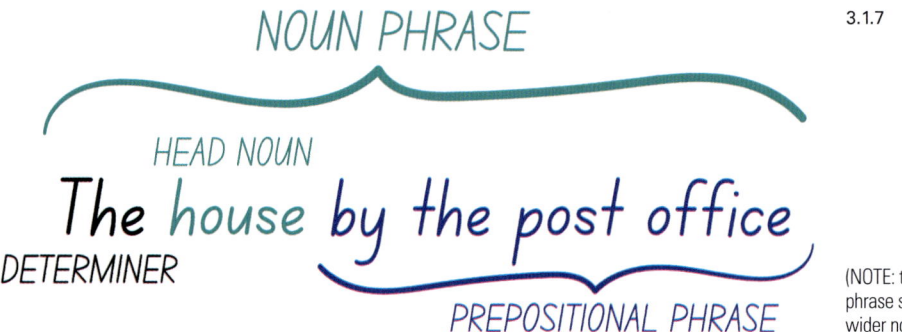

NOUN PHRASE

HEAD NOUN

The house by the post office

DETERMINER

PREPOSITIONAL PHRASE
POST-MODIFIER

(NOTE: the prepositional phrase sits inside the wider noun phrase.)

And within that prepositional phrase, there is a smaller noun phrase:

3.1.8

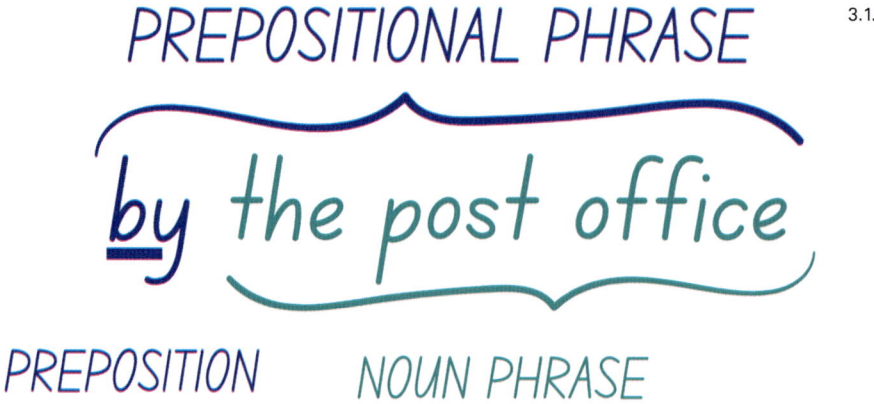

PREPOSITIONAL PHRASE

by the post office

PREPOSITION   NOUN PHRASE

And we can break this smaller noun phrase down into its determiner, 'the', and head noun, 'post office':

3.1.9

3.2.1

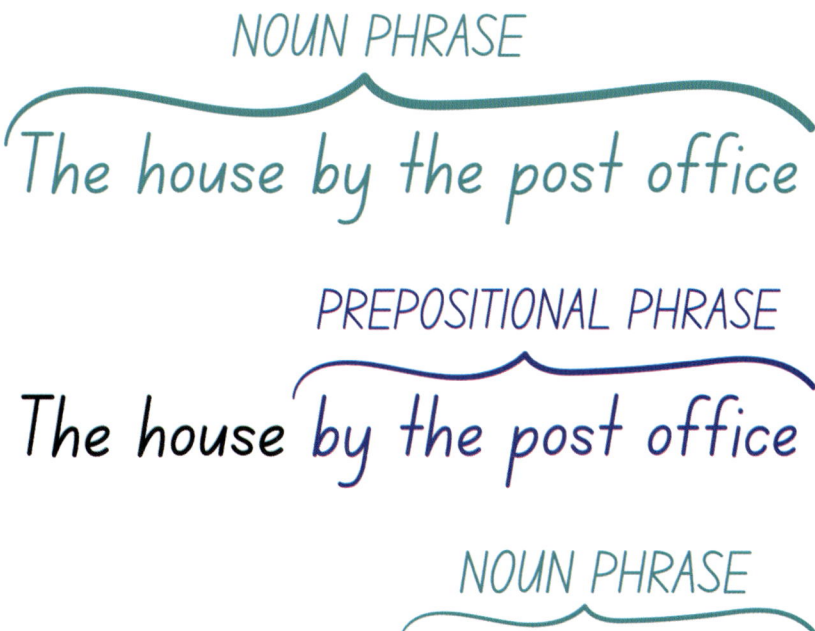

(NOTE: as you can see, almost like Russian dolls, phrases can be broken down and contain smaller phrases embedded within them. This noun phrase can be described as also containing a prepositional phrase and a noun phrase.)

> WARNING: this can cause confusion – it is not necessary to break every phrase down to its smallest components. Nor is it necessary to label everything you can see. What IS important is that we can label the things we want to talk about. If you want to talk about the use of the prepositional phrase, that's the label you should use, and leave the rest.)

Noun phrases may often be 'stacked' in a text to give a richer sense of description and to qualify a first noun phrase with a second one so as to show a relationship between the two. This is known as apposition. Look, for example at this extract from the beginning of *Great Expectations*, when Pip answers Magwich's question about with whom he lives:

3.2.2

| NOUN PHRASE 1 | NOUN PHRASE 2 | NOUN PHRASE 3 |
'My sister, sir, - Mrs. Joe Gargery, - wife of Joe Gargery, the blacksmith, sir.'
NOUN PHRASE 4   NOUN PHRASE 5

Here, the first three noun phrases are in apposition: 'my sister,' 'Mrs Joe Gargery,' and 'wife of Joe Gargery' all refer to the same person. In addition, 'wife of Joe Gargery' is a noun phrase with an embedded prepositional phrase 'of Joe Gargery,' consisting of a preposition 'of' and a further noun phrase 4, 'Joe Gargery.' Since noun phrase 5 'the blacksmith,' also refers to Joe Gargery, we can say that is also appositive in relation to noun phrase 4.

A verb phrase (VP) is built around head verbs. Verb phrases are often single words but, on some occasions, strings of verbs are built up around a head verb.

(NOTE: we talk more about apposition in Chapter 6 on pages 177–180.)

VP
I want a new car = want (lexical verb)
VP
I do like cars = do (primary auxiliary verb), like (main verb)
VP
I would like a new car = would (modal auxiliary verb), like (main verb)
I am driving my car = am (primary auxiliary verb), driving (main verb)

An adjective phrase is built around a head adjective.
Often this will be a single word and on some of these occasions the adjective is probably best described as part of the noun phrase, for example

Adj P

The old house = old (adjective phrase but probably best described simply as the pre-modifier in the noun phrase 'The old house'

At other times, an adjective phrase might be a stand-alone entity but still exist as a single word, for example following relational verbs:

Adj P

He was sad = sad (adjective phrase/single adjective)

On other occasions, however, adjective phrases can be much larger structures and be either pre- or post-modified

Adj P

He was very sad = very (pre-modifier) sad (head adjective)

Adj P

He was sad in lots of ways = sad (adjective phrase/single adjective), in lots of ways (post-modifying, prepositional phrase)

An adverb phrase is built around a head adverb

In a similar way to adjective phrases, adverb phrases are often single words but can sometimes consist of larger structures

Adv P

She ran quickly = quickly (adverb phrase/single adverb)

Adv P

She ran very quickly = very (pre-modifier), quickly (head adverb)

Of course across an example or extract, we can identify a number of phrases, for example in this extract from Chapter 5 of *Frankenstein*.

It was on a dreary night of November that I beheld the accomplishment of my toils.

It = NP
was = VP
on a dreary night = Prep P
of November = Prep P
[that]
I = NP
beheld = VP

the accomplishment = NP
of my toils = Prep P

Clauses and sentences

The next level of analysis is the clause level.

There are many ways to describe and label the various parts of clauses, and these all depend on what exactly you are trying to say about them. We have outlined a number of these:

1. Participant, process, circumstance
2. Subject, verb, object, adverbial, complement
3. Sentence types: declarative, interrogative, imperative, exclamative
4. Sentence complexity: single-clause and multi-clause sentences
5. Main and subordinate clauses: coordinating and subordinating conjunctions
6. Relative clauses
7. Fragmentation
8. Active and passive voice

1. Participant – process – circumstance

To begin with, we can describe a clause as a larger structure that is built around a verb phrase but contains more information such as who carries out a verb, who or what is affected by it, and the circumstances in which the verb takes place. This entire set of information is often called a proposition. In functional linguistics, a clause refers to the way in which we encode our experience of the world and contains participants, processes, and circumstances.

2. Subject – verb – object – adverbial

The broad labels of participant and process can be described more specifically to identify what are known as constituent parts that form particular functions within the clause,

3.2.3

PARTICIPANT   PARTICIPANT

The teacher gave out the books slowly

     PROCESS   CIRCUMSTANCE

participant: *who* carries out the verb, or
who or what is affected by the verb
process: verb
circumstance: *how* the verb takes place

3.2.4

SUBJECT   *VERB*   *OBJECT*

The teacher gave out the books

SUBJECT: generally the prime focus of attention in the clause and the main participant in the clause
VERB: the verb process
OBJECT: a secondary participant directly affected by a material, mental or verbal process

3.2.5

ADVERBIAL

The teacher gave out the books slowly

(NOTE: the ADVERBIAL is flexible in that it can occur in different positions in the clause.)

ADVERBIAL: the circumstances in which a clause takes place, often related to time, place or manner

Slowly, the teacher gave out the books

3.2.6

The teacher slowly gave out the books

3.2.7

A third alternative option seems intuitively more unusual but is possible. In this instance, however, a pair of commas helps to clarify that 'the books' is the object of 'gave out' and 'slowly' modifies the overall action.

The teacher gave out, slowly, the books

3.2.8

In some instances, for example following a relationship process, there is a different type of clause part:

SUBJECT   COMPLEMENT
The teacher was <u>pleased</u>

3.3.1

SUBJECT   COMPLEMENT
The teacher is <u>the head of sixth form</u>

3.3.2

COMPLEMENT: an attribute or identifying aspect of the subject

One interesting difference between an attribute and an identifying aspect is that generally it is easier to swap the identifying aspect and the noun it complements in a clause. So 'The head of sixth form is the teacher' seems as natural as 'the teacher is the head of sixth form,' but 'pleased was the teacher' is less usual (unless you are Yoda from Star Wars!)

(NOTE: the use of unusual syntax like this is called hyperbaton. We talk about it on page 184.)

3. Sentence types

We can also distinguish between different clause types, which follow a particular grammatical pattern and are typically used in a specific way:

Declarative clauses: used to make statements
Interrogative clauses: used to ask questions
Imperative clauses: used to give orders
Exclamative clauses: used to make exclamations

(NOTE: we talk more about declarative, interrogative, imperative, and exclamative clauses in literary texts and in writing in Section 3.)

4. Sentence complexity

Clauses form sentences.

A **single-clause sentence** contains one clause, while a **multi-clause sentence** contains several clauses joined together.

In multi-clause sentences, we can distinguish between coordinated clauses, linked by coordinating conjunctions such as *and*, *but*, and *or* which can stand independently and subordinated clauses which have a hierarchical relationship in that one is the main clause (a unit that can stand independently) with a number of subsequent subordinate clauses (units that depend on the addition of a main clause).

In older traditional grammars, the terms simple (single-clause), compound (coordinated multi-clause), and complex (subordinated multi-clause) sentences were often used but these have now largely been replaced in favour of the more straightforward and accurate singe/multi-clause distinction.

(WARNING: most people know terms like 'simple,' 'compound,' and 'complex' sentences. These aren't used very much in linguistics anymore because they aren't particularly accurate descriptors. Instead, use the simpler terms single-clause sentence (one clause!) or multi-clause sentence (more than one!).)

5. *Main and subordinate clauses: coordinating and subordinating conjunctions*

A coordinating conjunction is used when two INDEPENDENT clauses are being linked to each other. This means that each of the clauses could stand alone as single-clause sentence and still make sense. Here is an example of a sentence with two independent clauses joined by a coordinating conjunction:

3.3.3

co-ordinating
CLAUSE I (MAIN)   *conjunction*
The teacher gave out the books **and** wrote the date on the board.
CLAUSE 2

3.3.4

The teacher gave out the books.

[The teacher] wrote the date on the board.

Each of these clauses would make sense on their own. Think of it like a pair of books which are broad enough to stand upright on a shelf.

IN SHORT: Independent clauses are joined by a CO-ORDINATING conjunction - they are linked, but they don't depend on each other

A SUBORDINATING CONJUNCTION is used when the main clause is being linked to a DEPENDENT clause – that is one which depends on the main clause in order for it to make sense. This means that it is SUBORDINATE to the main clause. For example:

sub-ordinating
conjunction

3.3.5

MAIN CLAUSE
*The teacher gave out the books **before** writing the date on the board.*
SUBORDINATE CLAUSE

The teacher gave out the books.

[The teacher] writing the date on the board.

This clause does NOT make sense on its own. It is DEPENDENT on the first clause. This means that, rather than being a book standing on its end, it is leaning on the first one...

MAIN   *SUBORDINATE*
CLAUSE   *CLAUSE*

In this sentence, *before* is a subordinating conjunction because it joins a main clause to a subordinate clause.

Subordinating conjunctions can go in different places in the sentence and are often placed at the start, for example:

SUBORDINATE CLAUSE

3.3.6

__Before__ writing the date on the board, the teacher gave out the books.
sub-ordinating
conjunction
MAIN CLAUSE

(WARNING: in American English, they call these clauses INDEPENDENT and DEPENDENT clauses. In British English, we call them MAIN and SUB-ORDINATE clauses. The names don't really matter, as long as you know what you are trying to describe.)

(NOTE: to see an example of how to teach subordinating conjunctions for writing, see the visual strategy in Chapter 6, page 174.)

6. Relative clauses

A very common multi-clause sentence type contains a relative clause. A relative clause is a subordinate clause that is headed by a relative pronoun such as *who, whom, which,* or *that.* These pronouns link the clause they head to a previously mentioned noun (literally they relate back to it). Relative clauses may be restrictive in that they identify a specific noun referent or non-restrictive in that they provide secondary information.

3.3.7

The teacher <u>who</u> gave out the books **then taught the class**

MAIN CLAUSE

RELATIVE CLAUSE

(NOTE: this is a restrictive relative clause because it identifies or singles out a specific teacher (the one who is giving out the books) as its referent.)

RELATIVE clause: The teacher who gave out the books
MAIN clause: [The teacher] then taught the class.

THE YEAR 9 FOOTBALL TEAM, WHO HAD NOT LOST FOR FOUR YEARS, WON THE COUNTY CUP LAST WEEKEND

Clause 1 (relative clause): 'who had not lost for four years'

Clause 2 (main clause): The Year 9 football team [. . .] won the county cup last weekend

The relative pronoun 'who' refers back to the Year 9 football team.

In this instance, the referent is unambiguous and so the relative clause adds more information rather than identifying a referent as in the previous example. In writing, a non-restrictive clause is generally separated from the main clause with the use of commas.

A final, useful distinction to make is between finite and non-finite clauses. On the one hand, a finite clause is headed by a finite verb which specifies tense and thus draws attention to a full process occurring through time.

THE YEAR 9 FOOTBALL TEAM WON THE COUNTY CUP LAST WEEKEND

The finite verb 'won' specifies tense (the past) and draws attention to the entire process

On the other hand, a non-finite clause is headed by a non-finite verb such as an -ing present participle, an -ed past participle, or an infinitive to + the base form of the verb. Non-finite verbs only specify a part of a longer process: present participles identify an internal part of the process while a past participle focuses on the end of the process.

RUNNING WITH BALL, OUR MIDFIELDER DESTROYED THE DEFENCE

The non-finite present participle 'running' forms a non-finite clause 'Running with the ball' which omits the start and end of the verb process. The main clause is 'our midfielder destroyed the defence.'

FINALLY DEFEATED BY THEIR OPPONENTS, THE YEAR 9 TEAM'S RUN CAME TO AN END

The non-finite past participle 'defeated' forms a non-finite clause 'Finally defeated by their opponents' which focuses on the end of the verb process. The main clause is 'the Year 9 team's run came to an end.'

THE YEAR 9 TEAM VOWED TO BEAT THEIR OPPONENTS NEXT TIME

The infinitive 'to beat' presents a more general view of a process without identifying it as taking place through time. This example is interesting because here the non-finite clause 'to beat their opponents next time' headed by the infinitive 'to beat' functions as the object of the verb 'vowed' – you can test this by replacing it with a noun such as 'The Year 9 team vowed revenge.' Some grammars would therefore call this non-finite clause a 'noun clause' to show this function. Alternatively, this structure could be described as a single clause with two verb phrases 'vowed' and 'beat' linked by 'to.' This is actually a very good example of how language may not fit into one method of description!

Subject   Verb   Object (noun clause)   Adverbial
The Year 9 team vowed to beat their opponents next time

Subject   Verb   Verb   Object   Adverbial
The Year 9 team vowed to beat their opponents next time

7. Fragmentation

A fragment is a sentence that is missing either its subject or its main verb. In formal writing, we would say that a sentence isn't complete without both those components. However, deliberate fragmentation can be a highly effective device in writing in a number of forms.

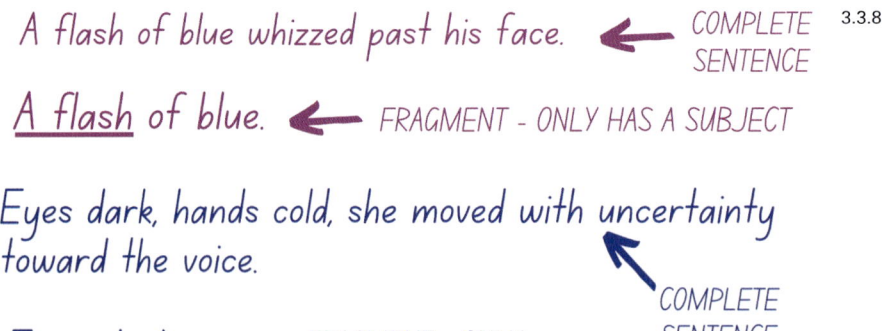

A flash of blue whizzed past his face. ← COMPLETE SENTENCE   3.3.8

A flash of blue. ← FRAGMENT - ONLY HAS A SUBJECT

Eyes dark, hands cold, she moved with uncertainty toward the voice. COMPLETE SENTENCE

Eyes dark. ← FRAGMENT - ONLY HAS A SUBJECT

NOTE: Fragments are *technically* grammatically incorrect, but can be used to great effect. <u>Nothing</u> is 'incorrect' if that's what the writer intended.

8. Active and passive voice

Chapter 2 (page 14) introduced the distinction between the active and passive voice which is one of the most important ways in which meaning derives from the organisation of a clause. As this was discussed in some detail there, we only provide a short summary of the differences in grammatical configuration here.

The key thing to understand is that VOICE identifies the relationship between who or what has AGENCY, and where that AGENT is positioned in the sentence.

Grammatical voice depends on which position the AGENT and PATIENT are in.

Active voice is when the AGENT is in the subject (initial) position in the clause, such as in the first example where the teacher is the subject.

Passive voice is when the PATIENT is in the subject (initial) position in the clause, such as in the second example where 'the books' are the subject.

This is important because, by writing something in active or passive voice, the writer can deliberately choose to place emphasis on something, to reduce the significance of something, or omit it altogether. For example:

Active voice:

> *Scrooge* signed it
>
> 'Scrooge' is the agent performing the action – he is foregrounded in the clause.

Passive voice:

> *The register of his burial* was signed by the clergyman, the clerk, the undertaker, and the chief mourner
>
> 'The register of his burial' is the patient (the entity affected by the verb), but it is in the subject (initial) position, so it is the main focus of the clause. The entities responsible for the action are introduced with 'by' and passivised through the use of 'was' and a past participle.

An effect is that the register of burial itself is foregrounded, rather than the signatories.

Agentless passive:

> *The register of his burial* was signed
>
> As previously mentioned, but there is no 'by . . .' and therefore no agent. An effect of omitting the agent entirely is that the action is foregrounded with no entity responsible for it.

(To see a more detailed exploration of how agency can work in media language, see 13–16.)

LEVELS OF ANALYSIS

Clause analysis can be undertaken in conjunction with analysis at different levels that we have covered in this chapter. For example we could analyse the following at each of the levels of word, phrase, and clause to provide a more detailed description of language. Here, for example is a section from the opening to *A Christmas Carol* showing analysis at word, phrase, and clause levels.

The register of his burial was signed by the clergyman, the clerk, the undertaker, and the chief mourner.

WORD LEVEL

> the = determiner
> register = noun
> of = preposition
> his = determiner
> burial = noun
> was = verb
> signed = verb
> by = preposition
> the = determiner
> clergyman = noun
> the = determiner
> clerk = noun
> the = determiner
> undertaker = noun
> and = conjunction
> the = determiner
> chief = noun
> mourner = noun

PHRASE LEVEL

> The register (of his burial) = noun phrase (with post-modifying prepositional phrase)
> of (his burial) = prepositional phrase (with embedded noun phrase)
> was signed = verb phrase
> by (the clergyman, the clerk, the undertaker, and the chief mourner) = prepositional phrase (with embedded four noun phrases)

CLAUSE LEVEL

The register of his burial was signed by the clergyman, the clerk, the undertaker, and the chief mourner = single clause

> Subject = The register of his burial
> Verb = was signed
> Adverbial = by the clergyman, the clerk, the undertaker, and the chief mourner.

Discourse

Traditional grammars tend to be clause-level ones; that is they are good at providing a framework for describing language at word, phrase, and clause levels but are not very useful for helping with the larger structure of discourse. As a term, 'discourse' can define different areas of study in linguistics, but here we use it to refer to the whole act of communication including, importantly, the context in which language gets used and understood.

As an example, look at the following text which appeared as part of a charity advertisement for Guide Dogs alongside a photo of a dog (called Pudding)

> Sponsor Pudding as the perfect gift this Christmas
> One day Pudding will transform someone's life. . . .
> . . . and you can be part of her journey this Christmas

We can do a straightforward grammatical analysis of this extract very easily, identifying for example the use of the imperative 'Sponsor' at the beginning, the modified noun phrase 'the perfect gift,' the use of the verb 'transform' to emphasise the dramatic effect that a guide dog will have, the use of the second person pronoun to informalise the text and involve the reader, and so on. These comments largely focus on specific words and phrases, why they might be used and what the possible effects might be but ignore how these language features fall into a broader sense of how a reader might make sense of the text.

So, here's a complementary way of thinking about this text.

The language of the text is understood by a reader with respect to a wider range of contextual knowledge that they hold. The word 'Christmas,' for example activates a schema (see page 7) that contains a vast array of knowledge about the event (when it is, what people generally do, its significance, and so on). 'Christmas' is, of course, a Christian celebration but more generally it is socially viewed as a time for thinking of others, charity, and families. So a big part of making sense of this text relies on readers drawing on a 'Christmas' schema (it's also why the word is repeated several times, why Pudding is called Pudding, and why in the photo she is sitting on a Christmas type rug surrounded by presents and tinsel. Equally, the use of the second person pronoun 'you' and two modal verbs 'will' and 'can' invites readers to take a mental leap and imagine a situation in which their donation results in Pudding changing someone's life for the better (and hence making it a perfect Christmas). As we saw earlier, one of the effects of modal verbs is that they project scenarios; here of course, the richness of the scenario that is triggered by the modality is likely to depend on the reader and the kind of background knowledge that they use to support their comprehension of the text.

We can also see that these schemas are constrained by the text itself, so that only relevant information is triggered and used by the reader to make sense of the message. At one level, this means that despite the vast range of knowledge that we have in our heads, only knowledge of Christmas, guide dogs, and charities is triggered, rather than say knowledge of football, cooking, summer holidays, etc. At another level, the text is specific enough so that although a reader's 'Christmas' schema will draw on a range of experiences of Christmas, this text specifically asks for a focus, through the demonstrative 'this' on the current festive period. And the invitation to be part of Pudding's journey triggers a schema of a particular kind of journey (probably both literally and metaphorically) associated with charities and helping rather than say a journey to the moon or to the Arctic Circle.

This kind of analysis is useful not only because it offers a view of language as a form of directing attention and analysing language as a way of explaining how writers and texts position readers to construct particular views of the world, but also because it helps students to understand that, on its own, a simple formal description of language is insufficient to describe the ways in which meanings get made. This more discourse-based approach has obvious value when it comes to thinking about literary texts. For example here's the opening to Wilfred Owen's poem 'Disabled':

He sat in a wheeled chair, waiting for dark,
And shivered in his ghastly suit of grey

Given Owen's status as a war poet, it's probably quite difficult for this poem not to automatically trigger a 'war poetry' schema in which readers will draw on the various kinds of knowledge that they have to flesh out and make sense of the opening description of the soldier. Some readers may have very detailed schemas whereas others will have less developed ones. And readers may also draw on more personal memories and stores of extra-textual knowledge to make sense of these opening lines. Perhaps the description of the soldier reminds them of something they had read or seen that isn't war related or connects to a family or friend being injured and so on. All this information provides an important context for thinking about, in conjunction with formal features, how meanings get made.

A discourse approach to grammar can also highlight the importance of the situational aspect of meaning. By this we refer to how the *where*, *with whom*, and *why* something gets read influences how readers might respond to a text. Think, for example about how readers might interpret Owen's poem in the school classroom in front of their peers and a teacher compared to say an individual reading to an anonymous post on a reading group blog. The context in which a text gets read plays an important role in how readers respond to language and demonstrates the importance of context in language production, reception, and interpretation.

4 Teaching grammar

From encounter to mastery

How might we explain grammar to our students? In general, we are wary of analogies because they have tend oversimplify complex ideas and can lead to misconceptions which need to be unpicked somewhere down the line. The following analogy, however, is useful as a way of explaining what 'grammar' does for writing, perhaps because it's such a nebulous set of ideas.

> Grammar is just a really broad term which describes <u>how</u> a text is constructed. When that construction is successful, it is like the music in a film soundtrack; you don't really notice it, but it influences the way you feel about the story or ideas being presented. A film music soundtrack can direct your attention to something specific, warn you that something is coming, or remind you of an idea, all without you really being aware of it; a subtle change from major to minor is enough to tell an audience that things are getting serious. Expertly crafted writing can do the same thing – it's not just the 'plot' which creates meaning, it's the way the writer uses, for example, sentence structure to build ideas, make us pause, or push us forward.
>
> If the film soundtrack is badly written, it can take us out of the moment and spoil our enjoyment. I always say to my students that accurate use of punctuation, appropriateness of word choice and carefully judged structures mean that the 'music' sounds right. Bad grammar gets in the way – it is jarring – it takes us out of the moment and makes our writing less enjoyable. Less persuasive. Less compelling.

This analogy creates a foundational understanding of grammar as something which supports art, just as the soundtrack in a film supports the action on screen and guides the emotions of an audience.

> (WARNING: if you were hoping that this book would provide lots of grammar worksheets, we are afraid you will be disappointed. That has been done – there are lots of worksheets and other resources out there (some really good ones, too) – but we feel strongly that effective teaching is about teachers themselves being the resource. You are the lesson. Your intellectual preparation is more powerful than any photocopying you could ever do. So instead of worksheets for students to fill in, this book focuses on helping teachers to craft really excellent explanations, make the complex concrete, and sequence grammar teaching over time so that gains are long lasting and woven into the fabric of what we do.)

DOI: 10.4324/9781003175261-6

TEACHING GRAMMAR TERMINOLOGY: KEY PRINCIPLES

There is a lot of terminology in grammar. As we've already mentioned, some-times one thing can have multiple 'correct' labels, and sometimes the definitions of things shift based on their context. This makes it very difficult to teach grammatical concepts without falling victim to misconceptions and confusion. The concepts in grammar are fundamentally *abstract*.

Principle 1: grammar terms aren't absolute – they shift according to *function*

What word class is 'man'? A noun? The trouble is, it's a noun most of the time, but it can also be a verb (<u>man</u> up), or modify another noun (<u>man</u> flu) and hence function a bit like an adjective. When we teach word classes, we often fall into the trap of saying that nouns are 'things,' and therefore begin to get confused when those 'things' don't behave like nouns.

A 'noun' isn't really a 'thing' – like other word classes, it's just a label to describe a word in a sentence when it's doing a particular *job*. For example we would usually feel safe with concrete nouns – they are safe and tangible. A concrete noun is a thing, person, or place which has physical existence in the world. A familiar example of this would be the word 'table.' We can use this word in a range of different ways, because words have form (word class) and function (the job they are doing in the sentence), and these can both shift.

For example:
The function of a noun is to denote a person, place, thing, or idea.

Put it on the <u>***table***</u>***.***

(NOTE: interestingly, this one is a form of grammatical metaphor – the verb 'table' is formed from the original noun 'table' and implies that you put something on a table, whilst you might not actually be putting anything on a table.)

In this sentence, 'table' denotes the *thing* which something is being put on. Its *function* is to denote a thing, therefore it is a noun.

The function of a verb is to show what action or process is taking place.
I plan to <u>***table***</u> ***a motion.***

In this sentence, 'table' is the thing which I am doing. Its *function* is to show the action being done and is therefore a verb.

The function of an adjective is to modify a noun (to give additional information or specify something about it).
Please remember your <u>***table***</u> ***manners.***

In this sentence, we are talking about manners, and the word 'table' tells us precisely what *kind* of manners we are referring to. Without the word 'table,' we would just be talking about manners in general, but the word 'table' adds important information which makes the sentence more specific. The *function* of 'table' in this case is to modify the noun 'manners,' so it is behaving *like* an adjective. However, nouns (and strings of nouns) can be used to modify other nouns. 'Table manners' is actually a compound noun, where 'table' has a kind of adjectival function.

Focusing on the *function* as well as the label for word class is helpful because this focuses us on thinking about the meaning being created by language, rather than just naming things. It is also much easier when students think about the *function* something performs, because it stops them from being limited by their idea of specific words being tied to specific things.

Principle 2: grammatical concepts are abstract and about *relationships* between things on the page

Grammar describes how language works in a particular text by identifying how features of a sentence, for example impact each other and create meaning. Look at this sentence:

The golden child ran through the towering sunflowers and laughed with warm delight.

In this sentence, the various elements have an impact on one another:

- 'The' (det., definite article) tells us that this is a child which the reader already knows something about. If we used the *indefinite article* instead, it might indicate that this is the first time we are seeing this child, e.g. *A child ran* . . .
- 'golden'(adj.) modifies 'child'(n.) but also relates to the colour yellow implied by 'sunflowers' (n.), which means these images combine to create a more powerful sense of colour and vibrancy. We might suggest that the word 'warm' (adj.) also contributes to these ideas of summer.
- 'ran' (v.) tells us what the 'child' (n.) is doing
- 'ran' and 'laughed' (v.) are both in the past tense, so they tell us that all these things have already happened
- 'through' (prep.) tells us where the 'child' (n.) 'ran' (v.)
- 'sunflowers' (n.) tell us what the 'child' (n.) can see and tell us what time of year this must be, as well as evoke ideas of summer, the colour yellow, flowers as a symbol of youth and beauty, etc.
- 'towering' (adj.) tells us that the 'sunflowers' (n.) are very tall but also gives us a sense of them being imposing and impressive, like towers. Though the word 'towering' (adj.) is functioning adjectivally in this phrase, it is also a present participle which gives us a sense of immediacy which we would not feel if it were written as a past participle instead: *the sunflowers towered*.

There are other details in this sentence which we might mention, but you can see how these examples indicate the way in which various language features *interact* with one another. Discovering the correct label for something in grammar is about understanding how it sits alongside other things; 'towering' is only an adjective because it comes directly before the noun 'sunflowers.' It is the relationships which are key.

If grammatical concepts are about relationships, then we must find simple ways to indicate those relationships and connections between things. This is not as simple as giving definitions in other areas of English knowledge. For example we might define sibilance as *the repetition of 's' sounds*. Sibilance isn't different if it is at the start of a poem or at the end, or if it's in a speech or in a novel. It is always sibilance. Though the effect of sibilance and our interpretation as readers might be different in each case, it remains true that sibilance is sibilance. Not so with grammar – terminology shifts with each new situation.

HOW DO I TEACH GRAMMATICAL CONCEPTS?

Teaching grammar is just like teaching anything else because learning is learning, no matter the content.

Learning is a complex long-term process which relies on clarity of instruction, connections with prior knowledge, repetition, and retrieval. Efrat Furst (2018) explains this in four stages: KNOW, UNDERSTAND, USE, PRACTISE to achieve MASTERY.

In the English classroom, this might represent the first time a teacher exposes students to the concept of *modality*. They might use the word when speaking to students, or they might encounter it through reading, for example.

4.1

KNOW

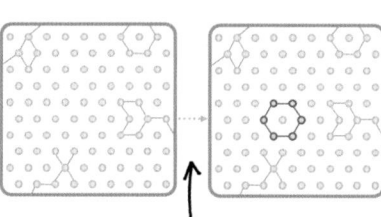

This panel represents the learner's brain before a concept has been encountered.

This panel represents the new concept where 'connections (edges in turquoise are formed among activated nodes to create a small network.' (Furst, E)

New concept encountered
(word, object etc.)

4.2

UNDERSTAND

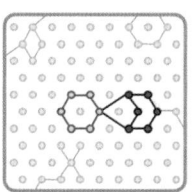

We know that the brain seeks to make connections with prior knowledge in order to create meaning. Furst explains that the 'understand' stage is where the concept is explained, and that 'meaning is generated when the new concept (turquoise) is associated with other concepts that the learner is already familiar with (dark grey).'

At this point, students KNOW that a thing called 'modality' exists, but that is all.

In our modality example, the teacher might write the word down for students to see, give a simple definition and some clear examples, e.g.

Modality: an expression of how certain, possible, or necessary something is, or how willing or able someone is to do something.

Example:

Shakespeare is possibly suggesting that Lord Capulet is a violent father.

Shakespeare is clearly suggesting that Lord Capulet is a violent father.

Shakespeare is undeniably suggesting that Lord Capulet is a violent father.

The words possibly, clearly, and undeniably are **modal** words which indicate how certain it is that Shakespeare is suggesting something.

After giving this simple definition and example, students might be at a point where they 'UNDERSTAND' the concept – they have made connections between this new concept and the things they already know about sentences and how vocabulary works to convey meaning. They have also begun to appreciate how these kinds of words might be useful to them in their English work.

Fiorella and Mayer's theory of 'Generative Learning' (2016) is based on the principle that, once students have been taught something initially, they embed and consolidate that knowledge through generative activities where they must process that information and think hard about it. Willingham said of memory: 'it's the residue of thought' and that 'the more you think about something, the more likely it is that you'll remember it later' (2008). The next step in learning,

4.3

USE

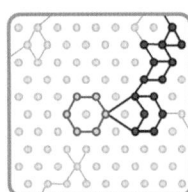

Furst says that 'acquiring information by taking it inis not the same action as trying to take it out, or actively retrieve it We tend to be overconfident about functionality when something merely "makes sense".'

The USE stage is about being able to access the concept and use it in meaningful ways. When students are asked to apply the concept, to process knowledge, they make more connections with existing knowledge and, as Furst puts it, 'build pathways' in the brain.

once students KNOW and UNDERSTAND, is to USE (to apply) that concept in situations in which they will have to think about it.

In our modality example, this might mean that the teacher facilitates opportunities for the students to process the concept. For example they might use some of the following activities:

- **Retrieval practice** – students are quizzed on the definition
- **Variation** – students look at a range of examples and non-examples of 'modal' language and identify which ones *are* modal and which are not
- **Questioning** – either live and verbal, or independent written responses, where students have to articulate their understanding in their own words
- **Application** – students re-write a set of statements to include appropriate modal language choices
- **Justification** – students look at a range of examples of modal language and consider which are appropriate for a particular type of writing and which ones are not; for instance, is the word 'undeniably' ever an appropriate choice in academic writing? Or is it too strong to enable the writer to maintain academic distance?

Each of the previously mentioned activities would require students to think hard about the concept, creating more connections and bigger neural pathways.

4.4

PRACTISE to achieve MASTERY

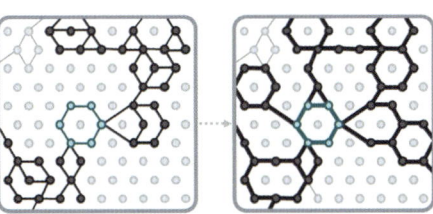

Through repeated practice, application and retrieval, we build larger and more complex networks of information in the brain. These networks are called "schema."

Furst talks about PRACTICE leading to MASTERY, saying that 'it takes a lot of effort to pave new pathways (left), but with repetitions, we manage to make these pathways more efficient (right): stronger and more robust.'

To support students to master the concept of *modality*, the teacher would deliberately return to the concept over time, applying it to a range of different situations, contexts, and tasks. In addition to the kinds of activities outlined earlier, they should also consider:

- How to move beyond that concept and add **greater nuance and complexity**, e.g. *modality* paves the way for specific word classes: modal *verbs*, modal *adverbs*, modal *adjectives*, modal *phrases*. These concepts can all be taught explicitly and linked to this concept and its schema.
- **Spaced and interleaved retrieval** over time – ensuring that spacing makes retrieval challenging, and interleaving forces students to distinguish between similar but different concepts, e.g. *modality* is not the same as *tone*, but the two concepts do interact and overlap. Students who are forced to retrieve definitions and practice subtle differences between linked ideas get the benefits of interleaved retrieval because it forces them to think hard.
- More **variation** – showing examples of modality in different contexts, different forms and genres. For example how does modality look different in descriptive writing when creating a sense of uncertainty and fear (see #1), as opposed to modality in literary analysis (see #2)?

  1. It *might* have been the wind. It *might* not. She wasn't so sure now . . .
  2. Owen *might* be indicating here that his own faith in God has deteriorated . . .

  Alternatively, you might get students to consider their writing *with* modal language and *without* modal language; ask them to make a choice about whether to use it or not, and to justify that choice in writing: **How would modal language alter the meaning? What choice have I made? Why?**

- **Frequent exposure** – the teacher ensures that their own use of language deliberately references the learnt concept in future lessons and that students have frequent opportunities to practice, identify, and engage with it in new contexts.

  For example months after learning about *modality*, the teacher might be reading aloud to the class from *An Inspector Calls* and come across the line where Mr Birling describes the Titanic as 'unsinkable, **absolutely** unsinkable.'

TEACHER: 'NAME, what type of adverb is this?'
STUDENT: 'Is it a modal adverb?'

TEACHER: 'It is a modal adverb. Excellent. How do you know that?'

STUDENT: 'It is saying it's definitely not going to happen.'

TEACHER: 'What's the precise definition of a modal adverb?'

STUDENT: [PAUSES. REMEMBERS.] 'A modal adverb indicates how likely, possible, or certain something is. Or how able or willing a person is to do something.'

TEACHER: 'Good – NAME [new student], why is this modal adverb particularly interesting?'

STUDENT: 'It shows Mr Birling thinks the Titanic won't sink.'

TEACHER: 'What do you think Priestley is indicating about his character here?'

STUDENT: 'That he isn't very intelligent . . .'

TEACHER: 'How would this line be different if he had said "probably unsinkable" instead?'

STUDENT: 'It would look like he wasn't completely sure. Maybe we would think he wasn't quite as foolish.'

TEACHER asks the whole class to rewrite the line using a range of different modal adverbs (ideally on mini-whiteboards for immediate assessment of the understanding of the whole class): to show he is 100% sure it won't sink, 75% sure, 50% sure, 25% sure, convinced that it WILL sink . . .

STUDENTS produce responses such as unsinkable, hardly unsinkable; unsinkable, ostensibly unsinkable; unsinkable, indisputably unsinkable . . .

These activities are just some examples of the sorts of strategies to ensure that students continue to revisit and strengthen their existing knowledge over time – there are countless methods to support this work.

By this point, you will probably be thinking that this section hasn't really been about grammar. You are right. Grammar is just one area of knowledge in English and one of the many tools available to us when we practice the skills of analysis, exploration, and composition in English. The key principles for learning which we have outlined about, borrowing heavily from the excellent work of Efrat Furst (2018), apply to the teaching of any concept in any discipline area. If we wish to teach grammar really well, it absolutely must be done in line with what we know about how the brain learns. For that reason, we have developed this model for teaching grammar in the English classroom.

This model breaks the learning process into three stages for the sake of ease, but don't let this fool you. It's not that simple. Learning is not linear. Alongside this process, it is imperative that we are constantly checking and monitoring student understanding and application so that we know where we need to go back, unpick, and consolidate.

TEACHING GRAMMAR:
from encounter to mastery

SHORT TERM: initial encounter and comprehension

1 **Simple, precise definition**
Focus the definition on the *function* which the device performs when it is part of a text.

e.g. an adjective <u>tells us what</u> a noun (a thing) is like, or <u>gives us information about</u> it

2 **Model examples.**
Simplicity first, then <u>in context</u>...

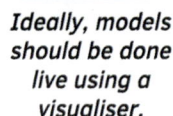

Show the simplest version of the concept first...

...then show another model, applying the concept in the context of what you are teaching (e.g. in a literary text, or in a sentence students might need to write).

e.g. The car
The <u>red</u> car
(the adjective 'red' tells us something about the car)

e.g. 'A solitary child' (the adjective 'solitary' tells us that the young Scrooge is lonely)

Ideally, models should be done live using a visualiser.

3 **Examples and non-examples**

Show students a range of examples and non-examples of the new concept. These could be where the device in question is present or absent, or where it is used accurately or inaccurately.

Students make a choice using a mini white board with a tick on one side and a cross on the other. The teacher can then diagnose how well students have understood the initial teaching of the concept.

Try to ensure the examples and non-examples are embedded within sentences so that students focus on function, rather than categorically labelling language out of context...

e.g. *Does the line use an adjective?*

'The raven himself is <u>hoarse</u>' ✓

'so <u>withered</u> and so <u>wild</u> in their attire' ✓

'the chimes were ringing' ✗

'phantom slowly, gravely, silently approached' ✗

'nothing but a <u>spectral</u> hand' ✓

4.6

MEDIUM TERM: subsequent re-exposure and repetition

4 PROCESSING: MAKE STUDENTS <u>THINK HARD</u>

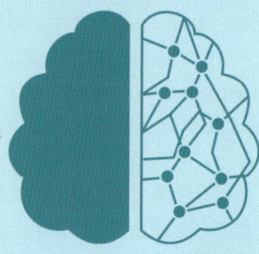

» Make explicit connections between new and existing knowledge
» Ensure that models increase in complexity
» Continuing to check for understanding and misconceptions
» Ensuring that activities are <u>generative</u>
» Retrieval practice: building stronger pathways in memory
» Spacing and interleaving
» Variation: context, use, purpose
» Deepening and refining: nuance, categorisation, connection
» Frequent exposure and deliberate use of precise language

Gradually increase the level of challenge: maintain healthy struggle

LONG TERM: moving towards mastery

Deepen and apply knowledge and skill with increasing sophistication and fluency...

READING: Identify concepts in context, privileging meaning over feature spotting

- What is this device?
- What is the effect?
- How does it alter the meaning of the text?

- If we changed X, how would that alter the meaning?
- Where else have you seen something like this before?
- How is it similar or different?
- What is the wider context of this text (purpose, audience, genre...)?
- How might that context have influenced the meaning or the effect of this device? etc.

WRITING: Craft language deliberately, selecting language devices with precision

- What do I want to achieve?
- What are the possible language features I could select to use?
- What are the benefits of X over Y?
- What are the conventions of this form and/or genre?
- What have I seen in style models which were successful, or which I would want to avoid? Why?
- Is my draft successful? How do I know?
- Are there elements I could edit?
- What difference have my edits made? Why?

Short term: initial encounter and comprehension

This stage is where a grammar concept is taught for the first time. Furst calls this 'KNOW' and 'UNDERSTAND' .

1. Simple, precise definition

Provide high-quality definitions and explanations of concepts from the outset. Try to achieve balance between being clear and simple, whilst also not making things so basic that you limit student understanding. For instance one common definition given to students is that a concrete noun is 'something you can touch,' whereas an abstract noun is 'something you *can't* touch.' This definition fits most concrete and abstract nouns, but for some it does not. For instance 'sound' is a concrete noun. So is light. Many students would think that because they don't think they can touch light, it must be an abstract noun. It would be more precise to define a concrete noun as 'something which can be experienced in the physical world via one or more of the senses.' This definition doesn't introduce limitations because it applies to every possible case of concrete nouns.

When creating definitions, it can be very helpful to discuss concepts as a department team and ask the question: what are the common misconceptions which our students have had about this grammar feature? Why might that be? How can we craft definitions and models which will help us to avoid them?

As mentioned previously, it is also important that our definitions centre on the *function* which features perform, e.g.

Determiner – *a word which gives us information about a noun such as the, a, some, her.*

This definition does a couple of problematic things. First, it is too general. Something which 'gives us information about a noun' could very easily also apply to adjectives. Second, listing those four words without any further explanation of *why* they are determiners and precisely what they are *determining* (i.e. their function) means that we risk students thinking that these words are always determiners. 'Her' can be a determiner, showing that the noun in question belongs to her. It can also just be a pronoun, as in: I love her.

A more precise, function-centred definition might be:

> **Determiner**– *a word which <u>specifies</u> something about a noun, such as the quantity or whether someone owns it or not.*

2. Model examples. Simplicity first, then in context

When modelling for grammar, it is very important that any modelling builds on and enhances student knowledge without trying to do too much too fast. There are many grammar terms which are close to each other yet distinct – unless you start modelling with very simple examples, similar terms may be elided together and student misconceptions may arise. For example if you are showing students how to modify a verb or a noun, use a very simple phrase first, such as:

The girl   ran
                (verb)

The girl	ran	quickly
	(verb)	(modifier)

This example may seem overly simplistic, but using something like this at the start enables students to have a sound grasp before trying to apply this concept in much more complex structures.

Once a simple model has been used, it is important to ensure that students are very quickly able to understand how this new concepts links to things they already know and, more importantly, that it is a key element of the wider topic they are learning at the time. Grammar is something which is so easy to sideline and view as distinct from the rest of the subject, but if we always demonstrate how knowledge of grammar is a fully integrated part of their learning in English, they are more likely to view it as important, whilst also actively building more neural 'pathways' as those connections are forged.

For instance if I am teaching the concept of modification as in the previously mentioned model, but it is during a larger unit on speech writing, I might use a model which demonstrates to students how modification can work in a speech. I would be careful to link this closely with something students already understand intimately – this is not the time to introduce a new speech topic. I might take the exact speech topic we worked on in the previous lesson and use that as a model, because this way they will expend the majority of their working memory looking at how I use modification, rather than being distracted by a brand-new concept which they must understand before they can attend to my model properly. Let's imagine that this is a line from a speech we looked at in the last lesson:

These young people have been forced to leave their homes.

I might model this sentence, and then write it again, using an adjective:

These <u>vulnerable</u> young people have been forced to leave their homes.

I would use simple questioning to elicit from the students ideas about what this word means; how the modifier changes the meaning of the sentence; how the modifier might make the sentence more powerful or compelling for the audience; what other options we might have for modifying elements of the sentence; and why each of those options might be effective. For example we could modify the word 'forced':

These young people have been <u>cruelly</u> forced to leave their homes.

. . . or the word 'homes'

These young people have been forced to leave their <u>family</u> homes.

Each of these options does something different, and these discussions with students enable them to see how modification is a valuable tool for a writer.

We might also consider what a combination of all those options would do to the sentence:

These <u>vulnerable</u> young people have been <u>cruelly</u> forced to leave their <u>family</u> homes.

Some might feel that using all three modifiers overbalances the sentence. Others might disagree. Grammar knowledge provides students with the power to make style choices, and it is good to show them that.

3.   Examples and non-examples

'Examples and non-examples' are sometimes called 'positive examples' and 'negative examples.' There is no space in this book, unfortunately, to fully do justice to the fascinating overlap between Variation Theory and Engelmann's work on examples in Direct Instruction (Engelmann and Carnine 1982). It will suffice to say that this part of the grammar teaching model is influenced by a number of different studies.

Once you have modelled a new concept in the context of the topic you are teaching, you can then deepen and refine students' understanding of what that concept can be, using more examples. When you use well-selected examples, it is possible to define the boundaries of what something *is* and what it *is not*.

For example if you have taught students what a subordinating conjunction is, you might then use a series of examples and non-examples and get them to discern which is which: (See page 37.)

> It is not only our duty to recycle, it is also imperative that we buy less plastic.
> Although it is our duty to recycle, we must buy less plastic, too.
> It is our duty to recycle and we must also buy less plastic.
> However much we recycle, we must also try to buy less plastic.

Notice that the topic of the example sentences remains the same, as does the order of clauses: 'recycle' followed by 'less plastic.' This means that students are able to see the defining properties of subordinating conjunctions, without being distracted by other features of the examples which aren't related to the concept at hand. They also get to see a number of different things which can constitute a subordinating conjunction – 'although . . . too,' '. . . not only . . . but also,' 'however much . . . also . . .'

The more examples students see, the broader and clearer their appreciation of the concept becomes because it is inclusive of more possibilities.

Variation can also be used as a springboard to discuss how language features have an impact on meaning. For example explaining why the use of an adjectival phrase placed at the start of a sentence might have a particular affect can seem a little abstract. By placing examples next to each other which vary from each other only slightly, we can highlight subtle but important language features and discuss how readers might experience them differently.

For example showing students a sentence *with* an adjectival phrase and then one without it (conceptual variation).

> **With:** *Absolutely mesmerising, the moon floated on the lake.*
> **Without:** *The moon floated on the lake.*

Or showing them the same sentence with one thing changed, such as putting the adjectival phrase at the end rather than at the beginning (rational variation).

> **Beginning:** *Exhausted and alone, the girl walked to the bus stop.*
> **End:** *The girl walked to the bus stop, exhausted and alone.*

Or showing fronted adjectival phrases in two different sentences which are used for different purposes in different types of writing (contextual variation).

> **Example 1:** *Exhausted and alone, the girl walked to the bus stop.*
> **Example 2:** *Criminally negligent, the officers were charged with misconduct.*

Each of these examples provides opportunity to explore the ways in which the versions are different and why that is. Doing something as simple as writing a sentence and changing as little as one word can have a profound impact on the sentence – a change to a single word could, in theory, change the meaning, tense, voice, perspective, genre, or tone of the whole sentence. This is why redrafting is so powerful. Taking time over these choices, from the minutiae all the way up to the larger structures, can be powerful.

Medium term: subsequent re-exposure and repetition

Re-exposure and repetition are important because unless we use knowledge, we forget. Neuroscientists call this process 'synaptic pruning' – the brain literally trims synapses which it thinks it no longer needs. If we haven't thought about something or used it in application for a while, our brains will likely eliminate it. Use it or lose it.

> (REMEMBER, synapses are brain structures which allow electrical or chemical signals to be transmitted. You can think of them as the connecting threads which tie pieces of knowledge together. Where there are multiple connections between across and between a body of knowledge, and those connections are strong and well-used, that is called a schema.)

We can support students to 'use' it through a huge range of activities (honestly, there are as many ways to achieve this as there are teachers in the profession), but here are a few strategies which are practical and don't require any excessive preparation:

- **Make explicit connections between new and existing knowledge**
  Take every opportunity to link grammar knowledge to knowledge students will be learning in subsequent lessons. When the content you are covering in one lesson can be enhanced by things you have covered in previous

lessons, you should reactivate that prior knowledge to support students to make links, but also to support them to encode the new learning. Simple questioning, retrieval, or discussion can enable those links to be made.

- **Ensure that models increase in complexity over time**

   If you use models in your initial teaching of a concept, you will hopefully start simple (as we suggested earlier), but then build in complexity. The more confident and secure students' knowledge is, the more sophisticated your models can become. Grammar is such an enormous field, and the concepts in grammar can be applied in virtually any context where written or spoken communication takes place, that the possibilities for models are virtually endless. For instance the earlier examples which use adjectival phrases (page 63) are relatively simple because those sentences are relatively short, and the adjectival phrases are only two to three words long. From this foundation, we could increase the complexity in a number of ways, and each one would serve to deepen student understanding of what this feature can do, how it interacts with its context in different ways, and how it can have an impact on meaning and readers.

   For example John Le Carre wrote this brilliant line in *Call for the Dead* (1961):

   Short, fat, and of a quiet disposition, he appeared to spend a lot of money on **really bad** clothes, which hung about his squat frame like skin on a shrunken toad.

   This is a more complex example than those adjectival phrases mentioned earlier because the text in question is more detailed. The sentence is longer and there are lots of elements which are doing adjectival work. The adjectival phrase here is 'really bad' – 'bad' being the head adjective, and both words modifying the noun 'clothes'. The complexity comes because there are a number of adjectives in this sentence: short, fat, quiet, bad, squat, shrunken. These might confuse a student looking for something which performs the function of an adjective. Discerning between a single word performing that job and a phrase which does the same is potentially more difficult. This all goes without mentioning the very noisy distractor of a simile sitting there in the final clause, also performing an adjectival function. Ensuring that students can distinguish between features, particularly when they are both present and overlapping, is something which belongs in this later stage of learning, where strong schema are being formed.

(REMEMBER: grammar features are often 'quiet' and understated when viewed alongside their more 'noisy' literary devices – particularly similes. Everyone knows what a simile is . . .)

- **Continue to check for understanding and misconceptions**

  Understanding isn't stable. Even if students appear to have firmly understood something, it is possible that they will become confused later as
  complexity increases and as there are more elements interacting with
  whatever feature you are working on.

  (WARNING: as we said on page 51, grammar concepts are defined by their
  function in context, so they are very prone to misconception for students
  and teachers alike.)

  You can check for understanding in many ways. The important thing is that
  whatever activity you design to ascertain levels of understanding actually tells
  you that information. For example if you want to see whether students have
  understood the concept of modality (see pages 129–136), you could set an essay
  and then see if they have used modal language. However, that wouldn't necessarily tell you anything for certain. If they have used modal language, they haven't
  necessarily done it because they know it is modal. If they haven't, they may
  know what it is but have chosen not to use it for this particular piece of writing.
  Far better, then, to check for understanding by explicitly asking them things like:

  > *Write a sentence about this image using a modal adverb.*
  > *This would tell you whether they can use a modal adverb independently.*
  > *Which of these words is a modal verb? Be, might, say, are*

  This would tell you whether they can identify a modal verb – the incorrect
  options (in multiple choice questioning usually called the 'distractors') have
  been chosen to be quite difficult in this case because they are all verbs, and
  'be' and 'are' are auxiliary verbs, so they are used very similarly to modal
  verbs like 'might.' If I was at an earlier point in the teaching of this concept, I
  might use easier distractors until student understanding was more secure.

  Select the most appropriate modal adverb to complete this sentence:

  > *Browning . . . . implies that the Duke is an obsessive and
  > sinister character.*
  > *Hardly   skilfully   clearly   outrageously*
  > *Explain why this is the most appropriate choice.*

  This would tell you that they can select a modal adverb from amongst
  other adverbs. One of the distractors – skilfully – is one which could work
  in this sentence, so students would need to understand the difference
  between this and the correct modal choice – clearly. If this was the question, it is possible that a student would select the correct answer but still
  not fully understand. For instance they might think that 'skilfully' is modal
  but decide that 'clearly' is better in the sentence. You won't have an accurate picture of their understanding unless you probe further. You could add:

What is the difference between 'skilfully' and 'clearly'?
OR
Why are 'hardly' and 'clearly' modal, while 'skilfully' and 'outrageously' are not?

If students fully understand what modality means, they will be able to explain that 'hardly' and 'clearly' indicate how certain the writer is about their interpretation and are therefore modal adverbs. The other two adverbs describe the quality or nature of Browning's craft – that he has written skilfully, or that his work is somehow shocking and outrageous.

(See more about modal verbs on page 32, and about modality for writing on pages 127–131.)

Constant monitoring of student understanding is a hallmark of good teaching. This isn't always obvious or visible – sometimes it is as subtle as a teacher observing student faces as they encounter a new question – it is very easy to sense the confidence in the room if you are tuned in to it. Teachers who read student work, listen to responses, and ask questions which probe every possible area where a misconception might be lurking, are able to catch problems and adapt their teaching to address them.

• **Ensure that activities are generative**
Generative learning 'involves actively making sense of to-be-learned information by mentally summarising and integrating it with one's prior knowledge, thereby enabling learners to apply what they have learned to new situations' (Fiorella and Mayer, 2016 – 'Eight Ways to Promote Generative Learning'). The bottom line is that learning is an active process and relies on creating connections between new information and knowledge they already have in their memory. For activities to be truly generative, students should experience healthy struggle and consciously make links between new and existing knowledge. For instance summarising is a key activity recommended for generative learning. We might ask students to summarise what they have learnt about sequencing conjunctions. This activity has the potential to be effective, but this depends on the set-up and expectations which accompany it. For example:

> Student 1 writes a summary. They copy out the definition and examples they can see on the board. They also write a few bullet points of what they remember from when their teacher explained the concept.
> Student 2 writes a summary. There is nothing on the board. They write a definition in their own words and give a couple of examples in their own sentences. They then explain how sequencing conjunctions are similar or different to other conjunctions they know (such as those which create emphasis or indicate contrast (see *discourse markers* in Chapter 6, page 171)). They then explain how sequencing conjunctions might be very effective in certain types of text, such as when writing instructions or constructing points in an argument in a logical order.

Student 1 will get *some* benefit from their summary, but anything which largely involves copying lacks the necessary challenge to ensure that learning is taking place .

Student 2 is writing from memory. It will be important to check that this student has remembered the definition accurately and that their examples are correct. The most effective part of the second example, though, is the way the student makes deliberate connections between this new concept and other things which they know. This means that the new knowledge will be more easily integrated into existing schema. The student also talks about how this feature will be helpful to them in the context of their writing – this engenders a powerful sense of grammar knowledge being meaningful and genuinely useful.

The second summary is clearly excellent, but there is no reason why it cannot be scaffolded using prompts like these:

1. Define sequencing conjunction
2. Write three sentences which use sequencing conjunctions
3. What other types of conjunctions do you know?
4. How are sequencing conjunctions different to some other types of conjunction?
5. What types of text might benefit from using sequencing connectives? Why?
6. How could you have used sequencing conjunctions in writing you have done during this unit? How might you use them in a future piece of work?

(We have found the mapping of grammar concepts to be particularly powerful. Examples of visual models of grammar concepts and the relationships between them can be seen in all our student-friendly definitions, but this is also something we discuss at length in Section 3.)

In the longer term, you might aim to get students to habitually write notes which include a summary addressing: definition in my own words; my own examples; connections with other similar things I already know; how I might use this in the future . . .

Fiorella and Mayer (2016) recommend eight different activities which can be highly effective for generative learning: summary, mapping, drawing, imagining, self-testing, self-explaining, teaching, enacting .

- **Retrieval practice: building stronger pathways in memory**
  Huge swathes have been written about retrieval practice in schools – it is an area which has been thoroughly explained by people more expert than us. The bottom line is that information needs to be repeated and retrieved to avoid synaptic pruning and to strengthen neural networks. The more students are asked to retrieve knowledge from their long-term memory and bring them into their working memories for use in a task, the faster and stronger those pathways in the memory become.

(NOTE: we would recommend 'Make it Stick' and any of the brilliant *Retrieval Practice* books by Kate Jones.)

(REMEMBER what we said about repetition earlier. If the brain doesn't use something, it begins to trim away structures which it decides it doesn't need any more. This has the rather pleasing name: *synaptic pruning*.)

We can achieve gains through retrieval practice if these activities are:

Low stakes – lots of quizzes and questions which put students into a state of struggle are potentially damaging. Ensure that such quizzes are low stakes (i.e. you aren't placing undue pressure on the outcome by recording results).

Designed as **learning activities in their own right**, rather than for the purpose of assessment (i.e. it is the struggle of retrieving knowledge from long-term memory which is the point, rather than getting right answers).

Well designed – in the case of multiple-choice questions, distractors are well selected. In the case of questions, they are carefully worded and unambiguous.

(WARNING: A poorly written prompt or question, or badly chosen distractor, can render an activity pointless. We have mentioned distractors in particular throughout this section, because they can be selected deliberately to vary challenge, but can also be problematic when not fully thought through.)

Grammar teaching in the classroom – what is important?

Teaching grammar over time is about more than the activities you do in the classroom. It is about maintaining a culture of language awareness in the classroom. We should frequently expose students to grammar features in context, make deliberate use of precise language, and encourage students to do the same.

In the long term, we must move from students *knowing* things about grammar, to the meaningful application of that knowledge in both their reading of language, and their own crafting of language. Section 3 explores a range of practical applications of grammar in literary analysis, critical reading, and teaching writing in a range of forms.

Ultimately, classroom grammar teaching relies on really excellent and intelligently crafted curriculum. We will explore curricular mapping for grammar in Section 4.

Before we move into these areas, though, we have tried in the next section to make links between the academic definitions of grammatical concepts in Chapter 3, and the teaching principles we have discussed throughout Chapter 4.

4.7

Grammar is a bit like film music - it can direct our attention, influence the way we read, build and structure ideas, but it remains in the background.

Grammar terms aren't absolute - they shift according to FUNCTION.

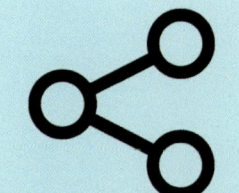

Language features interact with each other - grammar is really about the relationships between things on the page.

Teach concepts in grammar in the same way you would teach anything else. Look at Efrat Furst for a really excellent overview of how learning happens over time (https://sites.google.com/view/efratfurst/learning-in-the-brain?pli=1).

Maintain a culture of language awareness in the classroom: deliberate, explicit, precise.

Make grammar teaching an integrated part of a well-sequenced curriculum. (see Chapter 8)

QUICK SUMMARY: TEACHING GRAMMAR

SHORT TERM: initial encounter and comprehension

1 Simple, precise definition

2 Model examples. Simplicity first, then _in context_...

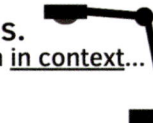

3 Examples and non-examples

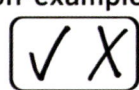

MEDIUM TERM: subsequent re-exposure and repetition

4 PROCESSING: MAKE STUDENTS THINK HARD

Gradually increase the level of challenge: maintain healthy struggle

LONG TERM: moving towards mastery

Deepen and apply knowledge and skill with increasing sophistication and fluency...

READING: Identify concepts in context, privileging meaning over feature spotting

WRITING: Craft language deliberately, selecting language devices with precision

SECTION 3

Reading and writing

English is, essentially, about giving students the knowledge and skill they need to *read* texts, and to *compose* texts. I say 'compose' rather than 'write' because communication isn't always written, and excellent speaking requires almost all the same knowledge of vocabulary, grammar, and context as does excellent writing. When we say 'composition,' we cover both speaking and writing.

Reading and composition are inextricably linked. Skilled and experienced readers have better language awareness (larger vocabularies, better knowledge of grammar and text structures, etc.), and are therefore often more skilled speakers and writers. In the same way, people who write fluently and speak with precision are better able to process the things which they read better.

In the subject of English Literature, we need students to be excellent readers. But it is more than reading in the sense of comprehension – we need students who are able to infer meaning from the way writers have used language. We have already shown a number of models where knowledge of grammar in particular enables extremely insightful analysis of literature. The clarity and accuracy which grammar can bring to the reading of literature is powerful, and we can draw on the best theories and models from linguistics to do so.

In this section, we will explore how grammar knowledge can act as a base for literary analysis and support critical reading. In the chapter which follows, we will look at the other side of the coin: grammar for composition.

5 Grammar for reading

STYLISTICS

Stylistics is an area of literary work which recognises the centrality of language to the study of literature. In this section, we highlight some of the key premises of stylistics and outline how they might be useful in the classroom.

As a starting point, it is sometimes useful to look at an example of what stylistics is not to see the benefits of using a language-centred approach for literary analysis. Here, for example a review in *The Guardian* (Adams 2020) on Martin Amis's novel *Inside Story* described it as

'this baggy, curious book'

On first glance, this might appear to be quite an original – and innovative – way of describing a book and, although this was taken from a newspaper review, it is not too dissimilar from the kind of comment found in mainstream academic literary criticism. But on close inspection, there are some very clear problems. Let's take each of the adjectives to see what these might be. First, 'baggy': what does this actually mean? How might a book be 'baggy' and why would this be an adequate way of describing a literary text? In fact, we can find out exactly how 'baggy' is used in English by consulting the British National Corpus (BNC), a dataset of over 96 million words from a range of different text types collected to show exactly how language gets used. Consulting a corpus like this is an easy and very useful way of looking at the contexts in which particular words or phrases get used. Searching for 'baggy' reveals 240 instances of the word with nearly all instances related to describing an item of clothing (i.e. as 'loose fitting'). The exceptions relate to uses of the term as a proper noun (the name of a person or a place) or, interestingly, in three instances as describing an eye or eyes. Put another way, 'baggy' has quite a fixed meaning and using it to describe a book is incredibly unusual. We can unpick this a little more to think about how a book might be 'baggy'? Is a book loose? In what way? The only explanation that comes to mind immediately is that it might have too many words or possibly too much description in places. Maybe the writing isn't 'tight' enough (whatever that means . . .). The problem is, of course, that we are working with a metaphor here and one that is hard to pin down and will inevitably draw different definitions and interpretations from different readers. The more I think about what 'baggy' might mean, the less I am sure about what it does mean and its effectiveness as an adjective in analysing literature.

To a lesser extent, a similar problem exists for 'curious.' Again, a quick search of the BNC reveals two common uses: to describe someone's desire to know more, e.g. 'I was curious'; and to describe something strange, e.g. a 'curious mixture.' Of the 2,115 instances of 'curious,' there are three instances of 'curious book' using the latter sense but all refer to 'book' in the academic sense rather than a novel. It's clear then, that describing a book as 'curious' is unusual in itself.

What can we make of all this? Well, it seems that 'baggy, curious book' is a very idiosyncratic way of responding to a text and one that brings with it lots of problems. What does 'baggy' mean if it is being used metaphorically? How can I understand the critic's points when how I interpret 'baggy' might be different to someone else? Why describe a book as 'curious'? Does this mean 'strange' (and if so, why not write 'strange') or does it mean something else? And so on. In effect then, this can become a very frustrating exercise in trying to work out exactly what the writer means; the rhetoric obscures the meaning.

Stylistics offers another – and better – way by being grounded in language analysis and presenting ideas not by attempting to be super innovative or rhetorical but instead by paying close attention to language and describing a text using clear and commonly understood terminology. As an example, here is the opening to 'The Tragedy of Pondicherry Lodge,' Chapter V of *The Sign of the Four* by Arthur Conan Doyle.

> It was nearly eleven o'clock when we reached this final stage of our night's adventures. We had left the damp fog of the great city behind us, and the night was fairly fine. A warm wind blew from the westward, and heavy clouds moved slowly across the sky, with half a moon peeping occasionally through the rifts. It was clear enough to see for some distance, but Thaddeus Sholto took down one of the side-lamps from the carriage to give us a better light upon our way.
>
> Pondicherry Lodge stood in its own grounds, and was girt round with a very high stone wall topped with broken glass. A single narrow iron-clamped door formed the only means of entrance. On this our guide knocked with a peculiar postman-like rat-tat.
>
> 'Who is there?' cried a gruff voice from within.
>
> 'It is I, McMurdo. You surely know my knock by this time.'
>
> There was a grumbling sound and a clanking and jarring of keys. The door swung heavily back, and a short, deep-chested man stood in the opening, with the yellow light of the lantern shining upon his protruded face and twinkling distrustful eyes.

Students often say that this opening is 'atmospheric,' but that doesn't get us much further than the claims that *Inside Story* is a 'baggy, curious book.' What we can do, however, is look at the grammar of the opening to *The Sign of the Four* for evidence of how this extract might be atmospheric and, in doing so, focus explicitly on the language responsible for this particular possible effect.

What we see in the first paragraph is the building up of the story through the setting of time, 'nearly eleven o'clock,' and the noun 'adventures,' which we could argue positions the reader to expect something exciting and mysterious. The paragraph then continues with a string of pre-modified noun phrases: 'damp fog,' 'great city,' 'warm wind,' 'heavy clouds,' all of which add more descriptive detail so that the background to the events that follow is presented clearly and evocatively (you can test this by simply deleting the modifying adjectives and thinking about what the effect might be). The atmosphere is also evoked in the way that movement is highlighted, in the verbs 'reached' and 'left' and the prepositional phrase 'behind us,' all of which track the journey of the narrator relative to space, thus again enriching the narrative world we are being asked as readers to imagine. This richness is amplified in movement of the wind, clouds, and moon and then the viewpoint we are positioned to adopt at the end of the first paragraph, imagining that we are looking out ahead with the characters, here helped by the side-lamp that shines through the dark.

(Read more about prepositional phrases on page 30.)

(REMEMBER what we said about modification on page 25.)

In the second paragraph, we see the continued use of modified noun phrases, 'a very high stone wall' and 'broken glass.' The further description of the door, 'A single narrow iron-clamped door' has three pre-modifying adjectives, which might be said to attract our attention; it is also interesting that the door retains the initial position, marked by the prepositional phrase 'on this,' in the final sentence of the paragraph rather than the more usual 'Our guide knocked on this.' The alliterative and onomatopoeic 'peculiar postman-like rat-tat' is also a strong attention-grabbing device to focus our attention on the event surrounding the door.

Finally, the atmosphere of the extract is heightened first by two instances of direct speech: the first has a reporting clause 'cried' but notice the noun phrase 'a gruff voice' that follows it is mysterious but the second represents simply the words spoken (we can call this free direct speech). As the door opens, the mysterious atmosphere is maintained through the onomatopoeic modifier 'grumbling' and the nouns 'clanking' and 'jarring' and then the attention that shifts first to the door and then to the man standing in the opening. Here too, pre-modified nouns, 'short deep-chested man,' 'yellow light,' 'protruded face,' and 'twinkling distrustful eyes' are significant in maintaining the atmosphere which has preceded this part of the chapter.

This analysis demonstrates that there are some clear patterns emerging in the grammar of this extract: language that orientates the reader in a particular time and place, sustained pre-modification of nouns in noun phrases, and the shifting of attention between particular aspects of the scene being described such as the travelling carriage, the door of Pondicherry Lodge, and, following the opening of the door, the man who appears behind it. The way that we as readers are encouraged to imagine this fictional world seems a crucial part of Doyle's craft here, and we can discuss it in an open and, we would argue, enabling way through the close attention to language rather than our own simple impressionistic remarks.

We can encourage this same kind of enquiry and practice easily enough in our classrooms by encouraging students to focus on the language of texts and draw on their understanding of language concepts. Paying close attention to the grammar of a text can provide real insight into the craft of literature. We would also argue that it makes for a much better type of literary criticism for the following reasons:

1. If students are confident in their linguistic knowledge and comfortable using it, then they will naturally be more confident at analysing literature. This means that they will naturally be less reliant on the teacher or pre-taught interpretations of texts.
2. Students will be less likely to 'feature spot.' Having a good knowledge of how language works enables students to pick out the most salient language features and the ones that are likely to support higher-level responses and interpretations.
3. Linguistic and grammatical knowledge enables a student to show their 'working out' and so responses will naturally have evidence to back them up.
4. Linguistic and grammatical knowledge generally results in a better clarity of expression. The key to stylistics is explanation in commonly agreed terminology and in a way that is easily followed and understood by anyone reading it. Students will aim for this kind of writing instead of obscure, pseudo-academic jargon that may sound impressive but offers little in the way of presenting an analysis carefully and precisely.

In stylistics, one way of thinking about the affordances of language-centred work on texts is captured in Paul Simpson's idea of the 3Rs (Simpson 2014). We like these because they highlight for us what we feel should be present in students' work.

1. Rigorous: the analysis should be clearly framed in established and commonly agreed methods and terms for describing language.
2. Retrievable: the analysis should be clear and presented in a way that anyone reading it can understand and follow the argument.
3. Replicable: the analysis should be such that someone else could use the same tools and ideas and reach the same interpretation of a text (although this does not mean that it is the only possible interpretation).

These are basic principles that underpin good text analysis (of non-literary as well as literary texts), and we will continue to draw on them throughout the rest of this chapter.

Grammar and poetry

In this section, we present some ways in which teachers can draw on grammatical ideas to explore different texts, focusing on extended case studies from poetry and from media and non-fiction writing. We start with a grammatical/stylistic analysis of each of the texts before presenting some ideas on how teachers might approach these in the classroom. We begin with 'Exposure,' a poem by Wilfred Owen:

Exposure

Our brains ache, in the merciless iced east winds that knive us...
Wearied we keep awake because the night is silent...
Low drooping flares confuse our memory of the salient...
Worried by silence, sentries whisper, curious, nervous,
   But nothing happens.

Watching, we hear the mad gusts tugging on the wire,
Like twitching agonies of men among its brambles.
Northward, incessantly, the flickering gunnery rumbles,
Far off, like a dull rumour of some other war.
   What are we doing here?

The poignant misery of dawn begins to grow...
We only know war lasts, rain soaks, and clouds sag stormy.
Dawn massing in the east her melancholy army
Attacks once more in ranks on shivering ranks of grey,
   But nothing happens.

Sudden successive flights of bullets streak the silence.
Less deadly than the air that shudders black with snow,
With sidelong flowing flakes that flock, pause, and renew,
We watch them wandering up and down the wind's nonchalance,
   But nothing happens.

Pale flakes with fingering stealth come feeling for our faces –
We cringe in holes, back on forgotten dreams, and stare, snow-dazed,
Deep into grassier ditches. So we drowse, sun-dozed,
Littered with blossoms trickling where the blackbird fusses.
   – Is it that we are dying?

Slowly our ghosts drag home: glimpsing the sunk fires, glozed
With crusted dark-red jewels; crickets jingle there;
For hours the innocent mice rejoice: the house is theirs;
Shutters and doors, all closed: on us the doors are closed, –
   We turn back to our dying.

> Since we believe not otherwise can kind fires burn;
> Now ever suns smile true on child, or field, or fruit.
> For God's invincible spring our love is made afraid;
> Therefore, not loath, we lie out here; therefore were born,
>   For love of God seems dying.
>
> Tonight, this frost will fasten on this mud and us,
> Shrivelling many hands, and puckering foreheads crisp.
> The burying-party, picks and shovels in shaking grasp,
> Pause over half-known faces. All their eyes are ice,
>   But nothing happens.

There's plenty that could be discussed in terms of the language and grammar of this poem but here, we want to focus on two particular aspects of this text that we think a grammatical analysis offers very interesting insights into: agency and the use of space.

Agency in the poem

This poem is interesting in how it highlights agency (i.e. who or what has the ability to undertake actions). We can explore patterns that emerge through looking at the grammar connected to two sets of agents: first, the soldiers, identified through the first person plural pronoun, 'we'; and second, the various elements of the landscape, including the weather and machinery of warfare, in which the soldiers find themselves.

(Read more about agency on pages 13–16, and pages 40–42.)

    The aspect of grammar we'll use is the distinction made in Chapter 3 (page reference) between types of verb processes: material (verbs denoting action); relational (verbs denoting states of being, appearing, or seeming); mental (verbs denoting cognitive processes); and verbal (verbs denoting actions that involve speech). So what we can do is take each of the clauses in the poem and identify the subject and the type of verb. If we do this for first, the soldiers, and second, the landscape, we find the following (in each instance, the verb has been underlined):

Soldiers:

> Our brains <u>ache</u>
> sentries <u>whisper</u>
> we <u>keep awake</u>
> we <u>hear</u>
> We only <u>know</u>
> We <u>watch</u>
> We <u>cringe</u> [. . .] and <u>stare</u>
> we <u>drowse</u>
> our ghosts <u>drag home</u>
> we <u>turn back</u>

we <u>lie</u>
their eyes <u>are</u> ice

Landscape:

iced east winds [. . .] <u>knive</u>
flares [. . .] <u>confuse</u>
the night <u>is</u>
mad gusts <u>tugging</u>
gunnery <u>rumbles</u>
dawn <u>begins to grow</u>
rain <u>soaks</u> and clouds <u>sag</u>
Dawn <u>massing</u> [. . .] her melancholy army/<u>Attacks</u>
bullets <u>streak</u>
air [. . .] <u>shudders</u>
flakes that <u>flock</u>, <u>pause</u>, and <u>renew</u> [. . .] <u>wandering</u>
Pale flakes [. . .] <u>come feeling</u> for our faces
this frost <u>will fasten</u>/<u>Shrivelling</u> many hands [. . .] <u>puckering</u> foreheads crisp.

What becomes apparent then, is that the soldiers are largely presented in ways that downplay actions and instead emphasise their static nature against the background conditions in which they find themselves or else are simply presented in various stages of thinking and feeling, as passive observers rather than active participants. Even in the two clauses that do present actions, 'our ghosts drag home' and 'we turn back' offer negative representations of the soldiers and their movements.

In contrast, the landscape is full of agency, often animated and suggestive of violence. The weather is often personified so as to be presented as acting *on* the soldiers and aspects of warfare such as the 'gunnery' and 'bullets' are equally given subject position within the clause as they assume actions. The effect then is a grammatical reversal of what we might normally expect: the human soldiers' agency is downplayed, and the landscape and machinery of war is highlighted as powerful and dangerous.

Grammar and space

A second interesting pattern is how space is presented in the poem. Here we can draw on our knowledge of prepositions to explore how Owen presents the relationship between the soldiers and the natural world. Since prepositions show the relationship between one thing and another in terms of space or time, again we can map out all examples in the poem and then interpret the significance of the patterns that emerge.

(Read more about prepositions on page 27.)

<u>in</u> the merciless iced east winds
the mad gusts tugging <u>on</u> the wire,
men <u>among</u> its brambles.

Dawn massing <u>in</u> the east her melancholy army
We cringe <u>in</u> holes, back <u>on</u> forgotten dreams,
Deep <u>into</u> grassier ditches.
<u>on</u> us the doors are closed, –
Tonight, this frost will fasten <u>on</u> this mud and us

Again, this simple observation reveals that 'in' and 'on' are the most frequently used prepositions. It's worth unpicking the meaning of prepositions a little more at this stage to show the significance of some of these choices. As we have already mentioned, prepositions present relationships in terms of space or time: 'in' shows a relationship that is a little bit like a container where one thing is enclosed within another. This can be literally, e.g. 'The toy is in the box' or meta-phorically, e.g. 'She is in love'; 'on' shows a different kind of relationship where one thing rests on top of another (the opposite is true of the preposition 'under'). It's useful to show these relationships (and others denoted by various preposi-tions) in a visual way as in Figure 5.1.

What becomes apparent from looking at the prepositions in 'Exposure' is that the soldiers are more often than not described as being enclosed and unable to move beyond the situation they are in. This sense comes about due to the use of 'in' but also because of similar prepositions 'among' (which denotes a similar kind of enclosure) and 'into' which shows the process of moving into an enclosed space. Equally, the two instances of 'on' show the soldiers at the bot-tom of the relationship – in other words, something happens (a door closing or the frost settling) that covers them.

How might we interpret these patterns? Well, one way would be to connect the grammar of prepositions to the grammar of verb types that we explored earlier. It seems plausible to suggest, and it can be supported with grammatical evidence, that the use of prepositions through which the sol-diers are presented as being enclosed within or underneath something else is another means by which their agency is downplayed – they literally and

5.1

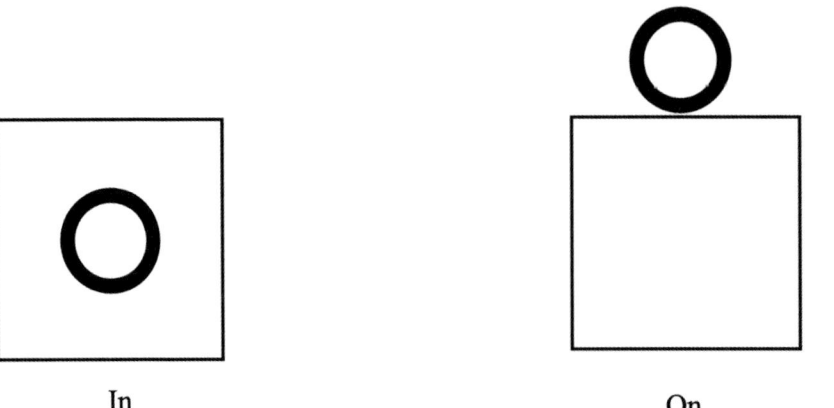

In   On

metaphorically are trapped. The poem's grammar then presents the soldiers as being denied space.

So far we have explored some of the grammar of the poem and connected specific language features to interpretative effects. These have highlighted some interesting ways in which soldiers are represented in the poem and could form the basis for extended discussion. Although we have focused on two key aspects of grammar (verb types and prepositions), it would clearly be possible to focus on some other aspects as well. For example you could ask students to examine Owen's use of abstract versus concrete nouns or adjectives.

It's also possible, of course, to use this language-focused analysis together with some wider contextual knowledge to enrich students' understanding of Owen's work. One of the perennial decisions to face when teaching literature is how much contextual information to present to students before they start looking at the text. This is tricky because on the one hand, providing background facts (e.g. on the historical, cultural, or social context, on the writer's life, or on the meaning of certain words) can provide valuable information that can help a student to start to make sense of a text; on the other hand, foregrounding this information too much can encourage students to fall back on facts at the expense of the text itself and their own interpretations with the result that any written response may end up looking more like a history essay than a literary one. There isn't the space in this book to set out a detailed set of ideas about how this conundrum can be overcome, but generally we would advise that background information should initially be kept to that which is essential for an overall sense of the text and to aid comprehension (e.g. difficult words) and that students should be guided to explore the text's language first and foremost.

With Owen's poem, then, it might be useful to provide some very basic context about the First World War and Owen's involvement in it as well as some information about conditions at the Front (although we could also assume that much of this information could be gained through reading the poem itself). It might also be useful to define any vocabulary that might be unfamiliar (although again, this could well come from reading the poem and drawing on the context in which words appear). It should also be clear, from our previous discussion, that paying close attention to the language of the text in itself might promote a renewed focus on context. For example the discussion of the ways in which the soldiers are passivised and insularised, denied both agency and space could quite easily lead to a discussion of conditions at the Front, to the abhorrent weather that soldiers had to endure, perhaps by studying first-hand accounts at the Front, and to other texts that identify similar situations, so that students read Owen's poem in the context of a broader set of texts that examine the soldiers and the landscape. There are plenty of poems, for example that focus on mud that could be read in conjunction with Owen's to get a broader sense of this kind of landscape poetry: see Mary Borden's famous 'The Song of the Mud', or the harrowing account of a soldier's death in Herbert Read's

'Kneeshaw Goes to War' (it would be interesting for students to analyse the verbs in this extract as well!).

> A man who was marching by Kneeshaw's side
> Hesitated in the middle of the mud,
> And slowly sank, weighted down by equipment and arms.
> He cried for help;
> Rifles were stretched to him;
> He clutched and they tugged,
> But slowly he sank.

Broadening out the biographical, literary, and cultural contexts, students could also explore the ways in which prepositions and other language features that suggest a sense of space in other Owen poems. For example the fragment 'Cramped in that funnelled hole,' thought to be an early version of one of his 'dawn' poems which influenced the writing of 'Exposure,' could equally be explored in terms of its prepositions and language of space.

> Cramped in that funnelled hole, they watched the dawn
> Open a jagged rim around; a yawn
> Of death's jaws, which had all but swallowed them
> Stuck in the bottom of his throat of phlegm.
>
> They were in one of many mouths of Hell
> Not seen of seers in visions; only felt
> As teeth of traps; when bones and the dead are smelt
> Under the mud where long ago they fell
> Mixed with the sour sharp odour of the shell

Finally, a language analysis could lead to exploring wider influences on Owen. First, the opening of 'Exposure' echoes Keats's 'Ode to a Nightingale,' 'My heart aches and a drowsy numbness pains/My sense,' and, in its depictions of a bleak and dangerous landscape, 'La Belle Dame Sans Merci,' 'The sedge has withered from the lake,/And no birds sing' and 'I saw their starved lips in the gloam.' By comparing the language of these poems, students can gain greater insight into Keats's influence on Owen and how for both poets bodily sensations are empha-sised, and the outside natural world is viewed as dangerous and giving rise to nightmarish visions.

Second, the way that agency is assigned to the landscape of war in 'Expo-sure' could be read against another key influence on Owen, Siegfried Sassoon. Here is part of Sassoon's diary entry from March 1916, four months after he had arrived at the Front. Again, an analysis of verbs and agency would help to understand the tradition in which Owen was writing.

Bullets are deft and flick your life out with a quick smack. Shells rend and bury, and vibrate and scatter, hurling fragments and lumps and jagged splinters at you; they lift you off your legs and leave you huddled and bleeding and torn and scorched with a blast straight from the pit.

Sassoon (1983: 48)

Overall, then, these final points highlight how holding back on context and instead making language the central focus of investigation can both allow the key aspects of the text themselves to be the initial centre of attention and naturally lead to other avenues of enquiry that connect with those language findings. In other words, what we are arguing for is that an analysis of grammar can often be a very good way of highlighting what contextual information may be worth pursuing and which can be downplayed to avoid less important knowledge dominating discussion at the expense of the text itself.

Using corpus tools

One really interesting way that teachers can encourage students to analyse grammatical patterns in texts is through the use of corpus tools. Corpus linguistics is the sub-field of linguistics that uses software to help analyse digitised versions of texts. The software can help to show patterns that would normally take a long time to draw out manually. In this section, we return to Wilfred Owen's poem 'Exposure' to show some simple ways that students could be encouraged to use corpus tools.

Initially, you'll need to download some corpus software. The software we are using here is called AntConc (Anthony 2022) and is free to download and one of the easiest tools to use. You'll then need to find an electronic version of the text (with Owen's poem, this is easy to find online) and save it as a txt. file. Once you have done that, you can enter it into the software.

We are going to use the corpus tool to support our initial work on the poem. In fact, an obvious use of such an approach is to provide evidence for what might appear to be initial hunches or intuitions about language in a text. For example we discussed the prepositions 'on' and 'in' in Section 2, but a corpus search of the ten most frequently occurring words in the poem reveals that these are in fifth and seventh places respectively.

What the corpus tool cannot do is analyse the significance of this frequency and this is an important point. So, any counting that the software can do will need to be accompanied by the kind of manual analysis of the text that we outlined in Section 2. But, and importantly, the software can draw your attention to patterns that you might not otherwise have seen and provide you with numerical evidence on which to develop analysis. In the case of the prepositions, we can see that their relative high frequency is potentially worth exploring.

We'll now turn to another word that scores highly in our initial frequency search, 'we.' Again, in Section 2, we discussed how we felt the grammar of

Rank	Word	Frequency
1	the	17
2	we	11
3	and	8
4	of	7
5=	on	6
5=	our	6
7=	in	5
7=	with	5
9=	are	4
9=	but	4
9=	for	4
9=	happens	4
9=	is	4
9=	nothing	4
9=	that	4
16	dying	3

Table 5.1

Word frequency in 'Exposure'

the poem presented the soldiers as passive or engaged in states of thinking or feeling whereas the landscape assumes a more active role. Again, the corpus tool can provide us with concrete evidence of this that can be used together with our manual analysis. Table 5.2 shows concordance lines (the occurrences of a word in the context in which they appear) for 'we.' Again, we can see that our initial observations about the types of verb that follow 'we' are supported by a thorough search of all the instances of the pronoun in the poem.

(Read more about pronouns on page 26.)

So far, we have looked at one single poem, but a corpus tool allows us to easily and quickly search for patterns across whole sets of texts in a way that simply would not be possible otherwise. So next, we look at some patterns in a whole collection of poems, taking the 1918 volume *Counter-Attack and Other Poems* by Owen's contemporary, Siegfried Sassoon. Again, this collection is easily available online to be entered into the corpus software.

There's plenty, of course, that we could discuss but we are going to focus on one particular feature to highlight how we can start with the patterns identified by the corpus tool and then build on those through grammatical/stylistic analysis. We'll start by using the tool to identify the two most frequently occurring nouns in the collection; a search tells us that 'war' and 'night' both appear 17 times. The frequency of 'war' might appear unsurprising in a collection of poems largely about the war, so we'll concentrate on 'night' and explore this word in context a little bit more to see what patterns emerge when we do a concordance search.

Table 5.2 Concordance of 'we' in 'Exposure'	blossoms trickling where the blackbird fusses. – Is it that	**we**	are dying? Slowly our ghosts drag home: glimpsing the
	doors are closed, – We turn back to our dying. Since	**we**	believe not otherwise can kind fires burn; Now ever
	flakes with fingering stealth come feeling for our faces –	**We**	cringe in holes, back on forgotten dreams, and stare,
	like a dull rumour of some other war. What are	**we**	doing here? The poignant misery of dawn begins to
	snow-dazed, Deep into grassier ditches. So	**we**	drowse, sun-dozed. Littered with blossoms
	curious, nervous, But nothing happens. Watching,	**we**	hear the mad gusts tugging on the wire, Like
	in the merciless iced east winds that knive us . . . Wearied	**we**	keep awake because the night is silent . . . Low drooping
	our love is made afraid; Therefore, not loath,	**we**	lie out here; therefore were born, For love of
	The poignant misery of dawn begins to grow . . .	**We**	only know war lasts, rain soaks, and clouds sag
	and doors, all closed on us: on us the doors are closed, –	**We**	turn back to our dying. Since we believe not
	With sidelong flowing flakes that flock, pause, and renew,	**We**	watch them wandering up and down the wind's

Table 5.3 Concordance of 'night' in *Counter-Attack and Other Poems*	'Thrushes'	Of dawn, and bold with song at edge of	**night,**	They clutch their leafy pinnacles and sing
	'Song Books of the War'	On summer morn or winter's	**night,**	Their hearts will kindle for the fight,
	'Repression of War Experience'	. . . I wish there'd be a thunder-storm to-	**night,**	With bucketsful of water to sluice the dark,
	'The Dream'	songs are full of odours. While I went Last	**night**	In drizzling dusk along a lane, I passed a
	'Break of Day'	Sussex lane in quiet September; slowly	**night**	Departs; And he's a living soul,
	'Invocation'	While dawn along the rim Of	**night'**	s horizon flows in lakes of fire,
	'Wirers'	coasts Gleams desolate along the sky,	**night'**	s misery ended. Young Hughes was badly
	'Prelude: The Troops'	The stale despair of	**night,**	Must now renew Their desolation
	'To Any Dead Officer'	, Moaning for water till they know It's	**night,**	and then it's not worth while to wake!)
	'Their Frailty'	him home again, She prays for peace each	**night**	Husbands and sons and lovers; everywhere
	'Banishment'	To those who sent them out into the	**night**	The darkness tells how vainly I have striven
	'The Triumph'	Beauty returned through the shambles of	**night;**	In the faces of men she returned;

(Continued)

'Twelve Months After'	who's out to win a D.C.M. some	**night;**	And Hughes that's keen on wiring	Table 5.3 (*Continued*)
'Together'	But at the stable-door he'll say good-	**night.**	Shaken from sleep, and numbed and scarce	
'In Barracks'	The bugle's lying notes that say, "Another	**night:**	another day." Come down from heaven	
'Break of Day'	of autumn in the air At the bleak end of	**night;**	he shivered there in a dank, musty dug-out	
'To Any Dead Officer'	Or been sucked in by everlasting	**night?**	For when I shut my eyes your face shows	

The corpus tool highlights some interesting patterns. For instance, 'night' appears four times as the head noun embedded in a prepositional phrase: 'edge of night' ('Thrushes'); 'end of night' ('Break of Day'); 'despair of night' (Prelude: The Troops), and 'shambles of night' ('The Triumph.' Often 'night' is quantified: 'last night' ('The Dream'); 'each night' ('Their Frailty'); 'some night' ('Twelve Months After'); and 'Another night' ('In Barracks'). In other places, 'night' is fully or semi-personified, for example in 'Break of Day' where 'night' has agency in the phrase 'slowly night departs,' and in 'Wirers' where the emotions associated with the soldiers in the wiring party are shown as being carried by the night itself, 'night's misery ended.' Only on one occasion, in 'To Any Dead Officer' is 'night' pre-modified by an adjective: 'everlasting night.' Put together then, we might summarise the following about Sassoon's use of 'night' in his collection:

* It is the most frequently occurring noun in the collection
* It is rarely modified by an adjective but sometimes forms the noun phrase within a prepositional phrase
* It is sometimes personified
* It is more often quantified either specifically or more generally.

Of course, how we (and students) might interpret these patterns and their significance is a task the corpus software cannot undertake – the analysis needs to come from the students, keeping in mind the central premises of what makes a good piece of stylistics.

Let's look at one final word in the collection, 'mud.' As we discussed in Section 2, the landscape of the Front is an important focus for First World War poets, and 'mud' in particular gets strong attention. So how does Sassoon use 'mud' in his collection? Table 5.4 shows the concordance of 'mud' in *Counter-Attack and Other Poems*.

The concordance shows that in five of the six occurrences, 'mud' is the noun embedded in a prepositional phrase, and that in four of these occurrences the preposition is 'in.' As we saw in Section 2, the preposition 'in' denotes one

Table 5.4

Concordance of 'mud' in *Counter-Attack and Other Poems*

'Glory of Women'	His face is trodden deeper in the	**mud**.	Dark clouds are smouldering into red
'Sick Leave'	I think of the Battalion in the	**mud."**	When are you going out to them again
'Attack'	And hope, with furtive eyes and grappling fists, Flounders in	**mud**.	O Jesu, make it stop!
'The Dream'	young Jones Stares up at me,	**mud-**	splashed and white and jaded
'Counter Attack'	And trunks, face downward, in the sucking	**mud,**	Wallowed like trodden sand-bags
'Together'	His hand will be upon the	**mud-**	soaked reins,

thing enclosing another. In these instances, we can look at the left context of the concordance lines to see just who is 'in the mud.'

> 'His face' ('Glory of Women') – an individual
> 'the Battalion' ('Sick Leave') – a group of individuals
> 'hope' ('Attack') – an abstract idea
> 'trunks' ('Counter-Attack') – a plural noun denoting a group

The fifth prepositional phrase is 'upon the mud.' 'Upon' is similar to 'on' in that it denotes a different kind of relationship between two things where one rests on top of the other. In this instance, 'mud' functions as a modifier for the noun 'reins.' In the final occurrence, 'mud' is used in a similar way, post-modifying the noun 'Jones.'

The pattern that emerges then shows that 'mud' as a single noun is wholly used in the prepositional phrase 'in the mud' but that Sassoon varies his description of who or what is 'in the mud,' most often referring to a group, but on one occasion specifying one individual and, on another, referring more broadly to an emotion or fear (although notice here the personification 'with furtive eyes and grappling fists'). Again, the corpus tool cannot interpret the significance of these patterns, but it would be a good starting point to discuss why Sassoon might use the idea of being 'in the mud' and why his descriptions largely focus on people (as opposed to say equipment). Of course, these findings could also be compared to another poem or set of poems to see whether 'mud' is used in a similar or dissimilar way and how the grammar of these texts can help us explain some of the patterns that emerge.

We think that this kind of work is exciting because corpus tools really do allow for the exploration of larger patterns of text. If you are looking to examine an even bigger set of texts than the poems we have looked at, then you might want to look at the Corpus Linguistics in Context (CLiC) tool which can be found at https://clic.bham.ac.uk/. You can access a considerable number of corpora of classic novels and novelists. It would be very easy to go to the 'Concordance' tab on the right-hand side, then select either a single text or a larger corpus and enter a word to see all the occurrences of that word in context. Students can then explore the significance of any patterns they see using their knowledge of grammar.

Grammar and non-fiction

As we saw in Chapter 2, grammar is central to the idea of representation (the way or ways in which a writer or speaker wishes to present a version of the world). In that chapter, we looked at how the distinction between the active and passive voice offers a way of thinking about how an event might be represented to draw attention to a particular aspect of it, for example responsibility for an action. Since the active voice foregrounds the agent in the clause, and the passive voice downplays or conceals agency, we can argue that analysing grammar is a powerful and enabling way of looking at some of the possible ideological motivations and effects of language choices. As we also saw in Chapter 2, news reporting can be a particularly good genre to explore since by its very nature, it is a genre where events can be framed very carefully (and often in contrast to other accounts of the same event) to foreground some aspect.

The next extract is taken from a BBC news (2020) report on fighting that took place in Delhi, following the introduction of a citizenship law.

> At least 37 people have been killed so far in the deadliest violence the Indian capital has seen in decades.
> The clashes first broke out on Sunday between protesters for and against a controversial citizenship law in north-east Delhi.
> But they have since taken on communal overtones, with reports of many Muslims being attacked.
> Even though the violence largely abated on Wednesday, there were reports of sporadic clashes in affected areas overnight and the city remains tense.
> www.bbc.co.uk/news/world-asia-india-51644861

We can use our knowledge of grammar to unpick some really interesting points about how blame is assigned (or not) here. First, let's set out all of the clauses one by one:

1. At least 37 people have been killed so far
2. in the deadliest violence the Indian capital has seen in decades.
3. The clashes first broke out on Sunday between protesters for and against a controversial citizenship law in north-east Delhi.
4. But they have since taken on communal overtones,
5. with reports of many Muslims being attacked.
6. Even though the violence largely abated on Wednesday,
7. there were reports of sporadic clashes in affected areas overnight
8. the city remains tense.

Initially, the report uses the passive voice, 'have been killed' (1) foregrounding the number of people killed but concealing any responsibility. Interestingly, the actions are then represented through the nouns 'violence' (2) and 'clashes' (3) rather than verbs; 'violence' describes the fighting generally without mentioning who the aggressor might be and 'clashes' works similarly, drawing attention to the fact that two sides were involved but without specifying who attacked whom (note that this could have been represented in a much different way to highlight who the aggressor was). 'Clashes' remains the referent of 'they' and therefore the subject of 'have since taken on' (4), which is followed with another passive form 'Muslims being attacked' (5) which again explicitly conceals agency. The pattern continues with the repetition of 'violence' (6) and 'clashes' (7) before 'the city remains tense' highlights the area rather than the people in it. In fact, this is an example of what is known as metonymy where one aspect of an entity is used to stand in for another; here the place for the people within it. Importantly, the effect seems to be to distance any sense of responsibility whatsoever. As we saw in Chapter 3, this can be a key effect of the passive voice. What we have here, in addition, is the use of nouns in place of verbs to further downplay agency, another form of what is known as *mystification*. Why might this representation be so dominant in this report? We can only guess, of course, but it seems that given the very sensitive nature of the conflict the BBC has been careful not to be seen to take sides and blame one party more than the other for the violence; the use of the passive voice and nouns rather than verbs helps them to achieve this aim.

Another powerful way that representations work is through metaphor. Metaphor can be a really enabling language topic to study since metaphors occur frequently across a wide range of texts (not just literary ones). They also tend to work in similar ways, by drawing on one domain of knowledge to help structure and represent another domain of knowledge. Our discussion of metaphor here draws on the classic treatment of metaphor by George Lakoff and Mark Johnson in their 1980 book *Metaphors We Live By*. Lakoff and Johnson explain that metaphor works by using a source domain (usually something concrete and familiar) to help us understand a target domain (usually something abstract and/or less familiar). Metaphors can be widespread and even near-universal, although clearly there are cultural and individual differences in how we think about concepts and ideas and express them through language. One very common example is how, in western culture, we tend to conceptualise our lives as a journey, captured in expressions such as 'I'll move on with my life,' 'I'm looking forward to what lies ahead' and 'That relationship came to an end' which represent life as moving along a path. Here the source domain of a journey (something concrete) is used to give structure to the more abstract idea of a life. The metaphor LIFE IS A JOURNEY (metaphors are conventionally written in small capitals) can be used by writers and speakers as a concrete way of explaining all the various aspects of life. Some of these are summarised in Table 5.5, with aspects of the target domain 'life' in the right-hand column given structure by aspects of the source domain 'journey' in the left-hand column.

Source domain 'journey'		Target domain 'life'
Travellers	⟶	People
Starting point	⟶	Birth
End point	⟶	Death
Events and actions experienced, and places visited	⟶	Episodes in life
Distance travelled	⟶	Progress in career, relationships, etc.
Deciding on a route	⟶	Making life choices
Obstacles on a journey	⟶	Problems in life to overcome

Table 5.5
Source and target domains for LIFE IS A JOURNEY (Originally in Giovanelli 2014: 70)

Let's have a look at how we might use metaphor to analyse some non-fiction writing. In this instance, we'll look at an extract from *The Crossing*, by Ben Fogle and James Cracknell, an account of the authors' involvement in a race across the Atlantic Ocean in a rowing boat called 'Spirit.' The following extract appeared on a recent GCSE paper:

I watched as a vast wave gathered behind the boat, soaring above the cabin, a wall of white water towering over our tiny boat. Once again I dug the oars in to propel us forward, but the wave was too big. For a moment it felt like we were moving backwards as we were sucked into the belly of the wave, the horizon disappearing as the churning surf enveloped the stern of the boat. I felt it lift, as a torrent of water crashed over the boat and I felt myself falling backwards. I was aware of the boat collapsing on top of me. I struggled to pull my feet from the stirrups to no avail. The world went black. I felt a weight on top of me and then a rush of cold water as my body was brutally submerged into the bottomless Atlantic Ocean. My feet were sucked from my shoes as I clung on to the oars for dear life, but then they too were dragged from my clasp. My mind went blank as I tumbled through the surf, spun around roughly like clothes in a washing machine.

(Fogle and Cracknell: 2006)

The authors initially use a metaphor in their representation of the wave's size relative to their 'tiny boat.' In this instance, we could argue that the metaphor is A WAVE IS A WALL. Here, although both are concrete objects, arguably a wall has more obvious characteristics that the writers appear to be drawing on to dramatically emphasise the wave. Some ideas for these characteristics are as follows:

Height: walls tend to be fairly or very high

Substance: walls tend to be built from a firm material

Strength: walls tend to be strong

Difficulty to overcome: walls can be difficult to overcome, e.g. due to height

Function (e.g. barrier): walls usually stop things coming in or going out

Problem: walls may be put up when there is a problem to solve

Drawing out some of the aspects of the source domain, 'wall,' would be a good starting point for exploring how this metaphor works in *The Crossing* and how effective it might be in representing the danger of the event Fogle and Cracknell find themselves in. Unpacking a metaphor in this way, rather than simply stating that it exists, can generate some interesting thoughts and insights that can be connected to other features of the writing (for example the alliterative use of 'w,' the ominous near personification of the wave that 'gathered behind the boat' and the choice of verb 'soaring' which suggests height, and because it is in the progressive form, a continual movement. A further metaphor, in the description of 'the belly of the wave' appears shortly afterwards. Waves don't have bellies, of course, so again the representation of the wave draws on a metaphor, here A WAVE IS A PERSON (personification can be understood as a specific type of metaphor). Again, unpicking some of the characteristics of the source domain 'person' could generate some interesting points; it seems the case here that being even more explicit and unpicking the characteristic that is specifically mentioned (a belly) would be very help-ful, for example a belly is where food goes once ingested, it's deep inside the body, hard to get out of and so on – indeed, this metaphor aligns with later representations of the ocean as deep and human-like: 'my body was brutally submerged into the bottomless Atlantic Ocean,' 'they too were dragged from my clasp.'

Finally, another metaphor in the extract occurs towards the end when the narrator describes himself as 'spun around roughly like clothes in a washing machine.' In this instance, the general metaphor A HUMAN IS AN OBJECT and a specific one A HUMAN BODY IS A PIECE OF CLOTHING is realised through a simile (a simile is a type of metaphor that uses 'like' or 'as' to introduce the comparison). We might even say that another metaphor THE OCEAN IS A WASHING MACHINE is also used here as part of the representation. Taken together, these metaphors really do provide a complex picture of the power of the ocean and the relative weakness of the human body at its mercy. Again, students can be encouraged to unpick these source domain characteristics and consider how readers might understand them to describe the situation in this extract.

As a final example, let's look at another extract again taken from a recent GCSE paper. This extract is from *Idle Days in Patagonia*, an account of travelling to South America by William Hudson.

> The wind had blown a gale all night, and I had been hourly expecting that the tumbling storm-shaken old steamship, in which I had taken passage to Patagonia, would turn over once and for all and settle down beneath the tremendous tumult of waters. For the groaning sound of its straining timbers, and the engine throbbing like an over-worked human heart, had made the ship seem like a living thing to me; and it was tired of the struggle, and under the tumult was peace. But at three o'clock in the morning the wind began to drop and, taking off the coat and boots, I threw myself in to my bunk for a little sleep.

The 'old steamship' that Hudson describes is personified mid-way in the extract through the phrase 'engine throbbing like an over-worked human heart.' Here we might say that there are two metaphors: the explicit AN ENGINE IS A HEART and the more general A SHIP IS A PERSON. Hudson extends these metaphors by explicitly stating that the ship 'is like a living thing to me.' Of course, these metaphors may be interpreted in different ways, but it seems that one significance of the person metaphor is that it portrays a sense of closeness between the narrator and the ship as they both suffer in the storm at sea.

CRITICAL READING

As we have shown in examples of political language in previous chapters, grammar has a significant role to play in supporting perceptive critical reading. We explained in Chapter 1 that some text features are 'noisy' and relatively obvious, while grammar features tend to be more subtle. One really useful strategy to support students to unearth the 'quieter' aspects of a text is to ask: 'what if . . .?'

Example passage – a charity campaign

> In 2016 we had no rain and our entire rice crop was ruined. We had no way to feed ourselves or our four children. I was scared. That winter we survived on a thin stew made from strained peas and the last of our grain. We couldn't have survived another year like that; the support we have received to manage our farm better has saved our lives and helped us to help our community, too.

This is written in first person. To get students to explore how this is effective as a text for a charity campaign, you could explore how the text would work in second or third person instead. Rewriting part of this text – either doing this as a teacher under a visualiser, live, or getting students to do it for themselves, or a mixture of the two – you can make clear comparisons, like so:

(Read more about first, second, and third person on page 191.)

We had no way to feed ourselves or our four children. I was scared.

Imagine having no way to feed yourself or your children. You would be scared.

She had no way to feed herself or her four children. She was scared.

These different versions are all highly emotive and explore the same ideas, but the way we engage with it as a reader is different in each one.

In first person, the text is immediate, personal, raw. There is an honesty to the line 'I was scared' which is arresting and might make a reader feel uncomfortable.

In second person, the reader is invited to empathise with the experience of this parent. They are directly challenged using the imperative 'imagine' and left considering how they might act in such a desperate situation.

In third person, the distance afforded by the pronoun 'she,' paired with the past tense, makes the account more abstract. The reader may feel a strong sense of sadness that some people experience such things, but there is no personal connection. We might argue that this is a less effective perspective from which to write if the purpose is to persuade the reader to part with their money.

Asking students to consider 'what if' we changed grammatical elements of the text enables them to see clear differences between the possible choices which writers make. We see similar things if we take a text from passive to active voice, or change tense. Such things can seem abstract for students until we really dig into direct comparisons such as this one to make the effect clear.

(NOTE: this is a really effective strategy to support students when they are looking at texts independently in situations akin to GCSE Language papers. Get them to notice the subtle features by thinking: if this word/phrase/sentence/section wasn't here, would it make a difference? If it was replaced with X, would it make a difference?)

WHAT COULD GRAMMAR-BASED ANALYSIS LOOK LIKE IN THE CLASSROOM?

Grammar-based analysis *looks* very much like any other analysis activity. We would always advocate live guided annotation of texts (using a visualiser, or on a board). The extent to which this is modelled by the teacher, or done independently by students and then shared, will depend entirely on the class: where they are in a sequence of learning and in their own grammar knowledge.

Just as you would explore language by identifying interesting words, images, and other devices, you can integrate grammar features where they are relevant. We find that the most powerful tool to support close language work in the classroom is to frame the text with questions – this way we can ask students things which will direct their reading of the text without giving them all the 'answers' from the start. We would look at the text and prepare those guiding questions or prompts in advance with the needs of our students in mind. Here is an example using a commonly taught poem:

My Last Duchess by Robert Browning

FERRARA

That's my last Duchess painted on the wall,
Looking as if she were alive. I call
That piece a wonder, now; Fra Pandolf's hands
Worked busily a day, and there she stands.
Will't please you sit and look at her? I said
"Fra Pandolf" by design, for never read
Strangers like you that pictured countenance,
The depth and passion of its earnest glance,
But to myself they turned (since none puts by
The curtain I have drawn for you, but I)
And seemed as they would ask me, if they durst,
How such a glance came there; so, not the first
Are you to turn and ask thus. Sir, 'twas not
Her husband's presence only, called that spot
Of joy into the Duchess' cheek; perhaps
Fra Pandolf chanced to say, "Her mantle laps
Over my lady's wrist too much," or "Paint
Must never hope to reproduce the faint
Half-flush that dies along her throat." Such stuff
Was courtesy, she thought, and cause enough
For calling up that spot of joy. She had
A heart – how shall I say? – too soon made glad,
Too easily impressed; she liked whate'er
She looked on, and her looks went everywhere.
Sir, 'twas all one! My favour at her breast,
The dropping of the daylight in the West,
The bough of cherries some officious fool
Broke in the orchard for her, the white mule
She rode with round the terrace – all and each
Would draw from her alike the approving speech,
Or blush, at least. She thanked men – good! but thanked
Somehow – I know not how – as if she ranked
My gift of a nine-hundred-years-old name
With anybody's gift. Who'd stoop to blame
This sort of trifling? Even had you skill
In speech – which I have not – to make your will
Quite clear to such an one, and say, "Just this
Or that in you disgusts me; here you miss,
Or there exceed the mark" – and if she let
Herself be lessoned so, nor plainly set

Her wits to yours, forsooth, and made excuse –
E'en then would be some stooping; and I choose
Never to stoop. Oh, sir, <u>she smiled</u>, no doubt,
Whene'er I passed her; but who passed without
Much the same smile? This grew; I gave commands;
Then all smiles stopped together. There <u>she stands</u>
As if alive. Will't please you rise? We'll meet
The company below, then. I repeat,
The Count your master's known munificence
Is ample warrant that no just pretense
Of mine for dowry will be disallowed;
Though his fair daughter's self, as I avowed
At starting, is my object. Nay, we'll go
Together down, sir. Notice Neptune, though,
Taming a sea-horse, thought a rarity,
Which Claus of Innsbruck cast in bronze for me!

We might use the following questions to frame our students' reading of the text:

- **Are there any repeated or linked words?**

  (NOTE: we might call this a *semantic field*.)

  This might reveal things which aren't grammar-based (such as lots of words linked to violence), but we might also identify things which are grammar-based. For example in this poem there are lots of pronouns/possessive determiners: 'my,' 'I,' 'her,' 'she.' This is significant because the identity of the Duchess is central to the poem – her name is omitted, and only the Duke and his 'nine-hundred-years-old name' is given prominence. The use of 'my' obviously emphasises his ownership and control over her, even in death, not to mention the repeated 'I' adding to our sense that the Duke is egocentric and considers his wife only in terms of her proximity to him. We might also be able to compare the personal 'I' and 'my' with the third person 'she' and 'her.' Her actions are being observed, monitored, judged, whereas his personal voice and feelings are being heard. The references to possession in this poem are a clear signifier of power.

  (Read more about pronouns and determiners on page 26.)

- **What are the verbs adding to this text?**

  This might sound a little silly, but verbs are genuinely a very useful place to start. Verbs are often (though not always!) the key to determining the action, movement, tone, and shifts in a text. For example in this poem, you might identify the verbs associated with the Duchess in the present tense – 'there she <u>stands</u>' repeated at the start and near the end. Then in the past tense: she 'thought,' 'liked,' 'looked,' 'rode,' 'thanked,' and 'smiled.' Her actions when alive were innocent, innocuous. In death, the Duke is able to keep her stationary – she 'stands' where he chooses .

- **Are there any unusually short sentence/lines or sequences of short clauses?**

  This might not always be a feature of the text you are looking at but can bear fruit. For instance, in this poem, there are frequent uses of clauses in parenthesis which give voice to the Duke's own thoughts, 'such stuff was a courtesy, <u>she thought</u>, and cause enough for calling up that spot of joy.' The clause in the centre here is not the Duchess's opinion, but the Duke's. The addition of 'she thought' makes it clear that this is a projection of his own anxieties and insecurities about his wife. Similarly, when he says 'thanked somehow – I know not how – as if she ranked . . .' the clause in the centre breaks the description of her behaviour with an expression of his own confusion. 'I know not how' is almost accusatory in tone – the use of this comment in parenthesis suggests that it is an aside where the Duke insinuates that something inappropriate happened. Again, Browning offers us nothing but the Duke's observations, and the use of this short clause adds to our impression that he is insecure without offering any credibility to his claims.

  (Read more about verbs on page 24.)

- **Who is explicitly named or mentioned in this poem, and how many other characters are implied?**

  Students will identify the names of the artists, Fra Pandolf and Claus of Innsbruck. They will identify the Duke and his Duchess who, though she doesn't get a name, is at least mentioned explicitly. There are other implied characters in the poem, though, and students will likely find reference to:

  'some officious fool'

  'men'

  Whoever the 'anyone' is who gave 'gifts' to the Duchess

  Whoever it is who was given 'commands' by the Duke

  'I gave commands'

  In this case, the Duke – 'I' – is the agent, 'gave' is the verb, but there is no patient. The sentence could have said: 'I gave commands to . . . NAME' – you could ask students to consider the difference between these options:

(REMEMBER: we talked about the agent and patient in Chapter 2, pages 13–16 and 40–42.)

I gave <u>her</u> commands

This would tell us clearly that he gave her commands and she 'stopped' 'smil(ing)'

I gave commands to <u>my Duchess</u>

This would do the same as earlier but would reiterate his possession of her by repeating the determiner 'my'

I gave <u>them</u> commands

This would imply that someone other than the Duchess herself was commanded to stop the smiles and would make it more apparent that some harm has befallen the Duchess

I gave commands to <u>my servant</u>

This might give a stronger indication that the Duke has given orders to his own people – the word 'my' suggests that whatever has happened to the Duchess is an extension of the Duke himself

Introducing a patient in each of these cases significantly changes the meaning of the line. The line 'I gave commands' is deliberately vague and adds to the sinister subtlety of the poem overall.

The framing questions mentioned could be given to students one by one – they could read the text (or listen to you reading it) and use the questions in turn to guide them to notice language features. The questions can be framed to reflect the needs of the group. For instance with some classes you might not need to be quite so specific – they might need more generalised prompts. With others, you might want to be far more direct in scaffolding their reading – that might include showing them where features are and asking questions about specific words, phrases, or lines. The extent to which you chunk or scaffold the text, and phrase the questions, can significantly change the level of challenge.

(REMEMBER: struggle is a prerequisite for learning, so it is important to have a strong understanding of how well your students have learnt concepts, and use that knowledge to ensure that your lessons are pitched at the right level . . .)

We hope it is clear from this short section that what we do with grammar-based analysis is the same as any other language analysis. This is the same as talking about metaphor and vocabulary, and it's often more interesting.

5.2

STYLISTICS is applying grammatical concepts to literary analysis.

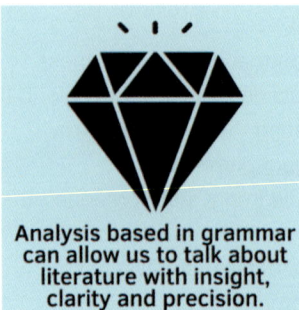

Analysis based in grammar can allow us to talk about literature with insight, clarity and precision.

Grammar knowledge can support students to read and interpret texts with greater confidence.

SIMPSON'S 3 Rs
Student work should be...

RIGOROUS: analysis should be clearly framed in established and commonly agred methods and terms for describing language.

RETRIEVABLE: analysis should be clear and presented in a way that anyone reading it can understand and follow the argument.

REPLICABLE: analysis should be such that someone else could use the same tools and ideas and reach the same interpretation of a text (although this does not mean that it is the only possible interpretation).

IN THE CLASSROOM...

Look at poetry, prose and drama through the lens of stylistics as well as what you might consider the more 'traditional' literary devices. Grammar concepts often provide more fruitful opportunity for close language work...

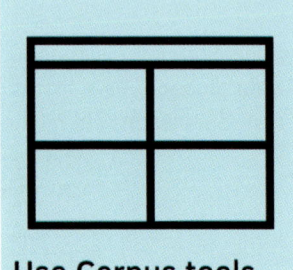

Use Corpus tools...

Frame text exploration with questions.

Consider ways in which non-fiction texts are shaped by grammatical choices. Remember - grammar directs *how* we read.

6 Grammar for writing

WHAT IS WRITING *FOR*?

Writing can be many things.

The obvious ones:

- **VERB**: *Writing* as a process so that students might apply their knowledge and improve their skill. That knowledge and skill is the subject of this chapter.

6.1.1

We write so that we can get better at writing.

- **NOUN**: *Written work* as a product which demonstrates evidence of learning. For instance when you ask students to write an essay about the poem you have studied, or write a speech during a speech writing topic, that written product is there for the teacher to read so that they can see how well the student has learnt and made progress. Writing can be used as 'evidence' of current student knowledge, understanding, and skill.

6.1.2

Teachers read students' written work to look at **progress** and further **areas for improvement.**

- **VERB**: *Writing* as a way to express and explore emotions. This can be a foundation for art, as well as a cathartic or therapeutic process in its own right. 6.1.3

We write to process and explore emotions.

Less obvious:

- **VERB**: Writing is a generative activity *in its own right*. The act of writing encourages the writer to process their ideas, to find clear and accurate language, to identify inconsistencies or gaps in arguments, to synthesise ideas, and ultimately, to generate new ones. No matter what your subject or topic, asking students to write about what they have learnt, to summarise or explain or connect ideas, is a powerful way to deepen and refine their understanding. 6.1.4

Writing brings clarity, supports better understanding and promotes the embedding of knowledge into long-term memory.

Even less obvious:

- **VERB**: When you *write* something down, you externalise it. The page becomes an extension of your working memory, and you essentially do your thinking *there*. This means that you have more capacity to think about complex things. Merlin Donald called this the 'external working memory field.' He posited that spoken information was transient (in that it immediately ceases to exist once the utterance is spoken), but that written expression allowed for 'longer trains of thought' (Donald 2017).

6.1.5

The page you are writing on becomes an extension of your working memory and effectively means you can develop more complex ideas and expressions.

- **NOUN**: Your thoughts as a written product make it possible for you to read them back, reflect, redraft, and refine both your expression and your understanding of something.
- **NOUN**: Your thoughts as a written product have the potential to form the basis of *other people's* thoughts. Made public, that written work can be subject to debate, development, scrutiny, as well as becoming combined with other ideas or applied to new contexts. Ideas which are written down have the potential to become part of a wider philosophy.

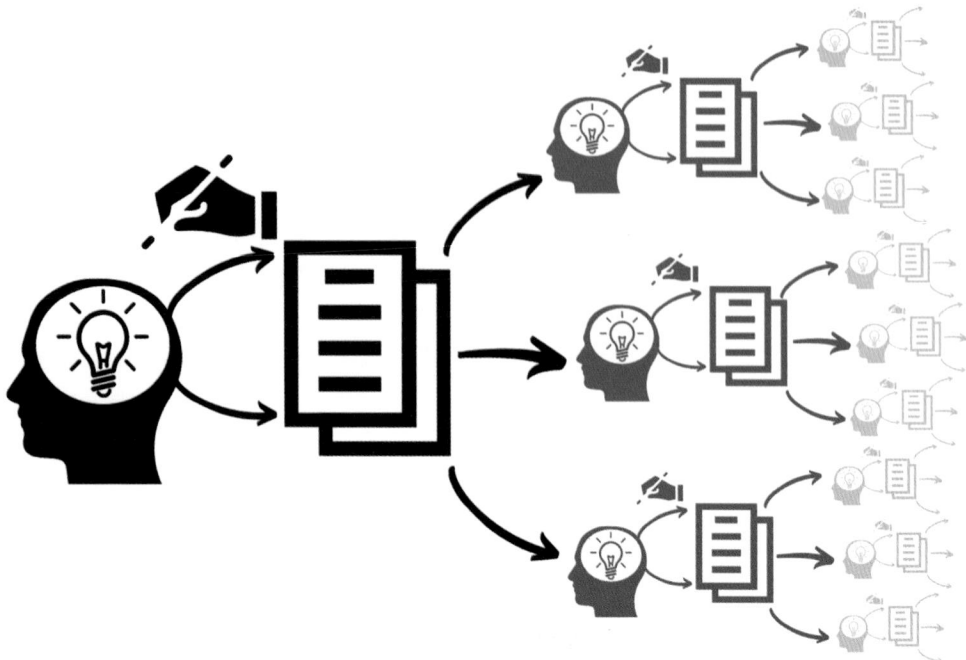

Written work can form the basis of the thinking and writing of other people. Ideas written down evolve through academic discourse, inquiry and debate. They prompt and influence more writing, and the process continues...

6.1.6

What does all this have to do with grammar*?*

We have just seen how writing can enhance not just what we say, but *how we think*. Our brains hold multiple ideas at once and can combine them in interesting ways, but this isn't always matched by our ability to reflect that complexity in writing. In English Literature analysis, for instance the best interpretations often come from combining concepts and exploring how different elements of texts influence each other. In order that students might think about things which are highly complex, they need to know how to write those things down. This is where explicit grammar instruction comes in. In his excellent introduction to Hochman and Wexler's *The Writing Revolution*, Doug Lemov explains the issues which arise from a lack of grammar knowledge for writing:

> Students [. . .] did not often have control of a sufficient number of syntactic forms and tools to capture and express complex thoughts. They could not express two ideas happening at once with one predominating over the other. They could not express a thought interrupted by a sudden alternative thesis. Their ideas were poor on paper because their sentences could not capture, connect and, ultimately, develop them [. . .] and because, as a result, they did not practise capturing and connecting complex ideas with precision in writing, they had fewer complex ideas.

The things which Lemov is referring to – those which enable students to write about 'two ideas happening at once,' to introduce an 'alternative thesis,' to 'connect' and 'develop' ideas – are all grammatical constructs. Subordination, modality, discourse markers, apposition, and the myriad other features which students might employ to express complexity must be taught explicitly in order that their writing *and* their thinking can soar.

In an interview with Edweek, Natalie Wexler defended her promotion of explicit grammar instruction in *The Writing Revolution*, saying:

> Writing is an extremely complex process, so if you're trying to think about the mechanics and master those at the same time you're trying to express yourself, you have less creativity left over to think about your content – what it is you want to say. But if you've got those tools of crafting interesting sentences under your belt so they become more or less automatic, then you can unleash your creativity and really focus your limited brainpower on what you want to say.
>
> (Loewus 2017)

In this section on writing, we will explore the areas of grammar knowledge which we feel enable brilliant writing in a range of forms, and we'll provide practical strategies for teaching this knowledge in the English classroom in a way which is done meaningfully and in the long term.

MODELLING

Writing: why model everything*?*
Modelling is one of the most powerful teaching strategies we have – all teachers model in some way or another, regardless of subject or student cohort. We talked about modelling as part of the process for teaching grammar concepts in Chapter X (pages X-X)– that was modelling to boost explanation of concepts during initial instruction.

Modelling for writing is different. When you model writing live, you demystify a *process*, taking it from an invisible miracle and moving it into the light of day where students can see the series of very simple choices, struggles, and ongoing revisions which produce the final product.

Live versus pre-prepared modelling:
the <u>instant miracle</u> vs. the <u>complex process</u> exposed

'Here's one I
made earlier!'

Exposed thinking: concepts,
structure, choices, artistry,
style, revision... a messy,
non-linear process.

6.2.1

Writing is immensely complex because much of the process of writing is invisible or private. The thinking happens in our heads, and the physical writing happens on our page. It's not like a movement in dance – we have to choose deliberately to showcase the physical and cerebral part of writing, or they remain a mystery.

There are literally thousands of decisions which writers might make about the words, positioning, phrasing, and structure of their work. By FIRST teaching students what these possibilities are and THEN showing them how to apply that knowledge through live modelling of writing, students can start to make those choices. *Should they use this word or this other word? Should they stop here and start a new sentence, or should they continue to modify and develop this image? Should they use this rather controversial example or be more measured? Should they phrase this as a series of questions or use a bullet point list?* The options are endless.

Ideally the teacher will hand-write under a visualiser, so that all students can see them constructing language in real time, and they will provide a live commentary (i.e. speak out loud) to explain what they are thinking and the choices they are making as they write. This isn't just a strategy for writing model paragraphs or essays. We can (and should) model writing at all levels, including planning writing; vocabulary selection; crafting phrases, clauses, sentences, paragraphs, and whole essays; proofreading for accuracy; acting on feedback and redrafting; reflection; and anything else you can think of.

How to model grammar for writing

1. **Set your intention**
   - What are you modelling *for*? For example if you want to show students how to use a complicated grammatical structure in their writing, you might choose to start by just modelling at sentence level so that you can keep the focus narrow and manage student cognitive load. On the contrary, if your intention is that students learn to skim read their work looking for fragmentation, you might do this on a larger piece of text.
2. **Use variation**
3. **Embrace imperfection**
   - Models shouldn't be perfect, especially writing models. Writing is a messy, gradual process and even the most fluent, accurate writers make errors or find better ways to express things on a second or third reading. It can be very helpful to deliberately model errors which students are making regularly – for example if you have given students feedback on sentence run-ons, you could continue to rehearse that proofreading skill by putting run-on errors into your own writing and getting them to identify them, and/or modelling how you would find and correct them.
4. **Annotation**
   - Unpick models and annotate their key features and successes so that those key learning points are clearly seen and understood by students. You might do this by writing your model live on lined paper in an exercise book but missing every other line so that you have empty alternate lines. You could then use a different colour to annotate key features and principles on the line directly below where you have written them.

Step 1

The teacher writes a model on every

other line on the page. Where

appropriate for the students concerned,

they write along with the teacher...

6.2.2

Step 2

The teacher writes a model on every
The teacher then goes on to annotate
other line on the page. Where
features of the model on the remaining
appropriate for the students concerned,
lines in a different colour...
they write along with the teacher...

6.2.3

Step 3

The playwright (clearly) shows their

modal adverb - shows you are making a judgement

(distain) for the upper classes

abstract noun - sophisticated vocabulary choice

in Edwardian society through his

prepositional phrase - adds necessary detail

(unflattering) depiction of Mr Birling.

adjective adds your judgement of the writer's craft

6.2.4

We have also seen this done using a rectangular commentary box drawn down the right-hand side of the page, or with numbers in circles with all the comments underneath the model with corresponding number labels. It doesn't matter which layout you use – what is key is that the commentary which sits alongside the model shows precisely how the model works and highlights your intended learning priorities for that model.

MODEL GOES HERE ↓   COMMENTARY GOES HERE ↓

The playwright clearly shows their distain for the upper classes in Edwardian society through his unflattering depiction of Mr Birling.	
	modal adverb - shows you are making a judgement
	abstract noun - sophisticated vocabulary choice
	prepositional phrase - adds necessary detail
	adjective adds your judgement of the writer's craft

6.2.5

5. **Metacognitive reflection**
   - Reflection is a critical part of the modelling process because it allows students to take their understanding of the model and its features and begin to apply it to their own writing. Questions you might ask to get students to reflect on grammar in particular are as follows:

Was there anything in the model I have seen before? Where? How was this version similar or different?

- *by making explicit links between the model and things they have seen before, students strengthen connections in the brain and create more robust schema*
- *by getting students to identify how things are similar or different to what they have seen before, they begin to see how their existing knowledge might change or be refined by seeing a new, different example*

Which features of the model do I feel most confident being able to apply in my own writing? How will I do that? What affect will it have?

- *By talking explicitly about confidence levels, students identify for themselves and for their teacher where their strengths and opportunities are.*
- *By making a deliberate plan for how they will apply their knowledge in their writing, students have a better chance of doing that successfully.*
- *By talking about the effect it will have on their writing, students affirm for themselves why this knowledge is powerful, whilst also ensuring that they are making an informed, deliberate choice to craft language – they have done it for a reason because they know what it will do.*

Which features of the model do I find daunting? Why? When was the last time I struggled with using a new grammar device? What happened? What did I learn from that?

- *By identifying what they struggle with, students are highlighting the thing which they need to focus their attention on. This is also useful for the teacher who needs to know where to direct their support.*
- *By asking students why they think they are struggling with something, you encourage them to independently diagnose the problem, which is the first step to resilience.*
- *By asking students to reflect on the last time they experienced this, we get them to learn from their previous behaviour, and to use that learning to inform their strategy moving forward.*

In my next piece of writing, what is the grammar device which will make the most difference? Why? How will I ensure that I use it accurately and meaningfully?

- *By asking students to think about their next piece of writing, we encourage them to plan for future success. This ensures that their experiences in the past and in the present can promote ongoing improvement in the future.*

We know that metacognition is a highly effective strategy for enhancing student progress (Quigley et al. 2018). Modelling writing is particularly fertile ground for metacognitive work because of the frequent opportunities afforded to students to stop, reread, redraft, and reflect. When you write something down, you can go back over and unpick it. This is part of the reason why writing is such a generative process – when we read back over what we have written, we are able to identify the problems or inconsistencies in our thinking. As a foundation for metacognitive processes, the written product provides an opportunity for us to identify successes and areas for development with real precision.

(REMEMBER what we said about 'generative' activities on pages 62–63.)

The modelling principles outlined earlier and elsewhere in this book are effective for all kinds of writing instruction, not just for grammar, and this is exactly the point. When we model writing, students see how all the required domains of knowledge come together. They can see, for instance how vocabulary choice is related to sentence length and how both of these influence tone. Writing is incredibly complex, but the modelling process enables students to see the synthesis of knowledge at the moment of composition.

What about scaffolds? Knowing your options, not learning 'the answer'

Sentence stems and other scaffolds are a mainstay of teaching writing. We are not here to damn or abolish them, but we do believe that they should act like stabilisers on a bike – they should enable students to practise in the early stages, with the ambition that they will quickly break free.

Have a look at some scaffolds in the context of academic writing for English Literature . . .

We will admit to using some of these sentence starters in our own classrooms:

WRITER'S NAME describes . . .
This suggests . . .
This could also mean . . .
This links to . . .

In English, these stems enable students to meet the requirements of external examination rubrics. These stems will enable students to write a suitable quantity and cover a range of points. However, these stems will promote only very simplistic writing, where students move from one simple idea to another and another. Each stem in turn introduces one idea and, though they are sequenced to move clearly through an explanation of their interpretation, these stems don't support any more advanced or complex thinking.

> **SHAKESPEARE describes** Romeo as impulsive because he makes sudden decisions, such as when he climbs into the Capulet gardens 'with love's light wings' to see Juliet. **This suggests** that he acted purely on his emotions because he was carried by 'love.' **The** image of 'wings' **could also mean** that he feels as though love has made him fly. **This links to** other uses of bird imagery in the play, such as when Juliet is likened to a 'snowy dove.'

There is nothing fundamentally wrong with this paragraph, but it moves from one simple sentence to another. Each sentence makes one point, and we rely on the determiner 'this' and the adverb 'also' to do the heavy lifting in terms of linking ideas together. These sentence stems don't allow for any kind of synthesis of ideas and students who write only using this kind of structure tend to produce very similar responses to each other because there is so little opportunity for variation. Remember what we said earlier about writing as a way of extending working memory onto the page? If students can compose sentences which express more complex ideas, they can *develop* more complex interpretations.

Mimicking a rigid paragraph structure might get students over the line in an exam, but it is not the answer to great writing in the long term, nor is it helping them to flourish as *thinkers*.

6.2.6

We support the teaching of sentence stems, phrases, and structures, but we would argue that, if you are going to teach students to copy something, it should at least be really, really good. Why get them to learn: 'This could also show' when, instead, you could teach them how to say: 'Whilst X is a viable interpretation, we might also consider Y . . '?

SKILL DOMAINS IN ENGLISH WRITING

There are many different written forms and genres for students to master in the English classroom. It is in the gift of English departments to decide which specific written forms are given real space on the curriculum, but it is important to do the following:

- Acknowledge that there are a LOT of text types which students could learn to write: everything from academic essays on Shakespeare tragedies, to stream-of-consciousness monologues
- Acknowledge that there are some core text types which students definitely need to be fluent in. These are, unfortunately, usually dictated by the text types required on examination syllabuses. This can often make us feel as though we are limited in the types of writing we can teach.

Regardless, writing is still writing. It actually doesn't matter what form students are writing in, because ALL writing supports their skills in all other written styles.

As an illustration of this, see this sentence from a literature essay:

Browning, a prolific writer of dramatic monologues, created many sinister and disturbing characters.

Now look at this sentence from a student's descriptive writing:

The house, a small dwelling on the edge of the town, held silence and pain behind its drawn curtains.

Now look at this sentence from an advertisement:

The Turkish Star Resort, a stunning pearl on the Aegean Sea, is available now for the family holiday of your dreams.

Each of these sentences is completely different in tone and meaning, but they share the same basic structure:

NOUN – APPOSITIVE PHRASE – VERB and detail.

When students do a unit on travel writing and create content for a hotel website, they are practising the application of their knowledge and writing skill in all other domains, too. The more they write, no matter what the form or genre, the better they will get. It doesn't matter what you are teaching – grammar is always relevant and there are always opportunities to make links with prior learning. In the previously mentioned case, you can see students might practise using apposition across a range of different units.

The vocabulary and phrasing across these examples are equally applicable to all forms of writing: *prolific, sinister, disturbing, small dwelling, silence, pain, drawn, stunning pearl, available, dreams.*

We might take some of these words and apply them to another writing form altogether – look at this example from speech writing:

> Children like us **dwell** in the shadow of our dreams. We share the same pavements, the same cities and towns, but we live in a different world to you – one where our voices are **silent**, while you enjoy up all the opportunities and **stunning** successes afforded by your privilege. 4.3 million children are living in poverty in the UK; if this statistic doesn't **disturb** you, doesn't cause you **pain**, then you are part of the problem.

So, every writing task is a powerful opportunity for repetition, retrieval, consolidation, and skill refinement. All writing supports all writing.

It is because of this interconnected web of knowledge and skill that this writing chapter has been fiendishly difficult to structure. We didn't want to divide genres of writing from each other, nor did we want to separate language features into silos; everything works in a fluid, integrated way. For the sake of our readers, however, we have tried to contrive a useful way to organise this content. We hope the system we have settled on is useful. Please just bear in mind the fact that there are no real rules for writing – yes, conventions exist but it is, essentially, creation, and the world is your oyster . . .

The rest of this chapter on writing is organised in the following way:

> You will find TWO sets of contents pages – this means that you can search for things EITHER by **domain**, or by **grammar feature** . . .
> For every section, we have also added the appropriate domain symbol to indicate where certain features are most suited.

A brief overview of the three broad writing domains

6.3.1

ACADEMIC WRITING: THE KIND YOU USE FOR WRITING ESSAYS . . .

There are set norms and conventions which rule student writing when they ana-lyse and explore texts. This is partly because essay writing, unlike some other forms, is a precursor to a highly controlled and regulated style which students might encounter if they move into the world of academia. If students study an essay-based subject at university or beyond, they will need to operate within systems which dictate norms for things like expression and citation. This is as close we come in this book for saying there are 'rules,' and that's because we recognise that these particular norms are there for a reason. Having a standard way to introduce references, to refer to specific reading you might have done, or to introduce ideas, means that the wider body of academic writing is as uniform as possible. The rules generally exist to ensure that academic writing is clear, unbi-ased, concise, and consistent across the board. Someone might write an essay in Hong Kong, and a fellow academic might read it in Mexico City and recognise in it the same standards and systems as they use themselves. This makes collegiate working easier. It makes comparison and influence easier. It makes the kind of philosophical sharing and building on the ideas of others which we discussed earlier, more possible.

It isn't necessary for secondary aged students to know all the complexities of academic writing at PhD level, but we have outlined the grammar for writing conventions we would recommend for this age group.

Academic grammar and punctuation accuracy
1. Using quotations and referencing . . . pages 117–120

Academic word-level choices
1. Tentative and modal language . . . pages 125–130
2. Verbs for academic writing . . . pages 131–152
3. Adjectives and adverbs for academic writing . . . pages 156–168
4. Discourse markers . . . pages 168–171

Academic sentence-level choices
1. Subordination . . . pages 172–178
2. Apposition . . . pages 178–181
3. Rhetorical structures . . . pages 182–189

RHETORICAL WRITING: THE KIND YOU USE FOR PERSUASIVE WRITING . . .

What we are calling 'rhetorical writing' is often framed in schools as 'transac-tional' or 'persuasive' writing. It is composition aimed at a particular audience to achieve a particular goal. This includes everything from a relatively formal job application letter to a rousing political speech. This form of writing has the

6.3.2

(NOTE: the four areas of classical rhetoric are ethos, pathos, logos, and kairos. This is not in the purview of this book, but we would absolutely urge any English teacher to make this part of their writing instruction and literature work. In this book, we are concerned with how language awareness can support students to have a wider range of choices when they write – this provides the foundations for the pillars of classical rhetoric described earlier.)

potential to be immensely powerful, entertaining, amusing, and challenging, but its most imperative function is *to get whatever it is that the writer wants*.

A job application letter should balance convention with persuasion and succeed in advancing the writer to the next stage of the appointment process. A speech should balance emotive language with personal credibility and logical argument and succeed in swaying its audience to agreement.

We really enjoy teaching rhetorical writing because of the huge potential for creativity and playfulness with language, particularly from a grammatical perspective.

Rhetorical conventions

1. Using quotations and referencing . . . pages 117–120

Rhetorical word-level choices

1. Tentative and modal language for rhetoric . . . pages 125–130
2. Verbs for rhetoric: establishing agency . . . pages 135–145
3. MODIFICATION: judgement and pathos: adjectives and adverbs for rhetoric . . . pages 156–168
4. Discourse markers for rhetoric . . . pages 168–171

Rhetorical sentence-level choices

1. Subordination . . . pages 172–178
2. Apposition . . . pages 178–181
3. Positioning and rhetorical structures . . . pages 182–189

CREATIVE WRITING: DESCRIBING, STORY-TELLING, EXPLORING, EXPRESSING . . .

6.3.3

'Creative writing' is a strange label. We tend to use this term in the English classroom to denote anything which is *not* a literature essay, or a transactional piece. That is anything which does not have a distinct purpose. This is problematic because some might argue that 'creative' writing is the most purposeful of all – it transcends the mundane everyday experience and functionality required to exist in the world and is, essentially, art.

The word 'creative' is also challenging because:

1. The word 'creative' implies that a person needs to possess a certain level of creativity to succeed in that field. We tend to think of great writers as being inspired by a muse; communing with ethereal entities, and of 'creativity' as something which you either have or do not have. This is rather discouraging for those who think they are not naturally creative.
2. The idea of creativity is often elided with *originality*. For a long time the words 'creative' and 'original' were part of the descriptors for writing on GCSE mark schemes. However much we might like to think that our favourite writers were *creating* from scratch, any English teacher knows that everything is a product of something else. Art begets art and nothing is entirely original.
3. The division between 'creative' writing and other forms implies that the act of writing in other domains, such as essays, speeches, letters, etc., is fundamentally *not* creative. This is obviously nonsense.

4. People often think that creativity is about freedom and being disconnected from rules and conventions of that form. That might certainly be the case for some writers, but to insist that it is a requirement of creativity is surely the same as introducing even more rules . . .
5. Wherever there is a conversation about rules and freedom, there are opinions about grammar.

There is a grammar debate raging in the liminal space where professional writing and English teaching converge. Among others, Michael Morpurgo has been extremely vocal about his opposition to teaching grammar in schools:

> How do you teach children to love literature? What you DON'T do is drill them with grammar and then test them on it. You read to them. You take them to see plays. You act them out. You get them writing. The grammar can come later when the fear has gone.
>
> (Mannion 2022)

The difficulty with this stance is that the argument has been framed based on the assumption that *knowledge* is an inherently bad or un-creative thing, but also that grammar is terrifying.

We know that:

- The more knowledge you have, the easier it is to learn new things. Knowledge in every domain makes the brain a better learner.
- Creativity has often been defined as a process which combines existing knowledge to engender novel concepts – knowledge is a prerequisite for creativity.
- Specific language knowledge is inherently democratic; it makes the structures of writing visible so that they can be learnt and mastered by *anyone*.

In a 2019 interview, Anna Abraham said, 'creative thinking involves the discovery of novel connections and is therefore tied intimately to learning' (Kaufman 2019).

Duff et al. said, 'creativity requires the rapid combination and recombination of existing mental representations to create novel ideas and ways of thinking' (2013).

(NOTE: we hope that the visual models throughout this chapter demonstrate how incredibly accessible that knowledge is.)

In simple terms, creativity depends on forging connections between existing knowledge in the brain. In the writing classroom, this might manifest as a student combining usually unconnected ideas to create a striking image. Jenny once had a student write the lines:

My tie
Cuts like a diamond
Folds like the week

We will risk ruining this striking group of lines by unpacking the 'creative' relationships between language, which stems largely from the novel use of vocabulary.

- Verbs: 'cut' and 'fold' – a tie can clearly be 'fold[ed],' but the notion that it can 'cut' is unusual
- Nouns: the shape of a 'diamond' has some similarity to the bottom of a necktie, but the idea that something could fold like the 'week' is unusual

This student's writing is undeniably 'creative.' That creation stems largely from a skilled and unique forging of connections between pieces of knowledge that student has.

So, knowledge is a basic prerequisite for creativity. We talked at the start of this book about grammar knowledge, language awareness, as an empowering force for good. In direct response to Michael Morpurgo's critique of grammar referenced earlier, Leah Crawford (author and education consultant) argued that 'you can play with language like putty and there's no fear. Just pattern seeking, riffing on patterns, innovating. We're okay doing this with numbers. We can with language too' (2022).

In this section on creative writing, we hope to capture this idea that we can 'play with language like putty.'

This third domain will be explored slightly differently because in creative writing, language choices need to be made in combination with each other. We will provide some reminders of key concepts from earlier in the book and look at how you can explore these holistically in the classroom.

(NOTE: to read more about the way knowledge and creativity are connected in cognitive science, this is a good place to start: Cavdarbasha and Kurczek (2017) Connecting the Dots: Your Brain and Creativity. Front. Young Minds. 5:19. doi: 10.3389/frym.2017.00019 or this: www.languagesciences.cam.ac.uk/news/iq-tests-cant-measure-it-cognitive-flexibility-key-learning-and-creativity.)

Language features which shape texts

Grammatical voice, person, tense and sentence
    types shaping meaning . . . pages 190–194
Positioning . . . page 181
Precision (selecting vocabulary) . . . pages 122–125
Modification . . . pages 152–155

Literary models and strategies to use in the classroom . . . pages 195–199

WRITTEN ACCURACY

a. Referencing conventions
b. Strategies to improve SPAG accuracy over time

We aren't going to outline all the rules for spelling and punctuation in this book – that's something you know and can find anywhere. However, we are all about empowering great communication, so we *will*:

- Outline conventions for quotations and referencing
- Suggest some ways teachers might support students to write with greater accuracy over time.

Referencing conventions

In academic and rhetorical writing, you will often need to reference people or texts to support the points you are making.

We always introduce and punctuate quotations and references according to these four rules:

1. **Embed in the body of the text**
2. **Use square brackets to alter the text**
3. **Use fragments of the quotation as a list or embed them**
4. **Use a colon to introduce longer quotations**.

This is a series of examples for an academic literature essay, but is equally applicable to rhetorical writing . . .

1. **Embed a quotation into the body of the text**.
   We want to avoid students saying things like:
   I know this **because it says in the play**, 'QUOTATION' . . .
   Or
   This **quotation** shows . . . 'QUOTATION'

   Part of the reason for this is fluency and style. If students seamlessly embed a quotation into the sentence they are already writing, that is faster than wasting time on a clunky introduction to that piece of evidence. The other reason is that we want students to treat all aspects of the text in the same way, so whether they are exploring a theme, a character, or a specific line in the text (which might use a quotation), they can do so without any bumps in the road. Compare these two examples:

   Browning's Duke complains about his wife; **for instance he mentions her** 'smiles' and **how** her 'looks went everywhere.' This implies that she has inappropriate relationships with the people around her.
   Browning's Duke complains of his wife's 'smiles' and 'looks,' implying that she has inappropriate relationships with the people around her.
   When we cut out the unnecessary words which introduce the quotation – 'for instance he mentions her' and 'how' – we are left with a far *smoother* sentence.

2. Sometimes, to embed something into our sentence, we need to **alter the text**. For instance:

   The Duke claims that 'I gave commands and all smiles stopped together,' demonstrating his power over his wife.

   This appears embedded, but the poem is written in first person, and the essay is in third person. To make the sentence grammatically accurate, we have to change the pronoun 'I.' When we make changes to a writer's original text, we put those changes in square brackets, like this:

The Duke claims that '[he] gave commands and all smiles stopped together,' demonstrating his power over his wife.

This might be even better if we swap the sentence around a little:

The Duke *demonstrates his power over his wife* by claiming that '[he] gave commands and all smiles stopped together.'

We can also use square brackets to indicate where we have taken something out of the text, for example:

Original line: *she ranked my gift of a nine-hundred-years-old name with anybody's gift*
Browning reveals the Duke's jealousy when the character explains that 'she ranked my gift [. . .] with anybody's gift.'

3. Sometimes we might want to use a number of words or short phrases from different parts of the text. We can simply do that by listing them with a colon, like this:

The Duke boasts throughout the poem about his wealth and connections to the art world: 'Fra Pandolf,' 'nine-hundred-years-old name,' 'Claus of Innsbrook.'

. . . or by embedding them into our sentence, like this:

The Duke boasts throughout the poem of his connections with the artists 'Fra Pandolf' and 'Claus of Innsbrook,' as well as ensuring that his listeners know that he has a 'nine-hundred-years-old name.'

> . . . 'Claus of Innsbrook'.
> This is a fragment of a sentence which cannot exist by itself as a full sentence. For that reason, we put the full stop after the final quotation mark.
> . . . 'she ranked my gift [. . .] with anybody's gift.'
> This quotation ends at the point where the line in the poem ends with a full stop already. For this reason, we put the full stop before the final quotation mark.

(NOTE on full stops: when your quotation is a full sentence in its own right and it would usually end with a full stop, you can put a full stop before the final quotation mark. If it is not a full sentence, put the full stop or other punctuation *after* the final quotation mark. See next:)

4. If we would like to use a longer quotation, we can do so using a full sentence, followed by a colon, like so:

In Browning's poem, he shows that the Duke quickly moves on to his
    next wife:
'no just pretense
Of mine for dowry will be disallowed;
Though his fair daughter's self, as I avowed
At starting, is my object.'

Note in this example that we have reproduced the lines of poetry the way
they are laid out in the original text. This is a choice – you could very easily
reproduce those lines consecutively instead:

'no just pretense/ Of mine for dowry will be disallowed;/ Though his fair
    daughter's self, as I avowed/ At starting is my object.'

Reproducing lines faithfully is, obviously, not necessary when quoting
prose:

Dickens opens his novel with a distinct focus on death and the macabre:
    'Marley was dead: to begin with. There is no doubt whatever about that.'

Note on quotation marks

*We use 'SINGLE QUOTATION MARKS' when we quote a text and "DOUBLE
SPEECH MARKS" when we report direct speech. For instance, if we are
engaged in rhetorical writing and we quote something someone has said
in an interview or a speech, we would use speech marks.*

Note on the word: quotation
It is important that students never feel the need to write the word 'quotation'
when they analyse a text. We discuss the subtle differences between the
writer, the text, and the reader as the agent on page X, but essentially, if we
give a quotation, we must be clear that the *writer* didn't use a quotation – it is
only a quotation because we made it one when we extracted it from the text.
    For example students might be tempted to write this:

The Duke demonstrates his power over his wife by claiming that '[he]
    gave commands and all smiles stopped together.' **This quotation
    shows that** . . .

It would be better for them to say something like:

The Duke demonstrates his power over his wife by claiming that '[he] gave
    commands and all smiles stopped together.' **This *line* implies that** . . .

Other words students might use to describe the text they have quoted include statement, image, moment, scene, word, metaphor (or other device) . . .
. . . anything, in fact, but: *this quotation!*

NOTE: if we aren't reproducing the words of a text or someone's actual utterances as a reference, but we are talking more generally about an argument someone has made, or an event which has happened, you would apply the same principles as mentioned earlier where appropriate and ensure that you try to embed your reference into the body of your writing as seamlessly as possible. For instance:

In her 1992 book on XXX, NAME argued for . . .
. . . such as the EVENT which took place on . . .
NAME has regularly advocated for XXX, for instance in their speech at
EVENT on DATE, and numerous articles in PUBLICATION NAME . . .

Strategies to improve SPAG accuracy over time

Accuracy is important. It supports both clarity of expression and credibility. The holy grail is a student who independently self-regulates: they are aware of what they are writing and consciously make corrections as they go.

We can recommend the following principles and strategies:

Student errors are usually a result of one of these things:

* Spelling mistake
* Punctuation error (usually stemming from a misunderstanding of clauses for commas and full stops, or from a misunderstanding of apostrophe rules)
* Fragmentation (where students accidentally write incomplete sentences)
* Students accidentally run one sentence into another without using a full stop where it was needed
* Tense inconsistency (where students accidentally switch tense part way through their writing)
* Syntax error (where students use words in an order which is wrong or obscures their intended meaning).

(See Fragmentation on page 40.)

What can you do in the classroom?

1. **Ensure that your feedback is precise**

   Teach students what *fragmentation* is, for instance, so that you can use that terminology when giving feedback. This creates a shared understanding and means that you can get students to deliberately look for fragments when they proofread their work.

2. **Proofreading is an explicitly developed skill**

   Train students to proofread systematically before handing work in. Ensure that they know what their own common errors tend to be in their written work so that they can look for those things, e.g. 'I know I usually spell these homophones wrong, so I'm going to check for those . . .'

3. **Live model for proofreading and redrafting – make it a visible part of the writing process**

   As well as live modelling writing, live model proofreading and redrafting. Comment on this as you do it so that students see and hear you crossing things out, asking yourself questions and normalising writing as a messy process.

   It can also be highly effective to deliberately model making an error which the class is struggling with, and correcting it live as part of that modelling.

4. **Live model marking a piece of student work (or your own work) under a visualiser**

   This process can enable students to see how SPAG accuracy will affect their grade, but also how it supports their clarity and tone overall.

5. **Live mark student work during lessons**

   Where possible and appropriate, move around the classroom and mark student work one-to-one. This can be a really useful way to notice accuracy errors (among other things), and to pre-empt issues you know particular students might make.

6. **Make feedback METACOGNITIVE**

   When you give students feedback, they might turn that knowledge of themselves and their work into a plan to help them to self-regulate, for instance: 'Before I hand my work in I will check that I've stayed in the past tense all the way through because this is something I have struggled with in the past.'

7. **Make feedback GENERATIVE**

   Avoid any feedback exercise where you, the teacher, are doing more work than the student. For instance if you circle every error with a red pen, or make all the corrections yourself, students might become quite passive. Instead, consider indicating where errors are (with something like a dot in the margin of the line, or a large circle in the general area) and ask students to identify and correct their own errors.

(Remember what we said about Generative learning on pages 62–63.)

(WARNING: make decisions based on your knowledge of students about what would be appropriate. For some students, identifying their own errors would be too overwhelming – consider what will provide a 'healthy struggle' for the students in front of you and adapt accordingly.)

8. **Ensure that you adapt your teaching based on their errors**

   Every time you encounter student errors and misconceptions, this is valuable information and feedback for you as a teacher. Consider that information and ensure that you plan future lessons and activities to meet the needs of students. For instance if some students are struggling with possessive apostrophes, ensure that you take the time to teach the class, or that smaller group, and support them through things such as low-stakes quizzing.

WORD-LEVEL CHOICES

Choice is everything in good writing. If students have lots of choices, they are empowered to write with precision. If, as we said earlier, they only know how to say something *suggests*, *shows*, or *links*, they will be limited in their interpretation. Similarly, if they can only say a character is *sinister* and *manipulative*, that will be the extent of their description. In the next few sections, we will move through lots of different word classes which will support students to have choices in a range of situations. This might seem like lots of impenetrable tables and lists, but the key is to see this as a resource – we lay this content out so that teachers can select what is appropriate for their students. We wouldn't advocate students learning lists and lists of words – that won't lead to a meaningful understanding of their language choices. We would, however, advocate learning clusters of words and supporting that learning with exploration of how word choices affect meaning. We outline specific classroom strategies for teachers as we go along.

a. Precision

Precise vocabulary selection is about being able to decide exactly how clear and specific your description of something is. For example:

The colour of the old car showed through the rust.
The red of the old car showed through the rust.
The scarlet of the old car showed through the rust.

Colour is a generic word – it could be any colour.
Red is more precise but there are lots of types of red, so this could be more precise.
Scarlet is a precise adjective because it tells us a specific shade of red.

All three of these choices might be the right one – it depends entirely on the intentions of the writer. They might, for instance want to be as precise as 'scarlet' because they are going to repeat that colour at other parts of the text as a motif. They might decide on 'red' because being slightly more vague allows them to play on the fact that the colour has faded and you only get a general sense of what it might have been. The word 'colour' makes the description a little less vivid and means, perhaps, that it is a *quieter* part of the overall picture being described – the car might not be the central focus, so by omitting to specify a colour, the writer might be keeping it on the periphery of the reader's notice.

There are many more reasons why a writer might make vocabulary choices, and often these choices combine over the course of a text to contribute to mood and atmosphere.

With students, it can be really powerful to consider the texts they are writing and look at precision as part of their editing and redrafting process. They might identify nouns, verbs, adjectives, and adverbs which might be more precise and can consider the connotations which some carry with them. For instance a student choosing to describe a car might decide that a Ferrari has very particular connotations of extreme wealth – this might be inappropriate for a scene where the car isn't the centre of attention, but, on the other hand, it might be exactly what the student wants. Similarly, an oak tree has connotations of strength and grandeur, but a silver birch might be more delicate. Look at some of the following examples:

GENERIC NOUN:
tree
PRECISE NOUN OPTIONS:
ash birch bonsai cedar maple oak pine poplar redwood willow

GENERIC NOUN:
car
MORE PRECISE NOUN OPTIONS:
sedan coupe sports car estate hatchback convertible
PRECISE NOUN OPTIONS:
Ford Fiesta Vauxhall Corsa BMW Volkswagen Mercedes Toyota Ferrari

GENERIC NOUN or ADJECTIVE*:
blue
PRECISE NOUN OPTIONS:
baby blue turquoise tiffany cyan cornflower azure neon blue ultramarine royal blue sapphire cobalt navy blue midnight blue

*Blue is a noun if we are talking about it as a colour. If we use it to describe something else, it is an adjective.

| GENERIC ADJECTIVE: |
| cold |

| PRECISE ADJECTIVE OPTIONS: |
| chilly |
| cool |
| freezing |
| icy |
| snowy |
| glacial |
| wintry |
| crisp |
| frosty |
| frigid |
| bitter |
| biting |
| piercing |
| numbing |
| sharp |

| GENERIC ADVERB: |
| quickly |

| PRECISE ADVERB OPTIONS: |
| expeditiously |
| hastily |
| hurriedly |
| immediately |
| instantaneously |
| promptly |
| rapidly |
| speedily |
| swiftly |

| GENERIC NOUN: |
| water |

| PRECISE NOUN – body of water: |
| river |
| lake |
| ocean |
| sea |
| pond |
| reservoir |
| pool |
| lagoon |
| canal |
| loch |
| creek |
| spring |
| tarn |
| gulf |
| shoal |

As with all other language choices students might make, there is no wrong or right, or worse or better. Let students experiment with the range of options, and then get them to make a choice based on their preference. What's important is that they are making an informed decision and that they can reflect on the choices they have made – *I am going to use this word instead of this one because* . . .

When students are in the habit of engaging critically with their own writing, they explore the effects which language choices have and thereby acquire a better understanding of these effects for when they are talking about literature texts. Crafting language consciously leads to better reading and vice versa.

b. Tentative and modal language

(REMEMBER: modal words are those which indicate the level of ability, possibility, obligation, or intention of something – see page X for more examples.)

Modality is a key element of academic and rhetorical writing because both are essentially about making coherent, informed judgements, and arguments. In academic writing, it is key that we demonstrate an understanding that our ideas aren't fact but are well-considered opinion. We must acknowledge the range of other possible interpretations which exist alongside our own. In rhetorical writing, we must be able to state opinions, but we often also need to indicate the degree of certainty, intensity, or severity of the issue we are discussing.

When our students write essays and arguments, we should explicitly teach them how to use modal verbs, adverbs, and adjectives to ensure that their writing is speculative and balanced rather than overly direct and making sweeping unsubstantiated claims.

e.g.
This line means that Owen is afraid of the sound of the wind.
This line **might** mean that Owen is afraid of the sound of the wind.
The use of the modal verb 'might' makes this statement more tentative – it shows that this is a possible interpretation.
We could change this even more to include other elements of tentative language:
e.g.
This line **means** that Owen is afraid of the sound of the wind.
This line **might suggest** that Owen finds the sound of the wind disturbing.
In combination with the modal verb 'might,' we can see that the word 'suggests' distances this interpretation further. It is no longer asserting opinion as fact, because it doesn't 'mean' this, instead, the writer is merely, possibly, *suggesting* this. We might also notice how the phrase 'is afraid' has been replaced by 'finds [. . .] disturbing.' The very definite 'is' has been changed to 'finds,' and the word 'disturbing' is a far more nuanced word than 'afraid' and is more closely supported by the text.

Modal verbs
Modal verbs act as auxiliary verbs – that means that they modify the modality of other verbs.

VERB

↓

The girl walks.

VERB

↓

The girl might walk.

↑

MODAL VERB

6.3.4

VERB

↓

Angelou implies...

VERB

↓

Angelou might imply...

↑

MODAL VERB

6.3.5

(NOTE: in the case of creative writing (✊), modal verbs can subtly impact tone by changing the level of certainty or safety, for example: *She knew what she was doing was dangerous.* Is different to: *She* <u>would have known about the risk if she had listened</u> . . .)

This is important, as we have previously explained, when we make assertions about literature texts.

We would use the most tentative modal verbs in literary analysis, such as could, may, might. We can, however, be more forceful in rhetorical writing if we so wish. For instance a student might write a persuasive letter and say that something **must *change***, or that someone **should *reconsider*** . . .

MODAL ADVERBS AND ADJECTIVES

Modal adverbs and adjectives when used to write about literature usually describe how certain we are of a particular interpretation. A list of modal adverbs and adjectives follows. We have also added, where appropriate, the related noun. We will explain why this is, a little later!

Table Note 1 – for some of these words, there are possible adverb, adjective, or noun forms. Some of these are appropriate for academic writing, but some aren't, because academic writing usually requires more distance than rhetoric. Where a word isn't really appropriate for academic form, we have put an asterisk beside it, because it is perhaps better suited to rhetorical or creative writing.

For instance, <u>inescapable</u> can work really well, as in:

The sense of impending doom is <u>inescapable</u> by this point in the play.

However, the adverb form, <u>inescapably</u>, is harder to use meaningfully in a literature context, so it has an asterisk.

Table Note 2 – You will also see that there are some noun forms which are a little silly. We have given those a double asterisk** to act as a warning! Just because you CAN turn an adjective into an abstract noun doesn't mean you SHOULD . . . see <u>indisputableness</u>**.

Table Note 3 – as with other moments in this book where we provide lists, this is just one way of presenting this information, and it's just our opinion. If you have other ideas, that's fine!

Modal adverb	Modal adjective	Related noun
actually*	actual	actuality*
apparently*	apparent	
arguably	arguable	argument
at first glance		
certainly	certain/uncertain	certainty/uncertainty
clearly	clear	clarity
conceivably	conceivable	concept/conception
conditionally*	conditional upon	condition*
debatably	debatable	debate
definitely	definite	definiteness*

Modal adverb	Modal adjective	Related noun
doubtlessly*	doubtless	doubtlessness**
essentially/in essence	essential	essence
evidently	evident	evidence
impossibly*	impossible	impossibility*
indisputably*	indisputable	indisputableness**
inescapably*	inescapable	inescapability**
inevitably	inevitable	inevitability
literally	literal	literalness**
loosely	loose*	looseness*
manifestly	manifest	manifestation
maybe		
necessarily	necessary	necessity
noticeably	noticeable	noticeableness*
observably	observable	observation
obviously	obvious	obviousness*
ostensibly	ostensible	
patently	patent	
perhaps		
plainly	plain	plainness**
plausibly	plausible	plausibility
possibly	possible	possibility
presumably	presumed	presumption
probably	probable	probability
reportedly*	reported	report
reputedly*	reputed	reputation
	rumoured	rumour
scarcely	scarce	scarcity
seemingly	seeming	seemingness*
surely	sure	surety
totally*	total	totality
transparently*	transparent	transparency
truly*	true	truth
undeniably	undeniable	undeniability
undoubtedly	undoubted	
verifiably*	verifiable	verification

HOW COULD I USE THESE LISTS IN THE CLASSROOM?

Teaching words in clusters can be extremely useful because it gives students *choices*. We can gradually increase student confidence and fluency in particular types of writing, by teaching a few simpler words first, such as perhaps, possibly, clearly, arguably

These words are simple because they indicate clear levels of modality:

perhaps/possibly = it might be the case, but it might not
clearly = it is obvious, and we know because the observable information indicates it (something has made it clear)
arguably = there are reasons why you might say it is or it isn't true

We might then move on to teach more nuanced words, such as patently, scarcely, essentially

patently = the same as clearly, but a less commonly used word
scarcely = hardly at all. This implies that you have a complete knowledge of this thing, and that you are judging that it is present, but just barely.
essentially = reduces a concept or idea to its core – its *essence*. This requires a sophisticated level of understanding and the ability to make a judgement about what something is *really* about.

We could ask students to write a sentence using one of the adverbs and then get them to change it so that it is in its adjective form:

Macbeth becomes **noticeably** more erratic as the final act progresses.
Macbeth's descent into erratic behaviour is **noticeable** as the final act progresses.
OR
Not only is Lady Macbeth metaphorically unable to rest because of her crimes, she is **literally** unable to sleep in Act 5.
Not only is Lady Macbeth metaphorically unable to rest because of her crimes, Shakespeare presents her **literal** inability to sleep in Act 5.

When students play with word classes and make subtle shifts like this, they can see a wider range of options for their writing.

(REMEMBER: what we said about Variation Theory on pages 58–60? Practising using words in different word class forms is using variation to refine student understanding of the potential of these words.)

Though they aren't technically modal words, the introduction of nouns in the third column of this table is useful when considering concepts which writers explore. When students write about key ideas in texts, they very often call them 'themes' or 'ideas.' This is fine, but if they have more choices, they can be more stylish and nuanced. Instead of discussing a 'theme' or 'idea,' they might call it:

an argument
a discussion
a concept
an observation
a debate

Dickens's **observations** of the divisions in Victorian society permeate the novel . . .

Priestley engages with the politics of his time, and the **debate** around workers' rights is clearly explored throughout the play . . .

This can be a really useful strategy in rhetorical writing because it allows the student to re-frame the subject. Rather than saying, for instance that they were 'appalled by the Politician's **speech**,' they could change the noun and call it: 'the Politician's **performance**' or switch in a derisive phrase, such as 'the Politician's **embarrassing stand-up routine**.'

DEVELOPING INTERPRETATIONS WITH GROUPS OF WORDS IN SHIFTING WORD CLASSES . . .

When students have made an interpretation of a text, they might have used an adverb, like this:

The audience **surely** sees that Mickey is a victim of an uncaring society, and Russell uses this **surety** to build sympathy for the plight of the Johnstone family.

This sentence moves from adverb to abstract noun. By using the word in its noun form, the student makes an additional point to develop their argument.

Dickens clearly argues that change is **possible**, and it is this **possibility** which provides hope in the novel.

As in the first example, the use of the word in its adjective form, followed by the noun, enables the point to be developed.

The playfulness of this type of sentence construction works well for rhetorical writing. The technical term for it is 'polyptoton' which we explore in more depth on page 185. This is something which is utilised heavily by writers like Shakespeare and can also work beautifully in creative writing because of the poetic potential for repetition and word play.

TENTATIVE LANGUAGE WHICH ISN'T *TECHNICALLY* MODAL . . .

As previously mentioned, there are some words and phrases which make our writing tentative which aren't modal verbs, adverbs, or adjectives. For the most part, these are verbs for talking about what a writer or text is doing (academic writing), or what a person, group, or idea is doing (rhetorical). Look at the following options:

DIRECTLY says X is true	INDIRECTLY says X is true/definite	INDIRECTLY says that X might be true
argues	reveals	insinuates
states	displays	intimates
proclaims	demonstrates	implies
critiques	signifies	suggests

These verbs can all tell us what someone or something is doing, but they vary in terms of how direct they are. If we are claiming that a someone or something 'argues' for something, we must be careful because we mustn't make unsubstantiated claims. In literary analysis, we might teach students to save words like 'argues' and 'proclaims' for writers where there is some real clarity about their opinion; for instance, we can say that Dickens **argues** in favour of reform in Victorian society, because his campaign work to improve the lives of the poor is well documented. Using direct, definite verbs in that case is far safer than, for instance making assertions about writers where we know far less.

In rhetorical writing, these verbs can be particularly powerful because they can indicate an opponent's lack of reliability. For instance: *The gentleman has* **insinuated** *that we can't be trusted, but where is his evidence?* OR use two words in opposition: *They* **proclaim** *their good intentions, all the while* **revealing** *nothing but contempt for the common people.*

c. 'Verbs are king'

Verbs are, arguably, the most powerful class of word for creating meaning in writing. The vast range of options available to us empower us to create atmosphere in creative tasks, indicate agency in literary analysis, and create pathos in rhetoric. Award-winning author, Jacob Ross, said 'verbs are king,' arguing that a well-selected verb can achieve far more than other more complicated constructs (Ross 2020).

Verbs > similes

One of the features of similes is that, by virtue of the fact that they make links between the subject you are talking about and something completely new, they introduce ideas which can be useful, but also distracting. For example we might be writing about a tense and moody walk down a dark street:

They walked slowly, picking their way through discarded litter. The silence between them was palpable. Each longed for the other to speak, but neither was willing to break first.

Now consider how a simile might distract our eye from this scene:

> They walked slowly <u>like tortoises</u>, picking their way through discarded litter. The silence between them was palpable. Each longed for the other to speak, but neither was willing to break first.

This simile appears out of place in this description and therefore breaks the tension – think of it like watching a horror movie and suddenly they play an S Club 7 song for no reason in the soundtrack. It's incongruous and distracting.

Obviously, similes can be done really well, and they *can* absolutely support brilliant writing. We would argue, however, that verbs have the potential to be more powerful.

For instance:

> She *ran like a cheetah* down the street.
>
> vs
>
> She <u>flew</u> down the street.

Or

> He *moved from lesson to lesson like a wounded soldier*.
>
> vs
>
> He <u>hobbled</u> from lesson to lesson.

It can be a really useful activity to get students to look at similes they have written, replace them with really precise verbs instead, and then decide which they prefer and justify the choice they resolve on making. We have listed some verb options for various types of movement.

(NOTE: all metaphors – and a simile is a type of metaphor! – involve one domain of knowledge being used to structure and give meaning to another. In this example, the source domain (in this case, the tortoise) is used to help us understand the target domain (the people walking).)

(NOTE: as with all other tables in this chapter, this is just a small selection of the possible options – English is a language replete with verbs!)

(NOTE: some of the words in the following table are usually used as nouns, but they *can* be used as verbs. For example you can *boat* along the coast, or a child might *helicopter* around a buffet table . . . see what we said on pages 47–48 about the function of words.)

Verbs – things a character or group might do . . .		
amble	charge	fire
balloon	chuck	flap
barge	clamber	flick
bash	climb	fling
bat	clump	flip
bicycle	coast	flit
bike	coil	fly
blow	crawl	frolic
boat	creep	gallop
bolt	cruise	gambol
bounce	crush	glide
bound	dance	gyrate
bowl	dart	hasten
bus	dash	heave
break	draw	helicopter
canter	drift	hike
cast	drop	hit
catapult	fidget	hobble
cavort	file	hop

Verbs – things a character or group might do . . .

hurl	scramble	throng
hurry	scrape	throw
hurtle	scud	thrust
inch	scurry	tip
jerk	scutter	tiptoe
job	shamble	toddle
journey	shoot	toil
jump	shove	toss
kick	shuffle	totter
knock	sidle	traipse
leap	skate	tramp
limp	skedaddle	travel
lob	skip	trek
lollop	skitter	troop
lope	skulk	trot
lumber	slam	trudge
lurch	sleepwalk	trundle
march	slide	tug
meander	sling	turn
mince	slink	twirl
motor	slip	twist
move	slither	twitch
nip	slog	vault
nudge	slouch	waddle
pad	smash	wade
paddle	snake	waggle
parachute	sneak	walk
parade	somersault	waltz
pass	speed	wander
pedal	spin	whirl
perambulate	spring	whiz
pirouette	squirm	wiggle
pitch	stagger	wind
plod	stamp	wobble
prance	steal	wriggle
press	steam	yank
promenade	steer	zigzag
prowl	step	zoom
pull	stomp	
punt	storm	
push	stray	
race	streak	
ramble	stream	
revolve	stride	
roam	stroll	
rocket	struggle	
roll	strut	
romp	stumble	
rotate	stump	
rove	surge	
run	swagger	
rush	sway	
sag	sweep	
sail	swim	
sashay	swing	
saunter	tack	
scamper	tap	
scoot	tear	
scram	teeter	

Other groups of verbs you might consider collating or working through with students for creative writing might be:

Verbs for sound omission, e.g. bang, jingle, splash, zing
Verbs for light production, e.g. beam, flicker, glow, radiate
Verbs for facial expression, e.g. smirk, grin, beam, simper, grimace, pout, glare

Writing verbs and how meaning is created
We have explored a lot of types of verb already. We are calling these 'writing verbs,' though that's not a formal label, because these are very widely taught as lists of words which students can use to talk about either:

- What the ***writer*** does: says, implies, suggests, argues, etc.
- What the ***text*** does: explores, develops, shifts, etc.
- What a ***feature of the text*** (an image, a word, a line, a scene, a character) does: symbolises, represents, creates, evokes, echoes, etc.
- What the ***reader*** does: their active experiencing and interpretation of the text.

These verbs are clearly important vocabulary in English, but they are also the root of many common errors and misconceptions for students. Writing verbs are difficult to use correctly because, though we often present them as a long list of options which students can choose from when writing, they aren't interchangeable. Each one has unique written or unwritten rules about how and where it should be used. For example some academic verbs take prepositions and some don't. Some can describe what a writer does, and some can't. Some can be used to describe one form of writing but not another. Depending on the ideas being explored in a statement, there may also be judgements to make regarding the need for auxiliary verbs (is, may, has, might, could, being, etc.), or about other prepositions which need to come later in the sentence.

When teaching academic verbs, we should be careful to teach them alongside clear modelled examples of what those do to the subject of the sentence, whether they have specific, linked prepositions, and ensure that we give clear feedback on errors.

So, how do we teach students all about writing academic sentences using verbs? Start simple. Look at the next sentence:

Shakespeare	presents	Lady Macbeth.
(subject)	(verb)	(object)

This isn't an effective statement for two reasons:

1. It doesn't engage in any kind of interpretation. It just states that the writer has done something. This is tantamount to saying 'Romeo and Juliet is a play which exists.' It's meaningless.

2. Most of the verbs we use to talk about writers' craft are *transitive*. This means that they need a direct or indirect object to make sense. Many of them also take a preposition or a determiner.

For example we might try to complete the sentence like this:

Shakespeare	presents	Lady Macbeth	sinister.
(subject)	(verb)	(object)	(adjective)

We know, simply by reading this, that there is something wrong here. There are other verbs where this *would* be fine, such as 'calls': Shakespeare *calls* Lady Macbeth sinister . . .

But for the verb 'presents,' we need a preposition to make the sentence work:

Shakespeare	presents	Lady Macbeth	**as**	sinister.
(subject)	(verb)	(object)	(preposition)	(adjective)

We can also see this in the case of some verbs which require a further clause to be complete:

Shakespeare	implies	**that**	Lady Macbeth	is	sinister.
(verb phrase)			**(noun phrase)**		
(subject)	(verb)	(conjunction)	(object)	(verb)	(adjective)

There is no formal rule which dictates which verbs take a preposition, which require a further clause and which are fine by themselves – we simply have to learn them. Here are some lists of verbs and their accompanying frames which might be useful in an academic essay. *These are not exhaustive, nor are they the only ways these words can be used.* Words have an infinite number of possible combinations – this is an overview of some of those possibilities which might act as a foundation for students creating their own in the longer term.

We have arranged these verbs by considering **AGENCY** and FUNCTION . . .

Agency is a really valuable concept for writing about literature because it enables us to talk about *how* meaning is being created.

AGENCY: who or what is doing the action.

If the writer is presented as having agency, they are presented as the person using the text to create meaning and are generally the subject of the clause.

SUBJECT	VERB	OBJECT
Owen	**uses**	**this image to imply that** . . .

SUBJECT	VERB	OBJECT
The reader	**understands**	**this image to** . . .

But it isn't just the writer who can create meaning – reading is a two-way street. Readers bring their own experiences to texts, and their active exploration and interpretation can also create meaning. So when we write about literature, we can talk about the agency of the writer, but present the reader or audience, and even elements of the text itself having agency too, in which case they become the subject of the clause.

SUBJECT	VERB	OBJECT
The	poem presents	war . . .

Overall, then, the order of elements in a clause is really a way of <u>emphasising</u> whom we want to show as having agency for meaning: writer, reader, or text?

The following tables of writing verbs are arranged based on who or what the agent is in each case.

The **writer**

The WRITER is the agent...

6.4.1

SUBJECT   **VERB**   **OBJECT**

...the reader and the text may or may not be mentioned explicitly.

e.g. <u>Owen</u> describes...

OR

The **reader** – the **reader** can take an active part in interpreting the text.

The READER is the agent...

6.4.2

SUBJECT   **VERB**   **OBJECT**

...the writer and the text may or may not be mentioned explicitly.

e.g. <u>The reader</u> senses...

(NOTE: on subject-object vs agent-patient

These are pairs of terms which are often used to label parts of clauses or sentences. Although they overlap with each other significantly, the agent-patient label is reserved for dynamic verbs (verbs where there is a change of state because of the action, e.g. in "I ate the cake," the cake disappears when eaten!)

(NOTE: you can find more about agency on pages 40–42.)

OR

The **text** itself, or **features of the text** – as though it is actively doing something to the reader, or making a statement about something.

6.4.3

The TEXT is the agent...

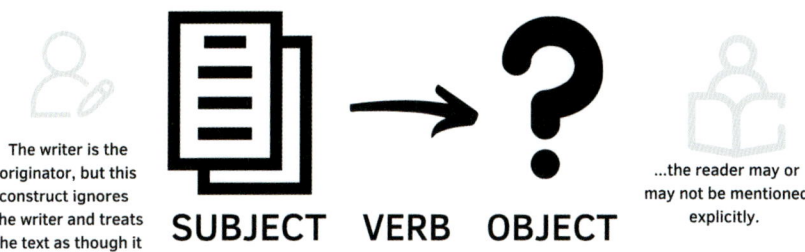

The writer is the originator, but this construct ignores the writer and treats the text as though it has the agency...

SUBJECT   VERB   OBJECT

...the reader may or may not be mentioned explicitly.

e.g. This line evokes...

It is really important that verbs match the subject you are using.

Have a look at this line:

Shakespeare symbolises Macbeth's guilt.

This sentence doesn't work because Shakespeare himself doesn't foreshadow anything. It is the features of the text which foreshadow things. We could say instead:

. . . this image symbolises Macbeth's guilt.

Some verbs can only be used if the subject you are discussing is the text itself, rather than the writer. Some of these are denotes, typifies, personifies.

(WARNING – this is a VERY COMMON student misconception because they often think that verbs are completely interchangeable. We have put an asterisk next to the verbs in the following tables which can sometimes be tricky . . .)

6.4.4

THE WRITER IS SAYING SOMETHING...

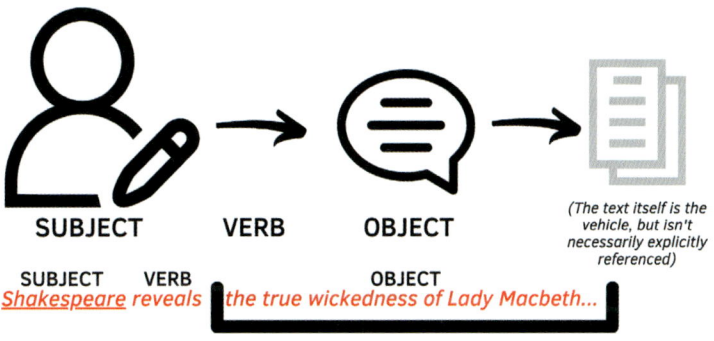

SUBJECT   VERB   OBJECT

(The text itself is the vehicle, but isn't necessarily explicitly referenced)

SUBJECT   VERB   OBJECT
Shakespeare reveals   the true wickedness of Lady Macbeth...

SUBJECT	VERB	
WRITER Use their name, e.g. Shakespeare, Angelou OR say: The writer, the poet, the playwright, the author, etc.	implies	that
	demonstrates	their
	argues	that
	signifies*	their
	states	that their idea/opinion/feeling that
	proclaims	the their
	reveals	the their that
	displays	their
	insinuates	that
	intimates	that

THE WRITER IS ENGAGING WITH AN IDEA...   6.4.5

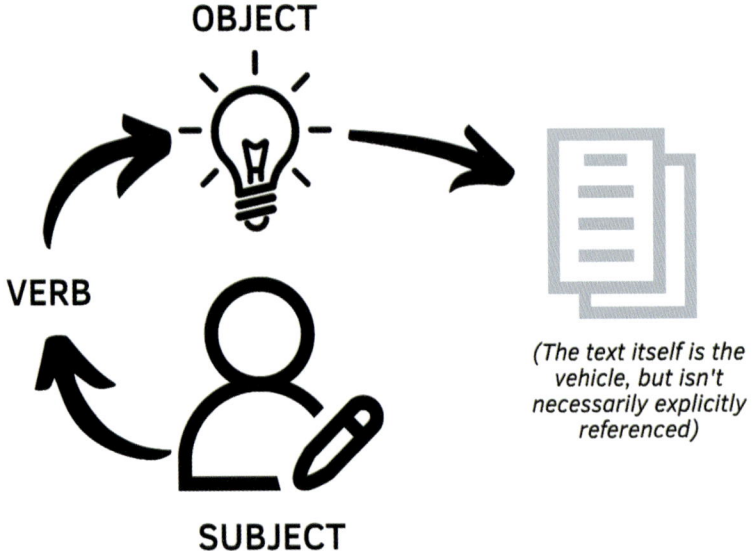

OBJECT

VERB

(The text itself is the vehicle, but isn't necessarily explicitly referenced)

SUBJECT

SUBJECT   **VERB**   **OBJECT**

Shakespeare emphasises the idea of guilt later in the same scene, when...

SUBJECT	VERB	OBJECT	
WRITER Use their name, e.g. Shakespeare, Angelou OR say: The writer, the poet, the playwright, the author etc.	poses	the question questions	of about/regarding
	articulates	the idea the possibility the/their belief	that/of that/of about/in
	emphasises	the idea ideas the possibility their belief their opinion	that/of of/pertaining to/linked to that/of in about/of
	strengthens	the idea the concept the argument(s)	that/of of for/against/surrounding
	promotes	the idea ideas the concept the opinion the argument(s)	that/of pertaining to/connected to of that/of of/for/against
	establishes	the idea ideas the concept the theme the motif	that/of of/pertaining to/linked to of of of
	addresses	the idea the concept the theory/theories	that/of of of/expressed by/posited by
	refutes	the idea the concept the theory/theories	that/of of of/expressed by/posited by
	critiques	the idea the concept the behaviour the decision(s) the theory/theories	that/of of of of/which of
	interrogates	the idea the concept the decision(s) the theory/theories	that/of of of/which of
	defends	the idea the theory/theories the decision(s) the argument(s) the belief their belief	of/that of/that/which of/to/which of/which that in
	validates	the idea the concept the assertion the theory/theories	of/that of that/by of
	reduces	the idea the concept the theme the argument the plot the character	of/that . . . to . . . of . . . to . . . of . . . to that . . . to/by to to

SUBJECT	VERB	OBJECT	
	diminishes*	the idea	of/that . . . to . . .
		the concept	of . . . to
		the character	to
	develops	the idea	of/that
		the concept	of
		the theme	of . . . by
		the motif	by
		the character	by
	draws out*	the theme	of . . . by
		the image	of . . . by
		the motif	of . . . by
		the tension	in . . . by
	substantiates	the arguments	for/in favour of/against
		the reasons	for/in favour of/against/why
	elevates	the idea	of/that
		the concept	of
		the argument(s)	for/against
		the reason(s)	for/against/why
		the theme	of
	raises	the point	that
		the possibility	that/of
		the potential	of/for
	supports	the argument	that/for/against
		the idea	of/that
		the theory/theories	of/which
	highlights	the idea	that/of
		ideas	that/of
		the theme	of
		the fact	that
		the notion	of
		notions	of

VERB	PREPOSITION	OBJECT
argues	for/against	the argument
advocates	for	the idea
counsels	against	the theory/theories
reasons	against	

6.4.6

THE WRITER DOES SOMETHING TO ALTER THE READER'S PERCEPTION OF SOMETHING...

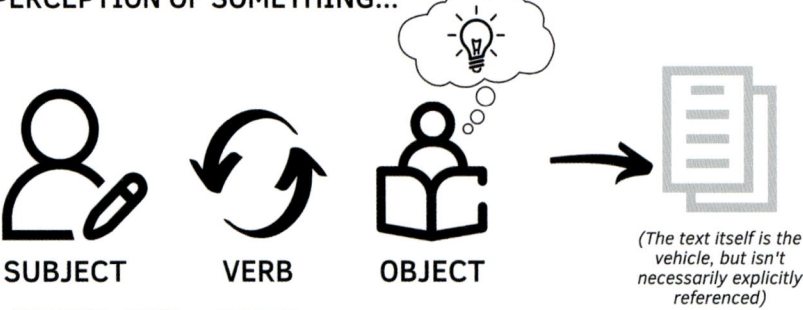

SUBJECT **VERB** **OBJECT**

(The text itself is the vehicle, but isn't necessarily explicitly referenced)

SUBJECT   VERB   OBJECT
Shakespeare forces the audience to re-evaluate what kingship truly means...

SUBJECT	VERB	OBJECT		
WRITER Use their name, e.g. Shakespeare, Angelou	poses a challenge to	the reader's the audience's our societal	understanding ideas opinion(s) belief(s)	of about towards
	strengthens		understanding impression(s)	of
OR say: The writer, the poet, the playwright, the author, etc.	challenges			about
	propels provokes	the reader the audience us		through towards	a/the realisation that . . . the moment of . . .
	persuades forces persuades fascinates amuses enthrals thrills stirs			to consider to re-evaluate to empathise of/to/that by/because by/because by/as by/because by

6.4.7

THE TEXT, OR A FEATURE OF THE TEXT, COMMUNICATES AN IDEA...

SUBJECT　　　　　**VERB**　　　　　　　　**OBJECT**

SUBJECT　　　VERB　　　　　　OBJECT
This moment ⌐ *mirrors* ⌐ *the first death in the play...*

SUBJECT	VERB	OBJECT	
The text The novel The play	conjures*	imagery feelings ideas	of/about of/about of/about
The poem The line The word	alludes to	ideas feelings	of
The image The motif The theme The character	establishes	the idea the notion the theme	of
The moment The argument	evokes*	a sense imagery ideas feelings	of/that of of/about/connected to of

SUBJECT	VERB	OBJECT	
The statement	exposes	the truth	of/about
		the reality	of/that
The assertion		the fact	that
		the lies	of/which
The phrase		the fallacy	of/which
The utterance		the experience(s)	of/which
The description	characterises	the/a place	as/by
		the/a person	
The exposition		the/a group	
		the/a community	
The introduction		the/a atmosphere	
		the/a OTHER NOUN	
The conclusion			
	challenges	the idea	of/that
The rise/fall in tension		the notion	of/that
		the opinion	that
The ambiguity		the status quo	which
		the norm	which
Or ANY OTHER		the convention	of/which
FEATURE OF THE	instigates	the descent	of
		the decline	
TEXT	initiates*	the journey	
		the downfall	
		OR OTHER PROCESS	
	symbolises*	SOMETHING (an idea, an emotion, a place, a community, a time, an event . . .)	
	personifies*	SOMETHING (an idea, an emotion, a place, a community, a time, an event . . .)	
	foreshadows*	SOMETHING which will happen or change in the text . . .	
	illustrates	the idea	that/of
		the notion	that/of
		the concept	of
	typifies* epitomises* exemplifies*	SOMETHING relating to the conventions of the text, the time it was written, the genre or form, or the style of the writer	e.g. typifies the tragic genre
	mirrors echoes	something else in the text	

VERB		OBJECT
concludes culminates ends terminates	with/in	the idea/event

SUBJECT	VERB	OBJECT	
	shifts from in		idea/theme . . . to . . . tone/focus/mood/ atmosphere
	departs from		idea/theme/tone/mood

THE WRITER MANIPULATES ELEMENTS OF THE TEXT (BUILDING, SYNTHESIS, CONNECTION, USE...)

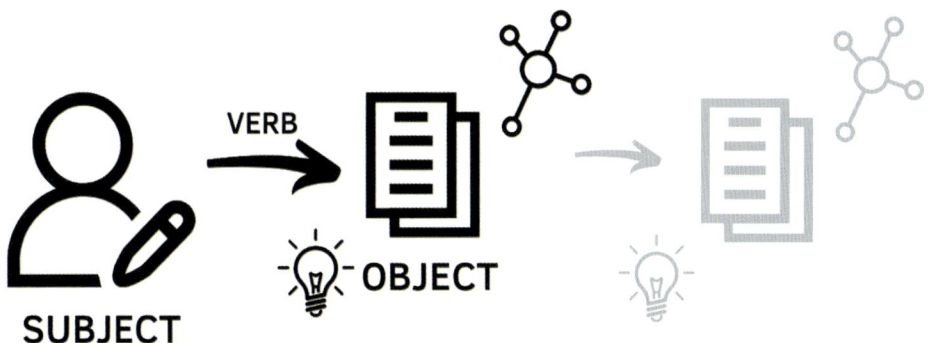

SUBJECT   **VERB**   **OBJECT**

1. *Shakespeare* *distinguishes between* *women who are nurturing* *and those who are violent and sinister.*

SUBJECT   **VERB**   **OBJECT**

2. *Shakespeare* *builds on* *the imagery of 'bloody execution'* *for the remainder of the play...*

6.4.8

SUBJECT	VERB			
WRITER Use their name, e.g. Shakespeare, Angelou	relates	idea A concept A character A moment A text element A	to	idea B concept B character B moment B text element B
OR say: The writer, the poet, the playwright, the author, etc.	integrates* synthesises	idea A concept A text element A	with	idea B concept B text element B
	compares connects contrasts juxtaposes aligns links	idea A concept A image A character A text element A	with to	idea B concept B image A character A text element B

SUBJECT	VERB			
	differentiates between distinguishes between	idea A concept A image A character A text element A	and	idea B concept B image A character B text element B
	expands on builds on responds to	the idea the notion the theme	that/of	
	concludes		by with	implying/suggesting the implication/the suggestion
	employs	FEATURE DEVICE	to	

THE READER ACTIVELY EXPERIENCES THE TEXT... 6.4.9

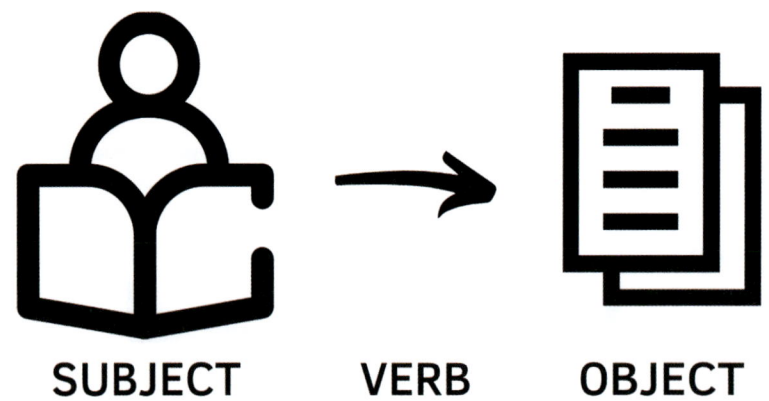

SUBJECT   VERB   OBJECT

SUBJECT   VERB

At this moment, the reader recognises that
there is no redemption for Macbeth...

OBJECT

SUBJECT	VERB	
The reader	infers	that/the
The audience	interprets	this/the
	reacts	to/by/with
	feels	that/the
	senses	the
	realises	that
	appreciates	the/that
	understands	the/that
	recognises	the/that
	knows	that
	envisions	the
	is conscious of	the
	discerns	the
	imagines	the
	acknowledges	that/the
	responds	to
	views	the
	regards	this/the
	distinguishes between	these
	identifies	THING A and THING B
	discovers	the
	observes	the/that
	experiences	the/that
	is aware of	the
	attends to	the/this
		the

There are a number of benefits to categorising verbs like this. Each of these options offers a subtly different meaning to the commonly used: suggests, says, describes, etc. The more options students have at their disposal, the more nuanced and complex their arguments can become. Here are some ideas for how to use these lists as a resource in the classroom.

Verb clusters

Give students three different openings for statements and ask them to complete each one using the verb to dictate the argument they are making.

Example:

Agard observes . . .
Agard raises . . .
Agard criticises . . .

This task requires students to identify the difference between an observation (something which is relatively neutral), raising an issue (being vocal about something, but in a relatively neutral way), and criticising something (an inherently combative act). Each option might become increasingly dynamic in tone:

Agard **observes** the Eurocentric nature of the school curriculum . . .

Agard **raises** the fact that here is a lack of representative black history in the curriculum . . .

Agard **criticises** what he sees as the deliberate rejection of black history in the curriculum . . .

You can easily create such tasks by selecting verbs in pairs or groups which offer different tones, such as:

encourages vs forces
acknowledges – responds – challenges
interests – amuses – thrills

Verbs by location . . .

The verbs you choose might differ depending on where in the text you are talking about. When you want to explore a particular *moment* in a text, it can be useful to think of it as a result of previous events, or as the originator of new ideas. We took inspiration from a strategy shared by Andy Atherton (2021), where he talked about the text extract at GCSE either being an *instigator* or a *culmination* of something.

We developed this idea and thought about how you might see a moment in a text in the context of the whole. For example if we look at Romeo and Juliet, we might map out the use of bird imagery, like so:

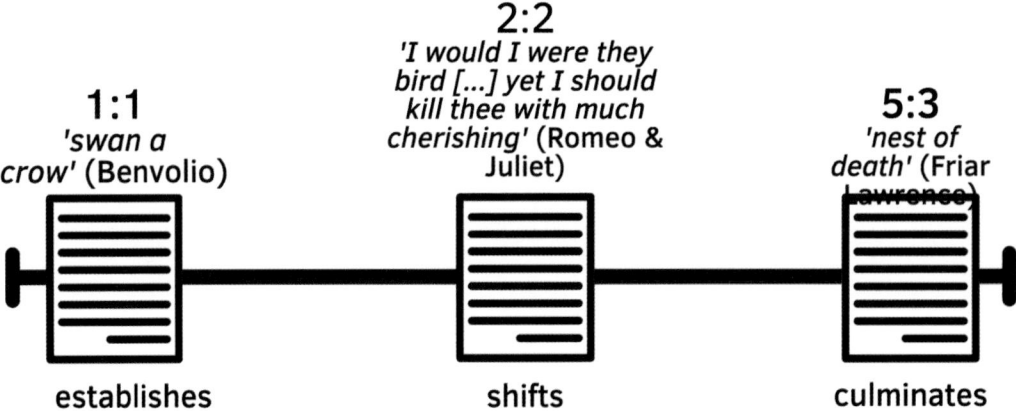

When we look at bird imagery in relation the whole timeline of the text, it is possible to identify the way in which a theme develops. This is an excellent way to look at literature in general, but it is actually very powerful for our academic writing if we also consider what this can do to support brilliant grammar choices.

We can look at these moments in the development of the bird motif and say that the image in 1:1 ***establishes*** the bird theme which runs throughout the rest of the play. We might also be able to say that the moment in 2:2 where Juliet says that she might 'kill' Romeo 'with too much cherishing' is a pivotal moment

6.5.1

because it clearly **shifts** the tone, suddenly becoming dark and prophetic. We might then describe the reference to the 'nest of death' a **culmination** of the bird motif which has built steadily over the course of the whole play. If we teach students to identify the PLACE where the particular text section or feature is coming from, and then identify useful verbs which will support interpretations which synthesise ideas with location, students might produce more nuanced writing.

6.5.2

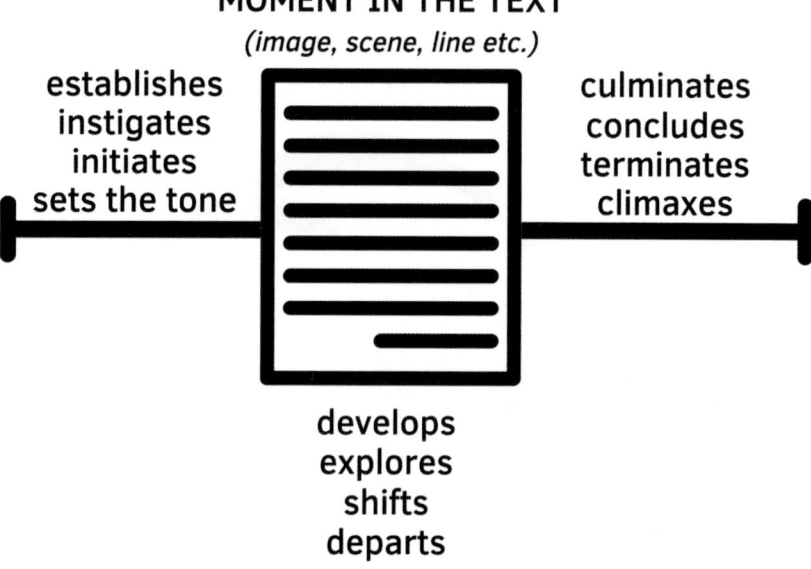

MOMENT IN THE TEXT
(image, scene, line etc.)

establishes
instigates
initiates
sets the tone

culminates
concludes
terminates
climaxes

develops
explores
shifts
departs

Get students to identify where the text or feature stands in the wider text.

For instance, if students are talking about how an idea is introduced, they might use verbs such as *established, initiated, instigated.*
Shakespeare **establishes** the theme of deceit and duality from the outset of the play.
A student might equally talk about how an idea builds over time: *develops, grows, is explored, intensifies, repeats, gains momentum, etc.*
Or about how something concludes: *culminates, reaches a climax, results in, reaches a high point, resolves by, etc.*

You might also get students to use the timeline visual to link other verbs, such as those which link specific events and ideas to each other, or place events and ideas in a hierarchy, or describe patterns.

This example might demonstrate how one part of a text influences another. Note how the addition of adjectives to describe the second extract enables us to link the relationship between elements of the text to their interpretation, e.g. thing A **precipitates** thing B, rendering it **inescapable**.

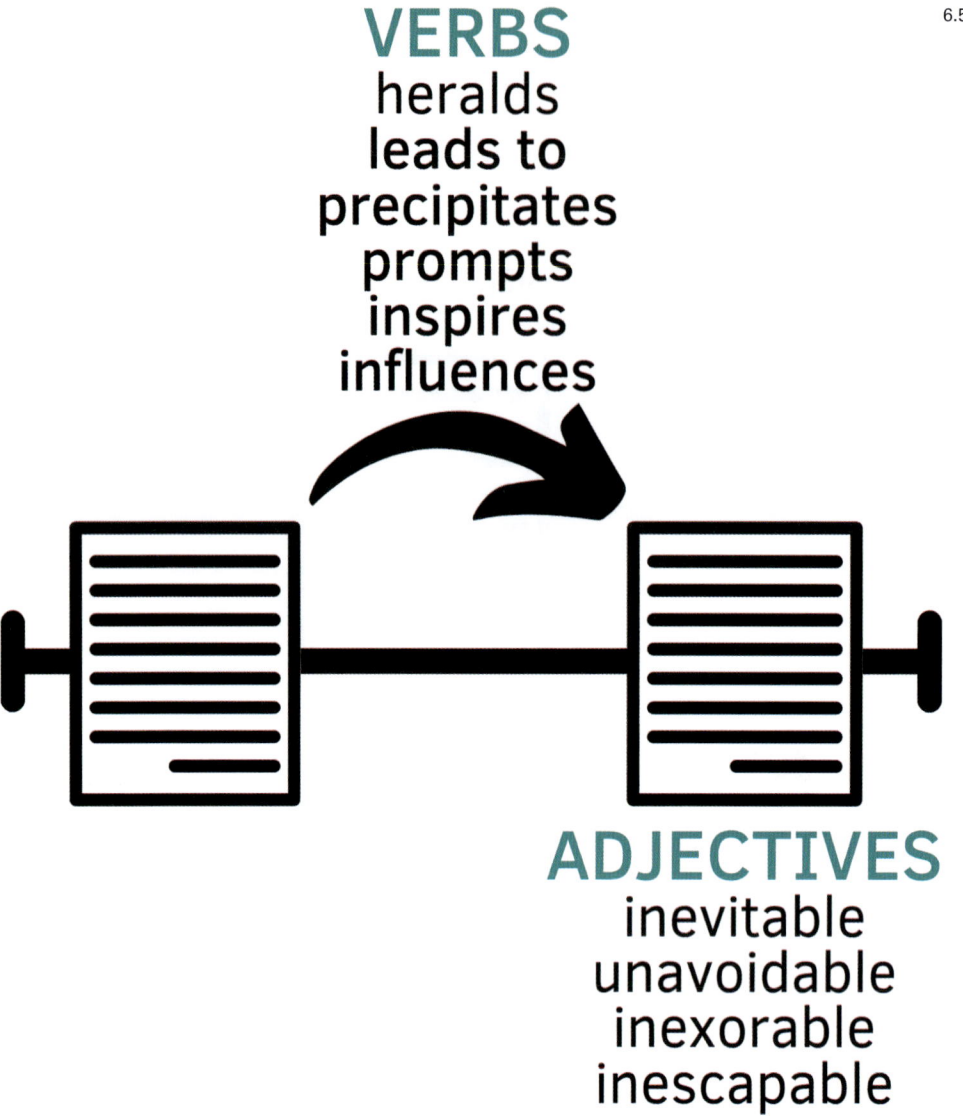

VERBS
heralds
leads to
precipitates
prompts
inspires
influences

6.5.3

ADJECTIVES
inevitable
unavoidable
inexorable
inescapable

Similarly, we might use a timeline visual and linked word classes to visualise the way in which an idea develops over the course of a text such as the next two which look at language you can use to explore how something *builds* or *wanes* over time. Explicitly talking about how we can group the verbs we use with linked adverbs, adjectives, or abstract nouns is also incredibly useful because it supports students to make far more sophisticated arguments. By using visual mapping in this way, and linking grammar choices to a visual, students can see how their awareness of word classes can support far more complex academic expression.

6.5.4

BUILDING over time . . .

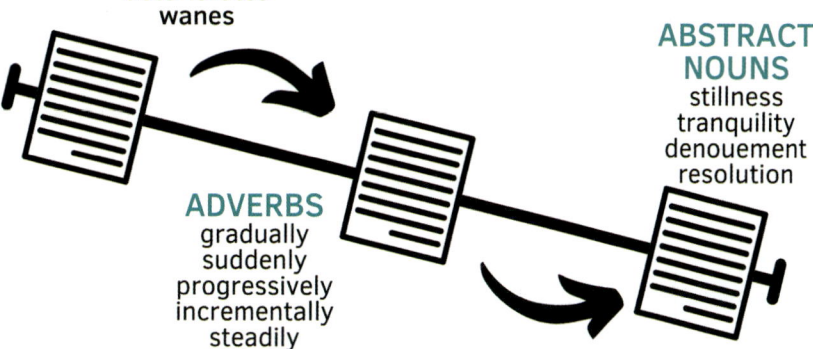

VERBS
intensifies
increases
escalates
surges

ADJECTIVES
acute
intense
severe
dramatic

ADVERBS
gradually
suddenly
progressively
incrementally
steadily

ABSTRACT NOUNS
culmination
climax
excess
height
apex

6.5.5

WANING over time . . .

VERBS
declines
reduces
deteriorates
wanes

ABSTRACT NOUNS
stillness
tranquility
denouement
resolution

ADVERBS
gradually
suddenly
progressively
incrementally
steadily

A NOTE ON *DUAL CODING* TO SUPPORT GRAMMAR FOR WRITING . . .

'Dual coding' has been a 'buzz word' in education for a long time, and has, in some cases, morphed beyond its original meaning. It is not about putting pictures next to information. ***It's about the visuospatial relationships between things on a page.*** Students might begin to understand complex concepts when they see the components of that concept represented in a way which clearly denotes the *relationships* between different pieces of information: visually above, below, alongside, branching from, leading to, influencing, similar or different, for example. This is important, because when we learn something and the information is presented visually, it is easier for the brain to encode that information. When we teach in a way which relies on explaining using words, this is more difficult to encode.

(NOTE: learning things using words is SEQUENTIAL – this is harder than learning something visually which is SYNCHRONOUS. 'Encode' just means to learn.)

When we accompany an explanation in words with the same information communicated visually, students learn that information more easily. The processes of transforming information from verbal to visual, and of translating those images back into words to express something, are highly generative.

For a long time, we have recognised the power of using visual aids in the English classroom. We might use mind maps to link ideas together, plot time-lines, character trees to show relationship and hierarchy. We do this a lot to demonstrate ideas in English, but we rarely use visual mapping to support the most complex part of our subject: writing. To be a great writer, a student must know the components of language and be able to apply this knowledge using procedural understanding of writing in practice: choosing the right vocabulary, devices, and content and deciding how to sequence information in the best way to meet the requirements of the task. This means that teachers must support students to understand how their knowledge translates into the actual skill of writing in the moment. This strategy which uses visual mapping of a text and links that explicitly to elements of grammar for student writing is a very powerful way to make the abstract concrete.

(NOTE: Oliver Cavaglioli explains this far better than us. We would highly recommend that you read *Dual Coding With Teachers*.)

Verbs for Pathos: Rhetoric

Many of the verbs previously outlined for academic writing will also be very useful in rhetoric. Another useful application of verbs in rhetorical writing is in creating pathos – an emotive tone which creates engagement, urgency, or care in the reader.

Look at this example from Churchill:

> And if which I do not for a moment believe, this island or a large part of it were **subjugated** and starving, then our Empire beyond the seas, **armed** and **guarded** by the British Fleet, would **carry on** the ***struggle***, until, in God's good time, the New World with all its power and might **steps forth** to the ***rescue*** and the ***liberation*** of the old!

The verbs subjugated, armed, guarded, carry on, and steps forth are all effective in that they conjure a militaristic, inspirational tone. The words *struggle*, *rescue*, and *liberation* in this extract act as abstract nouns in this context but are often used as verbs.

This example from Martin Luther King's timeless speech in 1963 does the same thing:

> I have a dream that one day down in Alabama, with its vicious racists, with its governor having his lips **dripping** with the words of interposition and

(NOTE: *'hew out of the mountain of despair a stone of hope'* – this is a brilliant example of the power of positioning – see page 181 – because it emphasises the work of 'hew[ing]' hope out of the mountain, implying that social change will be hard work, but that he is prepared for it.)

nullification – one day right there in Alabama little black boys and black girls will be able to **join hands** with little white boys and white girls as sisters and brothers.

I have a dream today.

I have a dream that one day every valley shall **be exalted**, and every hill and mountain shall **be made low**, the rough places will **be made plain**, and the crooked places will **be made straight**, and the glory of the Lord shall **be revealed** and all flesh shall see it together.

The participle form 'dripping' is particularly effective because it creates the sense that the governor in question is monstrous and distasteful. The repeated verb phrases 'be exalted [. . .] be made low [. . .] be made plain [. . .] be made straight [. . .] be revealed' create momentum in a sentence which gathers weight with every action and revelation.

Get students to consider how their verb choices can create impetus and a sense of urgency in their writing, but also how they might evoke their reader's or listener's sense of care or concern.

Some examples of simple verbs which might work well in a range of rhetoric tasks include the following:

Verbs		
listen	promise	revitalise
run	think	shimmer
scream	attack	shine
see	capture	unveil
shout	command	amplify
sing	crush	abound
teach	devour	bloom
touch	engulf	blossom
turn	ignite	laugh
walk	intensify	act
doubt	shun	create
ignore	oppress	listen
feel	poison	swell
hate	ruin	revolutionise
hope	scorch	rise
know	storm	soar
learn	cry	transform
look	break	transfigure
love	lie	accelerate
own	illuminate	build
remember	reverberate	

WHAT COULD I DO WITH THESE VERBS IN THE CLASSROOM?

- Get students to group the verbs according to whether they are positive, negative, or neutral. Or linked to conflict or creation. Or you could get them to identify a list of six which is linked to their writing topic.
- Get students to experiment with building statements around their chosen verbs, e.g. amplify

Amplify your voices!
I'm here to **amplify** what really matters!
Shout, scream, **amplify**!

- Get students to mimic the writing in a model, using their own verbs instead – e.g. using the previously mentioned Martin Luther King example:

I have a dream that one day every valley shall **be exalted**, and every hill and mountain shall **be made low**, the rough places will **be made plain**, and the crooked places will **be made straight**, and the glory of the Lord shall **be revealed** and all flesh shall see it together.
A student might mimic the repeated verb phrases and write something like:

We have **been ignored, been shunned, been oppressed** for too long!

d. Modification – adjectives and adverbs

We talked about modification on page 25. . . . It is when one or more words give information about another. The most common modifiers are adjectives and adverbs:
The **big white** van drives **slowly**.

Adjectives: *big, white*
Adverb: *slowly*

There are other types of modifier which can change the quality of a noun or verb:
Compound nouns: where a noun is used to modify another noun, and they form a compound together, e.g. firefighter
The noun *fire* tells us what kind of *fighter* this is.
It doesn't matter whether the compound noun is spelled as one long word, two separate words, or two words with a hyphen, e.g.

boy + friend = boyfriend
water + tank = water tank
six + pack = six-pack

Compound adjectives: where an adjective is used to modify another adjective and they form a compound together, e.g. pig-headed, laser-focused
Intensifiers: adverbs and adverbial phrases which strengthen the meaning of other things, e.g. absolutely, totally, so, sort of, really
Qualifiers: words which limit or enhance the meaning of another word, e.g. He is <u>somewhat</u> talented. She is <u>really</u> angry. This is the <u>heaviest</u> bag.
Quantifiers: words which specify a number either precisely or more generally, e.g. one, some, a few

(NOTE: many of these could also be described as MODAL words which we talk about on pages 125–130. Remember, there is a lot of overlap with grammatical terminology.)

(NOTE: some of these can also be described as MODAL words, and others could be described as superlatives – see page 25. There is a lot of overlap with grammatical terminology and the label you choose to use will depend on what you're focused on but, ultimately, the labels are less important than the making specific comments on the effect on meaning.)

(NOTE: we talk about quantifiers as a sub-type of determiner in Chapter 3, page 26.)

(NOTE: this is an example of asyndetic listing – that is listing without the use of conjunctions. If there were conjunctions, it would be called *syndetic* listing, and that might look like this – 'a squeezing and wrenching and grasping and scraping and covetous old sinner.')

(See what we have said about positioning on page 181.)

Listing modifiers: it is possible to stack modifiers on top of one another in a string of descriptive words. This is something which a number of writers do for effect, most notably perhaps is Dickens, 'a squeezing, wrenching, grasping, scraping, covetous old sinner.'

When you use a string of modifiers together, there is a conventional order in which they are usually used in English. That is **opinion, size, age, shape, colour, origin, material, purpose**.

e.g.

The <u>hideous</u> <u>large</u> <u>old</u> <u>green</u> <u>leather</u> chair sat by the fire.

OPINION	SIZE	AGE	SHAPE	COLOUR	ORIGIN	MATERIAL	PURPOSE
hideous	large	old		green		leather	

You can see in the Dickens line that the same pattern is followed:

a   squeezing, wrenching, grasping, scraping, covetous old sinner

OPINION	SIZE	AGE	SHAPE	COLOUR	ORIGIN	MATERIAL	PURPOSE
squeezing wrenching grasping scraping covetous		old					

As you can see, you can have multiple words in each category, but they go together. And you don't need to have a word in every category.

It's important to remember that, though this is the convention in English, writers can make whatever choices they like. There is no law about this order, and there is no reason why students might not play with this sequence, particularly in creative writing, where they might wish to position ideas differently.

Note – a modifier can be a phrase as well as a word. Anything which *modifies* **can be described as a modifier.**

Modifiers: the danger and the opportunity

As you can see from the previously mentioned Dickens line, it is possible to load a sentence up with a pile of modifiers – it is a style which can create a particularly abundant, rich feel. Excessively flowery or detailed description is something which characterises some writers. Some, on the other hand, choose to be more sparse and sparing. We have found that a useful way to explore this with students is using the image of sentences holding baggage . . .

If a sentence has no modifiers, such as that makes it relatively simple, e.g.

Sea and sky were a single thing, and there was a beach.

SENTENCE WITHOUT MODIFIERS

6.6.1i

The version of the next sentence has multiple modifiers:

Sea and sky were a single **ash-gray** thing and the sands of the beach, **which on March nights glimmered like powdered light**, had become a **stew of mud and rotten shellfish**.
(*A Very Old Man with Enormous Wings* – Gabriel García Márquez)

The sea and sky are modified with the colour 'ash-gray,' and the beach is modified by the relative clause starting with 'which . . .' and the noun phrase starting with 'stew . . .'

These modifiers create a richness to the description, but compared to the previous simpler version, this one is relatively 'heavy.' We use the image of modifiers as adding 'bags' of meaning to a sentence. The more bags, the more weighed down the sentence becomes, as in the following image:

6.6.1ii

This weight is increased with more descriptive detail. For example:

Sea and sky were a single **ash-gray,** *hazy, billowing* thing and the *grain-like* sands of the beach, **which on** *cold* **March nights glimmered** *and shone* **like powdered light,** had become a **stew of mud and rotten shellfish**.

And we might represent that added weight with this image:

6.6.1iii

The message to students here is that the level of descriptive detail, the extent to which you modify various elements of your sentences, adds complexity for the reader. This is neither a good thing nor a bad thing – it is about *choice*.

In some situations, we might prefer fewer 'bags.' We would argue that the second of the previous three sentences is more tasteful, but that is just our opinion. Depending on purpose, form, circumstance, and target reader or audience, a writer might choose to err on the side of simplicity, or load their prose up with multiple bags carrying layers of meaning. Dickens certainly preferred a maximalist approach.

(NOTE: that isn't a bad thing, necessarily, because it might be used effectively to reflect a sense of confusion or aimlessness in your text.)

In the classroom, using the 'bags' analogy can be useful to support students in crafting and editing work – get them to consider questions like:

- How many modifiers have you used?
- Are all your modifiers linked, or do they pull us in different directions?
- Do you have strings of sentences which are all heavily detailed? Or do you have a handful which are interspersed with more simple structures?
- What kinds of modifiers are you using? Do you have a mixture, or are you just relying on, for instance lots of adjectives?

(NOTE: again, there is no right or wrong here – we ask questions to support students to make informed, deliberate choices.)

Adjectives and adverbs for academic and rhetorical writing

We have talked extensively about verbs and, in some cases, linked them to other word classes. Judiciously selected adjectives and adverbs can heighten the tone and specificity of our writing. Thus far, we have looked at words which describe the actions, intentions, and effects of writers and readers. In reading literature, however, we also need to describe characters and events. When we are writing rhetorical pieces, we need to be able to describe our subject in a way which applies judgement and nuance. Next, we have outlined a wide range of words which can be useful for different sentence functions.

(NOTE: there are a lot of words in the English language. These are just a selection.)

(NOTE: we have tried to group these as with some of the others, so that the headings make it clear where certain words could be used for different functions.)

(REMEMBER what we said on pages 128–130 about lists of words – this is about having lots of choices, not necessarily about memorising lists of words.)

WARNING: *any word can be the wrong word in the wrong context.*

Adjectives and adverbs to describe *things* in texts: characters, events, tone, atmosphere, etc. and related nouns . . .
OR to express your opinion about ideas and issues in rhetorical writing . . .

ADJECTIVES	ADVERBS	NOUNS
aberrant		aberrance
abhorrent	abhorrently	abhorrence
absurd	absurdly	absurdity
accusatory	accusatorily	accusation
acerbic	acerbically	
adamant	adamantly	
admiring	admiringly	admiration
adroit	adroitly	
aggressive	aggressively	aggression
aggrieved		grievance
alienated		alienation
amazed	amazedly	amazement
ambitious	ambitiously	ambition
ambivalent	ambivalently	ambivalence
amused	amusingly	amusement
angry	angrily	anger
animated	animatedly	animation
annoyed	annoyedly	annoyance
anxious	anxiously	anxiety/anxiousness
apathetic	apathetically	apathy
apologetic	apologetically	apology

ADJECTIVES	ADVERBS	NOUNS
appreciative	appreciatively	appreciation
apprehensive	apprehensively	apprehension
ardent	ardently	ardour
arrogant	arrogantly	arrogance
assertive	assertively	assertiveness
astonished	astonishingly	astonishment
atrocious	atrociously	atrocity
atypical	atypically	atypicality
authoritative	authoritatively	authority
average		
awestruck/awed		
baffling	bafflingly	
baleful	balefully	
bellicose	bellicosely	bellicosity
belligerent	belligerently	belligerence
benevolent	benevolently	benevolence
bewildering	bewilderingly	bewilderment
bitter	bitterly	bitterness
boorish	boorishly	
brooding	broodingly	
brutal	brutally	brutality
calamitous	calamitously	calamity
callous	callously	callousness
calm	calmly	calmness
candid	candidly	candidness
caustic	caustically	
cautionary		
cautious	cautiously	caution
celebratory	celebratorily	celebration
charming	charmingly	charm
cheerful	cheerily/cheerfully	cheer/cheerfulness
chilling	chillingly	chill
cold	coldly	cold/coldness
comfortable	comfortably	comfort/comfortableness
comic	comically	
commonplace		
compassionate	compassionately	compassion
compelling	compellingly	compulsion
conceited	conceitedly	conceit
concerned	concernedly	concern

ADJECTIVES	ADVERBS	NOUNS
conciliatory	conciliatorily	conciliation
condescending	condescendingly	condescension
confined/confining		confinement
conformist		
confounding	confoundingly	
confused	confusedly	confusion
conservative	conservatively	conservatism
conspicuous	conspicuously	conspicuousness
contemptuous	contemptuously	contemptuousness
controlling	controllingly	control
conventional	conventionally	convention
courageous	courageously	courageousness/courage
critical	critically	critique
cruel	cruelly	cruelty
curious	curiously	curiosity/curiousness
customary	customarily	custom
cynical	cynically	cynicism
defamatory	defamatorily	defamation
defensive	defensively	defence
defiant	defiantly	defiance
demanding	demandingly	demand
demeaning		
depressed		depression
derisive/derisory	derisively	derision
desolate	desolately	desolation
desperate	desperately	desperation
detached	detachedly	detachment
determined	determinedly	determination
didactic	didactically	
dignified		dignity
diplomatic	diplomatically	diplomacy
direct	directly	direction*
disappointed	disappointedly	disappointment
disapproving	disapprovingly	disapproval
discontented	discontentedly	discontent
dismayed		dismay
disparaging	disparagingly	disparagement
dispassionate	dispassionately	dispassion
distressed		distress
dominant	dominantly	dominance/domination

ADJECTIVES	ADVERBS	NOUNS
drained		
dreadful	dreadfully	dread/dreadfulness
dynamic	dynamically	dynamic/dynamism
eager	eagerly	eagerness
earnest	earnestly	earnestness
eccentric	eccentrically	eccentricity
ecstatic	ecstatically	ecstasy
effulgent	effulgently	effulgent
egotistical	egotistically	Egoism
egregious	egregiously	egregiousness
embarrassed	embarrassingly	embarrassment
empathetic	empathetically	empathy
empowered		empowerment
empty	emptily	emptiness
enchanted	enchantedly	enchantment
enchanting	enchantingly	enchantment
encouraging	encouragingly	encouragement
endemic	endemically	
energetic	energetically	energy
enigmatic	enigmatically	enigma
enlightened		enlightenment
enthralled	enthrallingly	thrall
enthusiastic	enthusiastically	enthusiasm
envious	enviously	envy
equanimous		equanimity
erratic	erratically	
evasive	evasively	evasion
excited	excitedly	excitement
exhausted	exhaustedly	exhaustion
exhilarated		exhilaration
extraordinary	extraordinarily	
facetious	facetiously	facetiousness
faithful	faithfully	faith/faithfulness
familiar	familiarly	familiarity
farcical	farcically	farce
fastidious	fastidiously	fastidiousness
fatalistic	fatalistically	fatalism
fearsome	fearsomely	fear/fearsomeness
feckless	fecklessly	fecklessness
fierce	fiercely	fierceness/ferocity

ADJECTIVES	ADVERBS	NOUNS
flippant	flippantly	
forceful	forcefully	force/forcefulness
foreboding	forebodingly	foreboding
formal	formally	formality
frank	frankly	frankness
frantic	frantically	franticness
frequent	frequently	frequency
frightened	frighteningly	fright
frustrated	frustratedly	frustration
fulfilled		fulfilment
fulsome	fulsomely	fulsomeness
futile	futilely	futility
generous	generously	generosity
gentle	gently	gentleness
ghoulish	ghoulishly	ghoulishness
grateful	gratefully	gratitude
grim	grimly	grimness
guileless	guilelessly	guile
gullible	gullibly	gullibility
habitual	habitually	habit
harmonious	harmoniously	harmony
haunting	hauntingly	haunting
heartbroken		heartbreak
hesitant	hesitantly	hesitation
histrionic	histrionically	histrionics
hopeful	hopefully	hope/hopefulness
hopeless	hopelessly	hopelessness
horrible	horribly	horror/horribleness
hostile		hostility
hubristic	hubristically	hubris
humble	humbly	humility
humiliated		humiliation
humorous	humorously	humour
hypercritical	hypercritically	hypercriticality
hysterical	hysterically	hysteria
idiosyncratic	idiosyncratically	idiosyncrasy
idyllic	idyllically	idyll
impartial	impartially	impartiality
impassioned	impassionedly	passion
imploring	imploringly	

ADJECTIVES	ADVERBS	NOUNS
important	importantly	importance
impressed	impressively	impression
impressionable	impressionably	
inane	inanely	inanity
incendiary		
incensed		
inconsiderate	inconsiderately	inconsideration
incredulous	incredulously	incredulity
indifferent	indifferently	indifference
indignant	indignantly	indignance
influential		influence
informative	informatively	information
inscrutable	inscrutably	inscrutableness
insidious	insidiously	insidiousness
insolent	insolently	insolence
inspirational/inspired	inspirationally	inspiration
intense	intensely	intensity
interested	interestedly	interest
intimate	intimately	intimateness
intimidated		intimidation
intransigent	intransigently	intransigence
inveterate	inveterately	inveteracy
ironic	ironically	irony
irreverent	irreverently	irreverence
irritated	irritatedly/irritatingly	irritation
isolated		isolation
jaded	jadedly	jadedness
jocular	jocularly	jocularity
joyful/joyous	joyfully/joyously	joyfulness/joyousness
jubilant	jubilantly	jubilance
judgemental	judgementally	judgement
judicious	judiciously	judiciousness
laudatory	laudatorily	laudation
lethargic	lethargically	lethargy
liberal	liberally	liberality
liberated		liberation
lonely	lonelily	loneliness
loquacious	loquaciously	loquaciousness
loving	lovingly	love
luminous	luminously	luminosity

ADJECTIVES	ADVERBS	NOUNS
macabre		macabre
malevolent	malevolently	malevolence
malicious	maliciously	maliciousness
malign	malignly	malignity
mature	maturely	maturity
melancholic	melancholically	melancholy
metaphysical		metaphysics
mischievous	mischievously	mischief/mischievousness
mocking	mockingly	mockery
morose	morosely	moroseness
mournful	mournfully	mournfulness
munificent	munificently	munificence
murderous	murderously	murder
mysterious	mysteriously	mystery/mysteriousness
mystifying	mystifyingly	mystery
naïve	naively	naivety
narcissistic	narcissistically	narcissism
natural	naturally	nature
nauseated	nauseatingly	nausea
nefarious	nefariously	nefariousness
nervous	nervously	nervousness
nightmarish	nightmarishly	nightmare
nonconformist		nonconformity
nostalgic	nostalgically	nostalgia
notable	notably	notability
noticeable	noticeably	
numb	numbly	numbness
objective	objectively	objectiveness
obsequious	obsequiously	obsequiousness
obtuse	obtusely	obtuseness
ominous	ominously	ominousness
open	openly	openness
optimistic	optimistically	optimism
ordinary	ordinarily	ordinariness
outraged	outragedly	outrage
outspoken	outspokenly	outspokenness
outstanding	outstandingly	outstandingness
overwhelmed/ overwhelming	overwhelmingly	

ADJECTIVES	ADVERBS	NOUNS
painful	painfully	pain
passionate	passionately	passion
pathetic	pathetically	
patriotic	patriotically	patriotism
patronising	patronisingly	
peaceful	peacefully	peace/peacefulness
peculiar	peculiarly	peculiarity
pensive	pensively	pensiveness
pernicious	perniciously	perniciousness
perplexed/perplexing	perplexedly	perplexity
persuasive	persuasively	persuasion/persuasiveness
pervasive	pervasively	pervasiveness
perverse	perversely	perversion
pessimistic	pessimistically	pessimism
petulant	petulantly	petulance
philosophical	philosophically	philosophy
playful	playfully	playfulness
portentous	portentously	portent/portentousness
potent	potently	potency
powerful	powerfully	power/powerfulness
powerless	powerlessly	powerlessness
pragmatic	pragmatically	pragmatism
precipitate	precipitately	precipitation
predictable	predictably	prediction/predictability
presaging		presage
pretentious	pretentiously	pretention
preternatural	preternaturally	preternatural
prominent	prominently	prominence
prophesying	prophetically	prophecy
propitious	propitiously	propitiousness
prosaic	prosaically	
proud	proudly	pride
puzzling	puzzlingly	puzzle
quaint	quaintly	quaintness
rare	rarely	rarity
recalcitrant	recalcitrantly	recalcitrance
redolent	redolently	redolence
refreshed		refreshment
regretful	regretfully	regret/regretfulness

ADJECTIVES	ADVERBS	NOUNS
rejected		reject
rejuvenated		rejuvenation
relaxed	relaxedly	relaxation
relieved		relief
remarkable	remarkably	remarkableness
remorseful	remorsefully	remorse
resentful	resentfully	resent
resigned	resignedly	resignation
resilient	resiliently	resilience
resourceful	resourcefully	resourcefulness
restless	restlessly	restlessness
restrained		restraint
reverent	reverently	reverence
righteous	righteously	righteousness
routine	routinely	routine
ruminative	ruminatively	rumination
salient	saliently	salience
sarcastic	sarcastically	sarcasm
satirical	satirically	satire
satisfied		satisfaction
savage	savagely	savagery
scared		
scathing	scathingly	
sceptical	sceptically	scepticism
scornful	scornfully	scorn
sensationalistic		sensationalism
sentimental	sentimentally	sentiment/sentimentality
sincere	sincerely	sincerity
singular	singularly	singularity
sinister		sinisterness
sober	soberly	sobriety
solemn	solemnly	solemnity
sombre	sombrely	sombreness
spectral	spectrally	spectre
standard		standard
stressed		stress
strident	stridently	stridency
striking	strikingly	
subjective	subjectively	subjectiveness

ADJECTIVES	ADVERBS	NOUNS
sublime	sublimely	sublimity
submissive	submissively	submission
supernatural		supernatural
surprised		surprise
suspenseful	suspensefully	suspense
suspicious	suspiciously	suspicion
sympathetic	sympathetically	sympathy
taciturn		
tenacious	tenaciously	tenacity
tense	tensely	tension
terrible	terribly	terribleness/terror
terrified		
thankful	thankfully	thankfulness
thoughtful	thoughtfully	thoughtfulness
threatened		threat
timid	timidly	timidness
tolerant	tolerantly	tolerance
touched		
tragic	tragically	tragedy
tremulous	tremulously	tremulousness
trusting	trustingly	trust
turbulent	turbulently	turbulence
typical	typically	typicality
ubiquitous	ubiquitously	
unassuming	unassumingly	
uncanny	uncannily	uncanniness
uncaring	uncaringly	
uncomfortable	uncomfortably	discomfort
uncommon	uncommonly	
uncontrollable	uncontrollably	
unconventional	unconventionally	unconventionality
unearthly		
uneasy	uneasily	unease
unexceptional	unexceptionally	
unique	uniquely	uniqueness
unorthodox		unorthodoxy
unremarkable	unremarkably	
unusual	unusually	unusualness
urgent	urgently	urgency

ADJECTIVES	ADVERBS	NOUNS
vengeful	vengefully	vengeance
vicious	viciously	viciousness
vindictive	vindictively	vindictiveness
violent	violently	violence
virtuous	virtuously	virtuosity
voracious	voraciously	voracity
vulnerable	vulnerably	vulnerability
warm	warmly	warmth
weary	wearily	weariness
whimsical	whimsically	whimsy
willing	willingly	willing/willingness
withering	witheringly	
witty	wittily	wit/wittiness
wonderous	wondrously	wonder
worried	worriedly	worry
wretched	wretchedly	wretchedness
zealous	zealously	zealousness

What could I do with this in the classroom?

For academic writing . . .

Think about characters in key texts, for example Mr Birling in *An Inspector Calls*. Students might usually use the following words to describe him: *arrogant, ignorant, selfish*.

We could use the previous list of adjective options to select a wider range, but rather than just thinking about describing his character overall, we might consider how we might describe him at specific moments in the text.

For example at various points in the play, we might say he is *absurd, apathetic, authoritative*.

Give students a list of three words like this and ask them to recall parts of the play where they might be able to describe the character using those words. They might argue that he is *absurd* when he makes the claim about the Titanic being 'unsinkable'. They might say he is *apathetic* when he talks dispassionately about the fate of Eva Smith. They might describe him as *authoritative* when he first meets the Inspector and tries to establish his credentials as a previous Alderman.

You could also get students to use words in all three of the word class forms. For example you might challenge them to describe Eva Smith using the adjective *submissive*.

Eva's gender and position in life forced her to be <u>submissive</u> to Gerald Croft.

You might then ask them to write a similar statement where they use the adverb, and another with the abstract noun.

Eva <u>submissively</u> agreed to be Gerald Croft's mistress.
Eva's <u>submission</u> started with Gerald and ended tragically with Eric.

For rhetorical writing . . .

The previously mentioned adjectives and related words allow you to make more nuanced statements of opinion in rhetorical writing.

For instance a student might be writing a film review of a comedy and find a range of words to use instead of 'funny': witty, withering (to describe an insult), whimsical

As in the earlier example, they might use the different word classes to write using the adverb *whimsically*, or the noun *whimsy*.

When they write pieces which require strong statements of opinion, students might use those options to play with language choices. Look at this sentence:

The situation is stark: those who are duty-bound to help offer us nothing but scorn.

We might get students to play with this structure and make changes to sections of it . . .

Find three different ways to start a sentence using this structure:

The situation is <u>stark</u>: . . .
The situation is <u>chilling</u>: . . .
The situation is <u>desperate</u>: . . .

And consider different ways to frame the middle of the sentence:

: those who are <u>duty-bound</u> to help
: those who are <u>anxious</u> to help
: those who are <u>powerless</u> to help

Or different options for nouns which describe what is being offered:

. . . nothing but <u>scorn</u>.
. . . nothing but <u>ridicule</u>.
. . . nothing but <u>apathy</u>.

Students might end by changing this sentence:

The situation is <u>stark</u>: those who are <u>duty-bound</u> to help offer us nothing but <u>scorn</u>.

To this one:

> The situation is <u>desperate</u>: those who are <u>powerless</u> to help **can** offer us nothing but <u>sympathy</u>.

A really effective rhetorical device is to take the concepts in that strong statement and use them to build subsequent statements. For instance:

> The situation is **desperate**: those who are **powerless** to help **can** offer us nothing but **sympathy**. **Desperation** leads to drastic choices. **Powerlessness** leads to apathy. **Sympathy** leads to resent.

This playing around with language, translating words from one class to the other, pulling them through into new sentences, is the heart of rhetoric.

(NOTE: there are more ideas for rhetorical structures on pages 182–189.)

e. Discourse markers
Discourse markers are a form of connective which manage the flow of a text. This means that they can direct changes in direction, indicate moments of significance, and generally direct your reader where you want them to look. They are critical in all domains of writing and are incredibly simple to use.

Discourse markers for building arguments
It is critical that students appreciate the role discourse markers play in rhetoric and academic writing, because they act as the supporting structure which gives their opinion shape. Look at this example of an argument with the discourse markers in bold. The task was a letter to present a case about paying nurses a higher wage:

> I have outlined the practical advantages to increasing salaries for nurses but, **above all** these, we have a moral imperative. **Firstly**, we have a moral duty to recognise the value of people working in areas which require acts of sacrifice and selflessness. Nurses give of themselves emotionally and physically every day, **in contrast** to some better paid professions where people are able to maintain a distance and more easily preserve their mental and physical health. **In addition**, our poor treatment of nurses has led to a drop in training numbers, and we will **therefore** be unable to care for the most vulnerable people in our society because hospitals simply will not be able to staff their wards.

You can see in this text that the discourse markers perform a number of different functions:

> **Sequencing**: 'firstly' and 'in addition' place the arguments being made in a logical order and prepare the ground where new points will be made.

Emphasis: the phrase 'above all' implies that the 'moral' argument is the most important one which will be made. It places stress on this point and raises it above the others which have been made earlier in the argument.

Links and contrast: the phrase 'in contrast' makes explicit links between ideas. In this case, the discourse marker introduces an idea which is *different*, but some discourse markers identify similarities or parallels.

Conclusion: the word 'therefore' indicates that the arguments made so far will culminate in a final, logical interpretation.

We would advocate modelling the list of discourser markers live during writing, but also considering the use of simple visuals to indicate how they can be powerful. In this one, for instance the lightbulb represents the main idea, and the line beneath is the 'thread' of the argument. The idea is that discourse markers enable you to stick to your main argument all the way through, whilst giving you the tools you need to plan. The little series of arrows represent the broad type and function of these discourse markers.

6.7.1

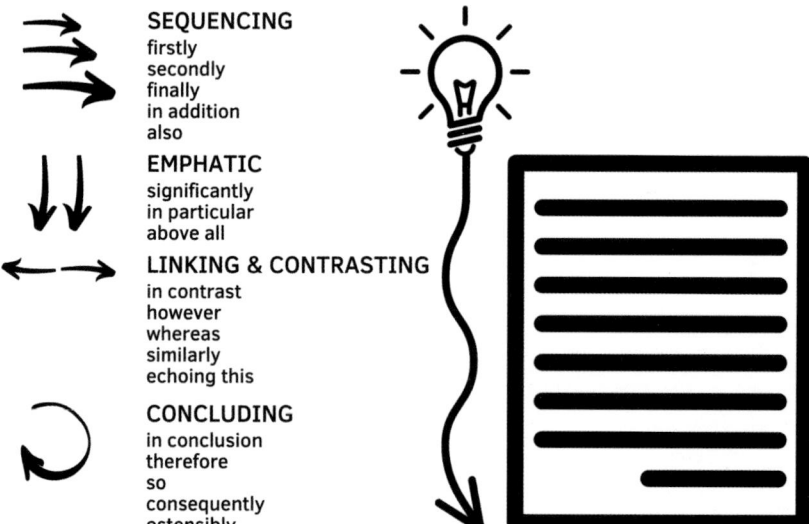

SEQUENCING
firstly
secondly
finally
in addition
also

EMPHATIC
significantly
in particular
above all

LINKING & CONTRASTING
in contrast
however
whereas
similarly
echoing this

CONCLUDING
in conclusion
therefore
so
consequently
ostensibly

What could this look like in the classroom?
You could model the argument structure under the visualiser by drawing the lightbulb and line down one side of the page. Then, as a class, co-create a really simple plan by writing down what your four(ish) main arguments will be – these will form the main paragraphs. Then alongside each paragraph you could decide what types of discourse markers you will need as you move through the argument. Students might decide that they want to introduce the

whole argument first, and then start their first point with a sequencing con-nective. They might use another sequencing connective each time they intro-duce a new idea. For some of their key ideas, they might want to emphasise the most important idea or implication of something by saying, 'significantly' or 'notably' (emphatic connectives). They might want to use contrasting con-nectives when they compare ideas to each other, or concluding connectives to show their reasoning. You would draw these symbols on the side of the visual plan and students would decide what language they would then use. The key benefit to working like this is that students learn how vocabulary choices affect the wider structure and building blocks of creating a successful argument. Drawing out an abstract representation of the argument overall and identifying *where* discourse markers would be useful help students to see the function which those words and phrases can perform, and the way they create links between different ideas.

(NOTE: this strategy uses visuospatial mapping, or 'dual coding.' You can read more about it on pages 149–150.)

Discourse markers and shifting focus in creative writing

Nothing is simple when it moves into the realm of creative writing. When you build an argument, you seek to guide your reader through a clear set of ideas. When you write a novel or a monologue, however, you may want to create ambi-guity, or multiple emotions at once. You might intend to make your reader feel uncertain or to surprise them with a sudden change. The basic discourse mark-ers such as those which add ideas, express cause and effect, etc. are clearly important elements of your toolkit.

And
But
Yet
Though
So
Because
If
Then
That

Though students may think these are really basic words, they can actually intro-duce profoundly effective moments in their writing. Shifts in tone or focus can happen gradually and subtly, or dramatically and suddenly. Look at the ways some writers have used these discourse markers:

Shakespeare frequently used 'and,' 'if,' or 'but' to begin the final couplets in his sonnets and indicate the change in tone or argument:

116: 'If this be error . . .'
15: 'And all in war with time . . .'
25: 'Then happy I, that love and am beloved . . .'

Browning used simple conjunctions to introduce the sinister moments of shift in his poems:

'and all smiles stopped together' *My Last Duchess*
'That moment she was mine, mine, fair,
Perfectly pure and good: I found
A thing to do, and all her hair
In one long yellow string I wound
Three times her little throat around,
And strangled her.'
- *Porphyria's Lover*

Get students to consider ways in which they might write a subtle shift in tone using a simple discourse marker, such as 'when' or 'and.' They might then contrast this with using something far more dramatic, such as *suddenly, in an instant, just then, swiftly, unexpectedly, without warning* . . .

Sentence-level choices

a. Sentence types
We have talked at length about the four sentence types and given examples of them in context

In the classroom, students should be aware of these choices but also remember that sentence types can have a significant impact on tone and, while there are no real 'rules,' there are some conventions and things they should be mindful of:

- **Imperatives** are powerful but are generally not appropriate in a formal register where giving orders or instructions might create a tone which is too forceful. For instance it would not be appropriate to end a job application letter with the imperative *Shortlist me*. A declarative would be more fitting: *I hope to be shortlisted so that I can show you my potential*.
- **Interrogatives** are very useful in certain forms but, just like imperatives, they require something of the reader or audience, which makes them quite forceful in tone. Use sparingly in rhetoric. In academic writing, it is usually not appropriate to ask a direct question of your reader – you should be more distanced than this. However, some people would argue that there are certain exceptions where individual writing style options might allow it,

  e.g. Is Macbeth overwhelmed by guilt or fear? It is both . . .
  Is this the moment Macbeth decides to commit murder? It is debatable . . .

- **Exclamatives** shouldn't be used in academic writing because it needs to be neutral and dispassionate. They are absolutely appropriate for rhetorical and creative writing, though.

b. Subordination

Subordination for building arguments

As we have already mentioned, we want to support students to express themselves with precision but also to handle complex and abstract ideas. One way of doing this is to use subordinating conjunctions.

(REMEMBER: there are two types of clause – main clauses and subordinate clauses are explained on pages 37–40.)

But how can this grammatical construct support argument writing? Let's imagine that I have the following goal:

Students will construct sentences which can handle **multiple concepts** at once, demonstrate and elicit **links**, and explore the **cumulative effect** of a number of things at once.

Here is an example using literature essay writing, but this could apply just as easily to rhetoric.

We have already referred to the kinds of sentence stems which limit students to writing a series of simplistic ideas: Shakespeare says . . . this shows . . . this also suggests . . . this might link to . . . etc.

(REMEMBER we talked about this on pages 107–109.)

This might support students to write things down, but these stems do nothing to scaffold really hard-working sentences which can do all of the things in the intention outlined earlier.

Look at these two sentences:

Blake's attack on the great institutions of British power is simultaneously furious and devastating. Not only does he convey a powerful sense of anger – 'every cry of every man' – but he also highlights the lived reality of the most vulnerable in society through reference to 'infants', child labour of 'chimney-sweepers' and the stark lives of young unmarried mothers.

Both sentences enable the writer to combine concepts. This is how a teacher might explore this in the classroom:

1.   Model the first sentence under a visualiser.

Then go back and highlight specific elements of the text. There are two adjectives at the end of this sentence, 'furious' and 'devastating,' which represent two separate interpretations. There is also an adverb: 'simultaneously,' which serves those two adjectives – the use of that word enables students to handle TWO ideas, rather than just one.

Blake's attack on the great institutions of British power is simultaneously furious and devastating.

6.8.1

2. Explain to students how this works.

The first section of the sentence is the 'thing' we are describing, and we must consider what two things we want to say. These interpretations should be things which will combine to enhance each other.

Blake's attack on the great institutions of British power is simultaneously furious and devastating.

ADVERB

What are we describing?

What two things do we want to say?

6.8.2

3. Explicitly teach the word 'simultaneously,' explaining to students that it is hard working because it will carry two (or more) interpretations at a time. This simple visual might illustrate this . . .

6.8.3

4. Introduce the subordinating conjunction.

This is a really useful grammatical feature because, much like 'simultaneously,' it sets up multiple ideas. A subordinating conjunction makes one clause subordinate to another. That means that a clause which might otherwise have been fine on its own, suddenly needs another clause to make sense. For example this is a full sentence:

Blake conveys a powerful sense of anger.

If, however, we began this sentence with a subordinating conjunction 'not only,' it would look like this:

Not only does he convey a powerful sense of anger

Suddenly, the sentence is rendered incomplete. It demands another clause to make it work. In the model, the completed version looks like this:

Not only does he convey a powerful sense of anger – 'every cry of every man' – but he also highlights the lived reality of the most vulnerable in society.

We could use this very simple visual to present this particular sentence structure for students.

6.8.4

Not only - - - - - - - but also - - - - - - - -

When teaching subordinating conjunctions as a general concept, we might also use the simple image of one book leaning on another, more stable book. We must stress at this point that it is not the pictures themselves which support students. It is the way the pictures represent relationships between different concepts. The leaning book denotes a relationship between clauses. We might talk to students about how the subordinating conjunction is almost like a hand which has pushed a book over into another, though this is far easier to explain in person using gestures!

(NOTE: please see what we say about dual coding on pages 149–150.)

5. **Move on to the word 'through,'** which introduces a series of linked ideas. By listing three pieces of evidence from the text rather than just one, we create emphasis – the strength of the interpretation swells with each additional reference, much like the wedge we have shown in the next figure. The pieces of evidence have been selected carefully because, though they are separate elements of the poem, grouping them highlights how they combine and have a powerful cumulative effect. In this case, by highlighting all the vulnerable people whom Blake mentions in the poem, we can heighten the reader's appreciation of this as a key theme in the poem.

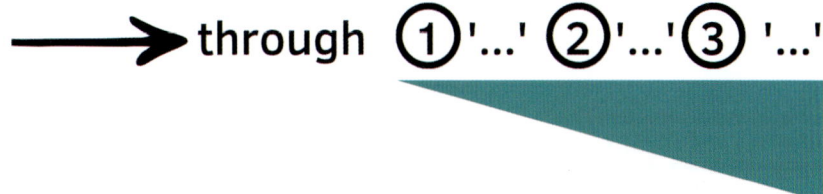

6. **The whole visual is here.** Part of the benefit of drawing this for students under a visualiser comes from the live action – students appreciate how it is constructed, what comes first, what direction the arrows are drawn in, etc.

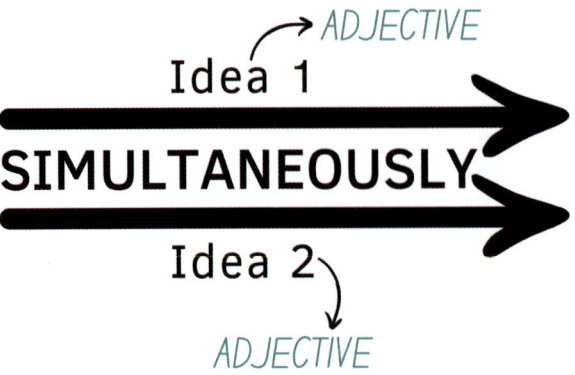

6.8.7

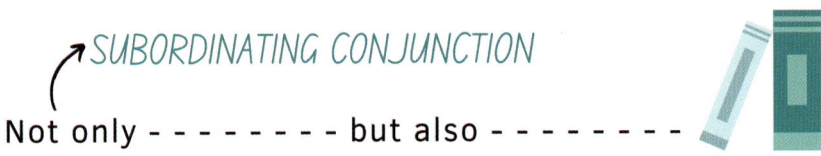

This could be condensed to an even simpler visual like so:

6.8.8

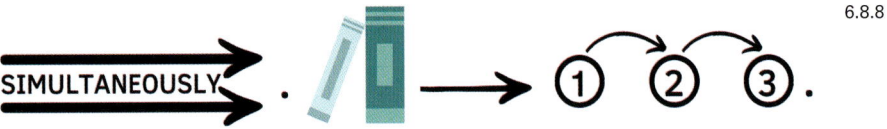

We might get students to use this visual in a range of ways:

- Recreate the larger and smaller version of the image from memory
- Annotate the visual with examples and explanations of what they represent, from memory
- Use them to recreate the original model
- Use them to create their own writing which uses the same structure.

Here is an example of this structure being used to write about a different text entirely . . .

6.8.9

Lady Macbeth is at once repulsive and endearing. Whilst we witness her unconscious confessions to murder and deceit, **we also** pity her vulnerability as she laments the brutal reality of her crimes: ① 'Banquo's dead'; ② 'the Thane of Fife had a wife'; ③ 'so much blood in him.'

In this example, you can see that the same level of complexity and sophistication has been achieved, but the content is completely different. You can also see that we have used 'at once' as an adverbial phrase rather than 'simultaneously.' Once students have a clear understanding of the *function* which that word or feature performs, they can swap things in and out to fit exactly what they want to say.

There are a huge number of possible options for subordinating conjunctions, some of which are listed in the section on discourse markers in the Rhetoric section on page X. A few other options which work particularly well for academic writing are here, with examples of *fronted* subordinating conjunctions.

(REMEMBER: 'fronted' means at the start, so these sentences all START with a subordinating conjunction . . . see page 184 for more on positioning.)

Whether they have been betrayed by their own government, or abandoned by God, it is clear that Owen and his fellow soldiers have lost hope.

Once Scrooge begins to cry in the face of his neglected childhood, the reader understands that his transformation has begun.

Until Stevenson reveals Dr Jekyll's final letter, the reader is left in a state of suspense.

> **Though** Tennyson describes a tragic 'blunder' in this poem, he clearly intends to promote it as a tale of heroism and patriotic triumph.
>
> **Because** Porphyria is such a classic example of feminine beauty and grace, her sudden brutal murder is even more disturbing.

c. Apposition (all three)

Apposition in academic writing

Apposition is when two or more words, phrases, or clauses are grammatically parallel and are talking about the same thing. By 'grammatically parallel' we mean that they perform the same function, e.g. a noun placed next to another noun, or a verb placed next to a verb phrase.

Most commonly, this involves nouns in the following structure:

6.9.1

For example this sentence starts with a noun:

NOUN   6.9.2

Dickens frequently featured orphans in his novels

We could add an appositive phrase like this:

NOUN   *NOUN PHRASE*   6.9.3

Dickens, a prominent campaigner against child poverty, frequently featured orphans in his novels

NOUN   *NOUN PHRASE*   6.9.4

Dickens, a prominent campaigner against child poverty, frequently featured orphans in his novels

PARENTHESIS

We could do this differently and place a noun phrase next to a different noun:

6.9.5

NOUN   NOUN CLAUSE

Dickens frequently featured orphans, children who have no parents,
in his novels

And although apposition is usually done with nouns, it actually just means units of equal grammatical value beside each other, so it could be done with other word classes, such as in this example:

6.9.6

6.9.7

VERB VERB PHRASE

Flying, sailing higher, **the kestrel played above us.**

And there is nothing to stop us from putting more than two units in apposition with each other . . .

6.9.8

6.9.8i

VERB VERB PHRASE VERB PHRASE

Flying, sailing higher, waltzing in air, **the kestrel played above us.**

Apposition works beautifully in academic writing because it enables students to include additional information without having to waste time on clunky extra sentences. They can casually slip in things like **Owen, a soldier who died in the trenches during World War One, describes the conditions of war with vivid and striking imagery** . . .

We find that using apposition is particularly useful for embedding elements of context or theory into sentences whilst still ensuring that the main work of the sentence is to explore the *text*, not to dump the student's wider knowledge.

How could this work in the classroom?

To use an appositive to demonstrate knowledge, students need to activate that knowledge. You could do the following:

1. Give students a noun you wish to explore. That might be a writer's name, a moment in a text, a concept or anything else linked to your study.

    e.g. Late 20th Century Liverpool

2. Ask students to do a brain dump (where they write down everything they can remember) about that noun.

    e.g. it's the setting for *Blood Brothers*, widespread unemployment, overcrowded social housing, new towns, Willy Russell grew up there, famous for music

3. Ask students to then use the material they have retrieved to create appositive phrases to expand this sentence:

    Late 20th Century Liverpool is the backdrop for the play.

Students might then write a list of sentences like this:

- Late 20th Century Liverpool, a city with widespread unemployment, is the backdrop for the play.
- Late 20th Century Liverpool, a city struggling with over-crowded social housing, is the backdrop for the play.
- Late 20th Century Liverpool, a place famed for its music scene, is the backdrop for the play.

Apposition can work in every type of writing. In rhetorical pieces, students might use an appositive phrase or clause to slip additional information into their sentence without losing the momentum or flow of an argument. In the previously mentioned literature examples, we have used apposition to add factual information related to text context. An appositive phrase, however, could be used to add statements of opinion or information which strengthens your argument. For example:

Reading, **perhaps the greatest human pastime on Earth**, is critical to the development of children.

d. Positioning

In language, positioning refers to how something is structured and where particular things are placed in relation to others. It is pretty straightforward, really:

Front = at the front
Mid = in the middle
End = at the end
Pre- = before
Post- = after

For example here is a line written in different ways:

'Beauty is an enormous, unmerited gift given randomly, stupidly'
(*And the Mountains Echoed* – Khaled Hosseini)

In the original, *beauty* is in the front position. *Gift* is a noun which is pre-modified by the adjectives *enormous* and *unmerited* which come before it, and the verb *given* is post-modified by the adverbs *randomly* and *stupidly* which come after it.
We could swap the whole thing around and write:

Enormous and unmerited, beauty is a gift given randomly, stupidly.
In this version, the adjectives are fronted, which perhaps takes the emphasis away from the concept of *beauty* and instead stresses the fact that it is an *enormous* gift.

We could equally write:

Randomly, stupidly, beauty is given as an enormous, unmerited gift.
This version is a little clunky, but you can see how the positioning now changes the emphasis to the adverbs *randomly* and *stupidly*.

The choices a writer makes about positioning enable them to guide their reader – they might place something at the very end so that it is the final idea a reader is left with. Or they might sequence images in a particular order to build tension. Or they might place two completely distinct ideas together to create contrast. The options are limitless.
You could get students to experiment with positioning by taking a piece of work they have drafted and asking them to experiment by:

*   Re-crafting a sentence so that a key image is in a different place (e.g. if it was at the end, put it at the start)
*   Taking a powerful word or image and finding a way to replicate it in other places in the piece of writing – can they start and end with that image? Or use it three times but in different ways?
*   Include the same sentence three times in their piece of writing but configured in a different way each time.

e. Playful structures

Related to what we have explored in terms of positioning, this selection of playful structures is all about looking at classic sentences, those which have been laid down in literature and rhetoric through the ages, and trying to apply them in our own writing.

For each of these structures you might:

- Get students to use them in the writing they are doing (in any form)
- Get students to use the same structure across different written forms and see what the difference is (e.g. use anadiplosis in a persuasive speech and in a description of a haunted forest)
- Ask students to write the same statement but in three different structures and see which they prefer
- Get students to identify these structures in the literature texts they read and explore how they create meaning.

It doesn't really matter what you do with them – the key is that you can be playful. We aren't reproducing classical rhetoric devices so that we can hammer terminology and sound clever. We don't really care whether students know what the Greek terms are or not. What's important is that these structures reflect playful patterns and artful manipulation of language which is empowering. The message for students is that language is your toolkit and you can do what you like with it.

POLYPTOTON

6i.1.1

DEFINITION: Repetition of words which all have the same root but are in different forms.

love is not love

which **alters** [VERB] when it **alteration** [NOUN] finds

nor bends with the **remover** [NOUN] to **remove** [VERB]

Shakespeare. Sonnet 116

More examples:

'**thank** me no **thankings** nor **proud** me no **prouds**' (Romeo & Juliet)

'The **rain** it **raineth** every day' (Twelfth Night)

'Give us this **day** our **daily** bread and forgive us our **trespasses** as we forgive them that **trespass** against us' (Book of Common Prayer)

6i.1.2

ANTITHESIS

DEFINITION: A pair of equal grammatical structures which are the opposite of each other.

To <u>err</u> is <u>human;</u> ⬅➡ to <u>forgive, divine</u>.

Alexander Pope, Essay on Criticism

More examples:

'Love is an ideal thing. Marriage is a real thing.' (Goethe)

'No pain, no gain.'

'One small step for man, one giant leap for mankind.'

6i.1.3

PROGRESSIO

DEFINITION: Saying one thing, then the opposite, and then continuing to the same repeatedly.

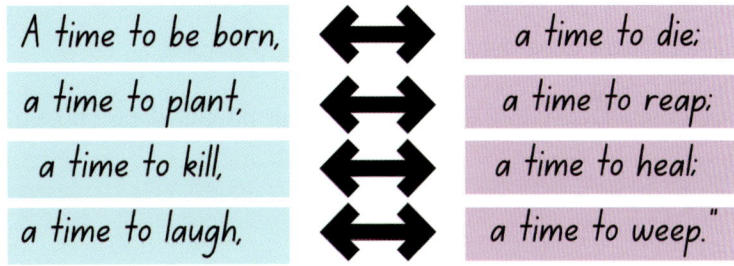

A time to be born, ⬅➡ a time to die;

a time to plant, ⬅➡ a time to reap;

a time to kill, ⬅➡ a time to heal;

a time to laugh, ⬅➡ a time to weep."

Ecclesiastes Chapter 3

Another example:

'It was the best of times, it was the worst of times, it was the age of wisdom, it was the age of foolishness, it was the epoch of belief, it was the epoch of incredulity, it was the season of light, it was the season of darkness, it was the spring of hope, it was the winter of despair."
(A Tale of Two Cities, Charles Dickens)

HYPERBATON

DEFINITION: Changing the natural order of words.
(HINT: think Yoda...)

Other examples:

'One swallow does not a summer make.' (Aristotle)

'Some rise by sin, and some by virtue fall' (Measure for Measure)

6i.1.4

ANADIPLOSIS

DEFINITION: Starting each successive clause or sentence by repeating the word or phrase from the end of the previous one.

Once you change your philosophy, you change your thought pattern.

Once you change your thought pattern, you change your attitude.

Once you change your attitude, it changes your behavior pattern and

then you go on into some action.

Malcolm X, 1964

Other examples:

'Suffering breeds character; character breeds faith; in the end faith will not disappoint.' (Jesse Jackson, 1988)

'The love of wicked men converts to fear;
That fear to hate; and hate turns one, or both,
To worthy danger, and deserved death.' (Richard II)

6i.1.5

PERIODIC SENTENCES

DEFINITION: A sentence where the main clause or predicate is at the end - you don't know what the main topic of the sentence is until the end.

After walking home, changing my clothes, feeding the cat and cooking dinner, _I finally got to relax._

MAIN CLAUSE

'To believe your own thought, to believe that what is true for you in your private heart is true for all men, _that is genius._'

'Self-Reliance' - Ralph Waldo Emmerson

MAIN CLAUSE

6i.1.6

186 ☐

6i.1.7

OXYMORON

DEFINITION: A phrase or pair of words which seem to contradict each other.

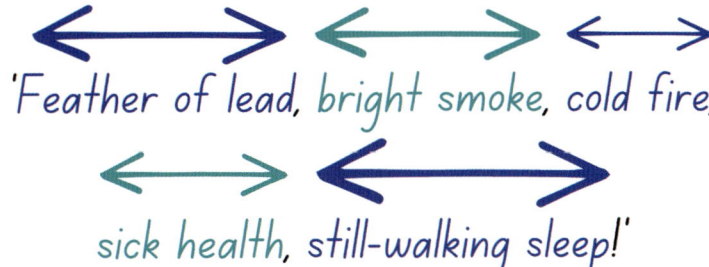

'Feather of lead, bright smoke, cold fire,

sick health, still-walking sleep!'

Romeo - Act 1, Scene 1

Other examples:

old news
deafening silence
bittersweet
organised chaos

6i.1.8

ZEGUMA

DEFINITION: When you use one word or phrase to modify two or more other words in different ways.

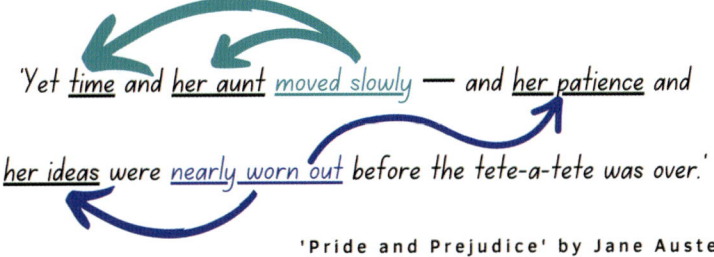

'Yet time and her aunt moved slowly — and her patience and

her ideas were nearly worn out before the tete-a-tete was over.'

'Pride and Prejudice' by Jane Austen

Other examples:

She broke my car and my heart.

The drive was so bumpy he lost his keys and his lunch.

He fished for trout and compliments.

APOPHASIS

6i.1.9

DEFINITION: When you raise an issue by claiming not to mention it.

<u>I won't mention</u> my opponent's <u>criminal past</u>...

CLAIMS NOT TO MENTION IT

MENTIONS IT

<u>I would never speak badly</u> of a fellow lawyer, especially one

who seems so <u>incapable of telling the truth</u>...

CLAIMS NOT TO MENTION IT

MENTIONS IT

POLYSYNDETON

6i.2.1

DEFINITION: The use of several conjunctions to join ideas in a list.

'There were frowzy fields, <u>and</u> cow-houses, <u>and</u> dunghills, <u>and</u>

dustheaps, <u>and</u> ditches, <u>and</u> gardens, <u>and</u> summer-houses, <u>and</u>

carpet-beating grounds, at the very door of the Railway.'

'Dombey and Son' by Charles Dickens

ASYNDETON

DEFINITION: The a list of items without conjunctions.

'A squeezing, wrenching, grasping, scraping, clutching, covetous old sinner.'

'A Christmas Carol' by Charles Dickens

6i.2.2

ISOCOLON

DEFINITION: Two or more clauses or sentences of equal structure

Roses are red..

Violets are blue..

My gorgeous palace for a hermitage,

My gay apparel for an almsman's gown,

My figured goblets for a dish of wood,

My sceptre for a palmer's walking staff,

Richard II, Shakespeare

6i.2.3

189 □

TEXT-LEVEL CHOICES

This section is mostly relevant for creative writing. Things like perspective and tense tend to be prescribed in academic and rhetorical writing because of the audience and purpose of each. Here, then, we are concerned with the grammatical choices which a writer can make, which enable them to create tone and atmosphere and provoke that ineffable reader sense of how things are, before they've even considered pathetic fallacy and other such 'noisy' devices.

'Should I write this in 1st person?'

English teachers are asked things like this a lot. We probably respond with something like, "it's your choice," but how confident are we that students are making those choices based on a real understanding of what they want to achieve?

For students, it is relatively easy to select vocabulary or use imagery because it is simpler to understand how these things create meaning. Understanding how writing in the third person can create distance, or how expressing something in the agentless passive might create ambiguity, is more abstract.

Voice, perspective, tense, and sentence type are things we have already talked about. In this section we are keen to show how incredibly useful these concepts are for writing, but without placing too much emphasis on having to label things. This is about exploration and students being able to try lots of different things to see what best matches their writing intention.

1. Voice
2. Person
3. Tense
4. Sentence Type

Brief reminders

Grammatical voice describes the relationship between AGENT (the thing which is *doing* something) and PATIENT (the thing which is being done to), and the VERB (the action, process, or state which is being described).

Grammatical person (perspective) distinguishes between something which is voiced from the perspective of a first-person speaker (I, we, me, us), addressing an audience directly in second person (you, your, yourself, yourselves), or talking to another person or people (he, him, she, her, they, them, it, its).

VISUAL first, second, third . . .

Grammatical tense expresses time relative to the moment of speaking. For example you might describe something which ***has* happened** in the past, something which ***is* happening** now, or something which ***will* happen** in the future.

Present simple: I do, I do do
Present continuous: I am doing

Present perfect: I have done
Present perfect continuous: I have been doing

Past simple: I did, I did do
Past continuous: I was doing
Past perfect: I had done
Past perfect continuous: I had been doing

Future simple: I will do
Future continuous: I will be doing
Future perfect: I will have done
Future perfect continuous: I will have been doing

(NOTE: don't worry about whether you can remember each of these – remember, this is about meaning, not labelling things . . . knowing present, past, and future is enough!)

Sentence types distinguish between whether a sentence functions as a statement of fact (declarative), a command (imperative), a question (interrogative), or an exclamation (exclamative).

(See examples of these on page 171.)

Though these four concepts are quite distinct from one another, they are all similar in that they contribute to the seemingly ineffable sense of tone and atmosphere in the texts we write. Have a look at this example from *The Princess Bride*:

My name is Inigo Montoya. You killed my father. Prepare to die.

- Spoken in first person (my)
- Active voice: '**You**   killed   **my father**'
                 AGENT   VERB   PATIENT
- Imperative: **Prepare** to die
- Past tense: **killed**

We could change some of these elements and have this instead:

My name is Inigo Montoya. My father has been killed.

By changing the second sentence to the agentless passive, we suddenly lose any element of blame for the death of his father.

We could instead go with:

'Prepare to die,' spat Montoya, 'my father is dead.'

This is now in third person, adds the verb 'spat' which gives additional information, and has taken us even further from the original direct blame, to say simply that the 'father is dead,' rather than ascribing any deliberate action which caused that death.

There are so many ways to play with language like this. Students might ultimately decide that the original version is the best but looking at these subtle variations can be incredibly helpful because it gives us a framework to make informed choices.

What could this look like in the classroom?

Iconic lines

1. Take brilliant lines from literature – these could be from a range of different texts, from something you are studying, or even something a student has written.
2. Ask students to identify things about the line: what is the tense, voice, person/perspective, sentence type?
3. Ask students to DO SOMETHING to change the line. You could provide one or more of these prompts:
   - Change the line so that it is in the past/present/future tense
   - Change the line so that it is written in the first/second/third person
   - Change the imperative/declarative/interrogative/exclamative into a(n) imperative/declarative/interrogative/
   - Change this statement so that it is written in the active/passive voice.

(NOTE: this step is optional and certainly shouldn't become a grammar labelling exercise!)

These prompts can and should be adapted so that they are more specific to the starting sentence. Here are some examples:

'Whatever our souls are made of, his and mine are the same.'
(*Wuthering Heights* – Emily Bronte)

- Change the line so that it is written in the third person
  Whatever their souls were made of, his and hers were the same.
- Change the line so that it is written in the second person
  Whatever your soul is made of, mine is the same.
- Change the line so that it uses interrogatives
  What are our souls made of? Are they the same?

You might then ask students to consider:

- How have these changes affected the meaning of the lines? The one in third person would have to be voiced by another character – who would that be? Why? What is the power of the original being voiced in the first person?
- How does the version with interrogatives change the tone at this moment in the story?

'He stepped down, trying not to look long at her, as if she were the sun, yet he saw her, like the sun, even without looking.'
(*Anna Karenina* – Leo Tolstoy)

- Change the line so that it is written in the first person
  I stepped down, trying not to look long at her, as if she were the sun, yet I saw her, like the sun, even without looking.
- Change the line so that it is in the first person and in the present tense
  She is like the sun; I am trying not to look long at her as I step down. Yet I see her, like the sun, even without looking.

(NOTE: in this example, we have also changed the positioning, which you can read about on page 181.)

(REF: The Essential Neruda.)

'The moon lives in the lining of your skin'

- Change the line so that it is in the passive voice
  In the lining of your skin lives the moon.

You could do this with a longer passage and look at the impact it has on the overall tone, such as in the opening to Moby Dick:

Call me Ishmael. Some years ago – never mind how long precisely – having little or no money in my purse, and nothing particular to interest me on shore, I thought I would sail about a little and see the watery part of the world. It is a way I have of driving off the spleen, and regulating the circulation. Whenever I find myself growing grim about the mouth; whenever it is a damp, drizzly November in my soul; whenever I find myself involuntarily pausing before coffin warehouses, and bringing up the rear of every funeral I meet; and especially whenever my hypos get such an upper hand of me, that it requires a strong moral principle to prevent me from deliberately stepping into the street, and methodically knocking people's hats off – then, I account it high time to get to sea as soon as I can. This is my substitute for pistol and ball. With a philosophical flourish Cato throws himself upon his sword; I quietly take to the ship. There is nothing surprising in this. If they but knew it, almost all men in their degree, some time or other, cherish very nearly the same feelings towards the ocean with me.

(*Moby Dick* – Herman Melville)

- Change this extract to third person and increase the *distance* between the character and the narrative voice so that there is less familiarity . . .

His name was Ishmael. Some years before, having little or no money in his purse, he went sailing. It was a way he had of driving off the spleen and regulating the circulation. Whenever he found himself growing grim about the mouth; whenever it was a damp, drizzly November in his soul, then he accounted it high time

> to get to sea as soon as he could. This was his substitute for pistol and ball. There is nothing surprising in this. Almost all men in their degree cherish very nearly the same feelings towards the ocean as Ishmael.

This version is far more direct and less conversational. Consider just the opening statement: 'Call me Ishmael.' It is an odd start which immediately gives the first person speaker control over what we call him, almost implying that this might not be his name, but that this is the one he is choosing to use. By using third-person instead, we start with certainty – 'His name **was** Ishmael.'

But is this creative writing? The act of manipulating text and interrogating the choices which writers make when they frame a narrative is incredibly helpful as a way of informing students' own choices, but also as a platform for new writing.

In the next section, we have included a range of further extracts from literature which might act as a foundation for playing with language.

MODELS AS A FOUNDATION FOR CREATIVE WRITING

Here are some other examples of lines and longer text extracts which can be useful for this kind of exploration. We have provided notes for each with some ideas for how you might frame these in the classroom, but these are just suggestions, and you might have other, better ideas.

'I took a deep breath and listened to the hold brag of my heart. I am, I am, I am.'
(*The Bell Jar* – Sylvia Plath)

(NOTE: it might be interesting to explore changing this one to second or third person, OR thinking about moving 'I am . . .' to the start of the sentence as something which her heart is *saying*.)

'Shoot all the blue jays you want, if you can hit em, but remember that it's a sin to kill a mockingbird.'
(*To Kill a Mockingbird* – Harper Lee)

(NOTE: this is written with imperatives 'shoot' and 'remember.' It could be rewritten as a memory by the character listening to this advice instead . . . past tense and declaratives. Or it could be written as a conversation with interrogatives.)

'And in that moment, like a swift intake of breath, the rain came.'
(*Other Voices, Other Rooms* – Truman Capote)

(NOTE: this might be interesting if it started in first person: 'I felt . . .' or something similar.)

'We shall meet in the place where there is no darkness.'
(*1984* – George Orwell)

(NOTE: this is in future tense – it could change to past, or it could be written as an interrogative: Will you meet me?)

'You forget what you want to remember, and you remember what you want to forget.'
(*The Road* – Cormack McCarthy)

(NOTE: this is a great example of chiasmus – students could look at the other rhetorical sentence structures on pages 182–189 and try to rewrite this in a different structure.)

'In our village, folks say God crumbles up the old moon into stars.'
(*One Day in the Life of Ivan Denisovich* – Aleksandr Solzhenitsyn)

(NOTE: this could be written using direct speech: "God crumbles up the old moon into stars," said the woman.)

'All we have to decide is what to do with the time that is given us.'
(*The Fellowship of the Ring* – J.R.R. Tolkien)

(NOTE: this is a declarative – it could be rewritten as an imperative.)

'Many years later, as he faced the firing squad, Colonel Aureliano Buendia was to remember that distant afternoon when his father took him to discover ice.'
(*One Hundred Years of Solitude* – Gabriel García Márquez)

(NOTE: this is a great example of an introduction to a character, where a memory is introduced with two prepositional phrases and then an unusual image. Could students mimic this structure for a character for their own? i.e. PREP PHRASE (DESCRIBE TIME), PREP PHRASE (DESCRIBE AN EXPERIENCE), X REMEMBERS . . . UNUSUAL IMAGE.)

'She had waited all her life for something, and it had killed her when it found her.'

(*Their Eyes Were Watching God* – Zora Neale Hurston)

(NOTE: this is written with 'She' as the agent in the first clause, and 'it' as the agent in the second clause. Could students change this so that the second clause is written in the agentless passive? e.g. she had been killed . . . – are there other things students can do to make the line more precise, e.g. rewrite it saying explicitly what the 'something' is. What difference does it make?)

'And the ashes blew towards us with the salt wind from the sea'

(*Rebecca* – Daphne Du Maurier)

(NOTE: this could be rewritten without reference to the wind from the sea – what difference would that make? Or students could change it and position the 'salt wind from the sea' at the front of the sentence instead.)

'The knife came down, missing him by inches, and he took off.'

(*Catch-22* – Joseph Heller)

(NOTE: this could be rewritten with 'him' as the agent – e.g. He rolled out of the knife's path . . ., or students could use this structure: The NOUN – VERB – ADVERB (DIRECTION), VERB – NOUN – PREPOSITIONAL PHRASE, CONJUNCTION – NOUN – PHRASAL VERB, to write their own short sentence description. E.g. The cake came out, tempting them with chocolate scent, and they tucked in.)

'It was a bright cold day in April, and the clocks were striking thirteen.'

(*1984* – George Orwell)

(NOTE: can students rewrite in different tenses: it is, it will be, or using modal auxiliary verbs: it should be, it might be? How does this change the overall meaning?)

'I must not fear. Fear is the mind-killer. Fear is the little-death that brings total obliteration. I will face my fear. I will permit it to pass over me and through me. And when it has gone past I will turn the inner eye to see its path. Where the fear has gone there will be nothing. Only I will remain.'

(*Dune* – Frank Herbert)

(NOTE: this is a great example of threading the same word through a series of sentences – see 'fear.' Students might rewrite this passage to enhance this motif, but also include the word fear in other forms – fearful, fearing, fearfulness, fearfully. They could also change this from first person to second ('You must not fear . . .') or third ('They/he/she must not fear . . .'). Explore the different effects of these choices with students.)

'It was the best of times, it was the worst of times, it was the age of wisdom, it was the age of foolishness, it was the epoch of belief, it was the epoch of incredulity, it was the season of Light, it was the season of Darkness, it was the spring of hope, it was the winter of despair, we had everything before us, we had nothing before us, we were all going direct to Heaven, we were all going direct the other way – in short, the period was so far like the present period, that some of its noisiest authorities insisted on its being received, for good or for evil, in the superlative degree of comparison only.'

(*A Tale of Two Cities* – Charles Dickens)

(NOTE: this is a great example of stacked clauses and repetition – anaphora to be precise. The repetition of 'it was' could be changed to 'was it' to make the passage one of questioning and uncertainty. How would that change the meaning?)

'I am a sick man. . . . I am a spiteful man. I am an unattractive man. I believe my liver is diseased. However, I know nothing at all about my disease, and do not know for certain what ails me. I don't consult a doctor for it, and never have, though I have a respect for medicine and doctors. Besides, I am extremely superstitious, sufficiently so to respect medicine, anyway (I am well-educated enough not to be superstitious, but I am superstitious). No, I refuse to consult a doctor from spite. That you probably will not understand. Well, I understand it, though. Of course, I can't explain who it is precisely that I am mortifying in this case by my spite: I am perfectly well aware that I cannot "pay out" the doctors by not consulting them; I know better than anyone that by all this I am only injuring myself and no one else. But still, if I don't consult a doctor it is from spite. My liver is bad, well then let it hurt even worse!'

(*Notes from Underground* – Fyodor Dostoyevsky)

(NOTE: this is a list of complaints framed as declarative sentences – some might call these exclamative. Students could extract the declaratives and rewrite some of them as a list of insults and imperatives, e.g. You are sick. You are spiteful. You are unattractive. Your liver is diseased. You know nothing about your disease. Don't consult a doctor, ever . . . while this will produce a rather strange piece of prose, it will highlight the incredibly negative and emphatic tone which Dostoyevsky creates in this section of the text. Students might consider how the writer uses this sequence of short, simple declarations to create a striking character.)

The studio was filled with the rich odour of roses, and when the light summer wind stirred amidst the trees of the garden, there came through the open door the heavy scent of the lilac, or the more delicate perfume of the pink-flowering thorn.

(*The Picture of Dorian Grey* – Oscar Wilde)

(NOTE: this is a great example of very elaborate description using modifiers. Students might identify where there are descriptive verbs, such as 'filled'; qualifying adjectives, such as 'rich,' 'light,' 'heavy,' and 'delicate' being contrasted against one another; precise adjective colours – 'lilac' and 'pink.' They might use this example to write using their own version of these images. They could take the same colour palette and the same four qualifiers and write a description of a different location using them, for instance. How does their new piece of writing differ from the original model? How is it similar?)

'You think because he doesn't love you that you are worthless. You think that because he doesn't want you anymore that he is right – that his judgement and opinion of you are correct. If he throws you out, then you are garbage. You think he belongs to you because you want to belong to him. Don't. It's a bad word, 'belong.' Especially when you put it with somebody you love. Love shouldn't be like that. Did you ever see the way the clouds love a mountain? They circle all around it; sometimes you can't even see the mountain for the clouds. But you know what? You go up top and what do you see? His head. The clouds never cover the head. His head pokes through, because the clouds let him; they don't wrap him up. They let him keep his head up high, free, with nothing to hide him or bind him. You can't own a human being. You can't lose what you don't own. Suppose you did own him. Could you really love somebody who was absolutely nobody without you? You really want somebody like that? Somebody who falls apart when you walk out the door? You don't, do you? And neither does he. You're turning over your whole life to him. Your whole life, girl. And if it means so little to you that you can just give it away, hand it to him, then why should it mean any more to him? He can't value you more than you value yourself.'

(*Song of Solomon* – Toni Morrison)

(NOTE: this is a series of statements and questions written in second person. Explore with students how these interrogatives and declaratives, and the personal pronoun 'you' combine to create a force of feeling and intensity. Students could rewrite this passage, or parts of it, from the perspective of the person being spoken to. They could do it as a stream of consciousness in first person and consider how the change from 'you' to 'me' makes the questions and statements more introspective and uncertain.)

Grammar knowledge can enhance the quality of writing, but ALSO the effectiveness of writing as a generative thinking process.

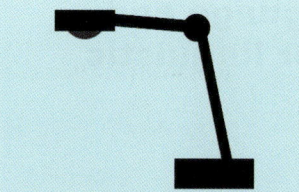

Live modelling, including opportunity for metacognitive commentary and reflection is a powerful tool for the teaching of writing.

Scaffolds should provide OPTIONS and support student cognitive load, rather than prescribing rigid structures.

THE DOMAINS OF WRITING IN SECONDARY ENGLISH

ACADEMIC
...for literature essays

RHETORIC
...for persuasive texts

CREATIVE
...for playing with language

All writing is writing. There are significant areas of overlap between writing in all forms and genres.

KNOWLEDGE IS POWER: if students know what is possible, they have more choices and therefore the greater potential for clarity and control over what they say and how they say it.

Nothing is 'wrong' if it's what the writer intends.

Create a culture where students manipulate texts - changing words and structures like artists shaping clay.

Remember that grammar knowledge is there to empower, not to restrict. Choice over all else.

6i.4.1

7 Attitudes to language and opportunities for linguistic investigation

ATTITUDES TO GRAMMAR

'Grammar' is arguably one of the most debated topics in education probably because the term carries with it a wealth of associations with ideas of 'correctness' and standards. In fact, judging the way that people write and speak and associating those behaviours with standards has, unfortunately, been around for a long time. Fortunately, this also provides an interesting topic for students to explore!

In language debates, 'grammar' is often connected to ideas around standard and non-standard varieties of English. Standard English, which is the variety (notice we are using this word rather than judgemental terms such as 'proper,' 'correct,' etc.) of English that has come to be used in formal contexts and is identified in the National Curriculum, for example as the variety that children should learn and be able to use in their speech and writing. Standard English itself, however, has an interesting history. As London began to develop as the political and cultural centre of England, professions working there needed a standardised form of language in which to communicate and keep records. In turn, the population movement to London from the east midlands brought with it a regional variety of English that quickly formed a 'standard.' Once the printing press arrived, this variety became fully standardised in writing and thus spread beyond London to different regions. Standard English, then, is really only one variety of English that gained prestige and became associated with power and correctness.

(REMEMBER what we said on pages 5–6 about different varieties of English?)

We haven't got the space to discuss the entire debate about Standard English in this book, but it's worth pointing out – in line with our overall approach which focuses on grammar as a way of describing actual language use rather than prescribing rules – that non-standard varieties equally have their own grammar; in other words, it's wrong simply to equate grammar with the standardised form. As an example of this, 'I ain't,' which occurs in many non-standard

DOI: 10.4324/9781003175261-10

varieties of English follows the pattern of negating a primary auxiliary verb by placing 'not' after it and then contracting it by removing the 'o' (the omitted vowel is marked by the apostrophe). Standard English actually has no form for negating and contracting 'I am'; 'I amn't' which would follow the pattern of 'You aren't,' He isn't,' and so on fell out of use many years ago. In fact, one theory about 'I ain't' is that it emerged from speakers eliding the 'm' sound in 'amn't' over time. So in fact the non-standard form has a fascinating and certainly grammatical past!

There are some other points about Standard English that are worth mentioning. First is the fact that Standard English can be spoken in any accent. Sometimes Standard English can be conflated with Received Pronunciation (sometimes known as the 'posh' accent), but Standard English is a dialect rather than a specific accent. Second, Standard English is, like any language variety, useful in specific contexts and not useful in others. For example we might want to use Standard English in a formal academic essay but not when communicating with friends. In effect then, the idea of Standard English being 'proper' or 'correct' can be replaced with the better idea of register, a term linguists use to describe a variety of language in a particular context of use. Standard and non-standard forms are best considered as different registers that writers and speakers draw on depending on the situation they find themselves in.

(NOTE: this is IMPORTANT. Our students can all speak in Standard English, whilst still retaining a regional accent. A young person in Newcastle can speak in Standard English just as well as someone from Surrey. Explicit teaching of the difference between *accent* and *dialect* is powerful.)

In terms of teaching, we feel that students should know the difference between standard and non-standard varieties and be aware of the history of Standard English and its function as one kind of linguistic resource. But they should also be aware that non-standard forms are not ungrammatical or incorrect or inferior in any way. In fact there is plenty to celebrate and explore with non-standard forms and this can be a really good springboard for students to explore their own language use and others' attitudes towards different varieties both of English and of other languages.

One key reason why this is so interesting is that language is inherently tied to identity. When we use language in any situation, we are effectively upholding or projecting an identity, a version of ourselves that we want others to see. Language is as much a marker of identity as the clothes we wear, the music we listen to and the books we read. Of course, identity is not fixed and we can move in and out of various identities that we have in different contexts. Just as we might change our clothes if we are attending a particular kind of event or if the weather gets warmer or colder, so we can adapt our writing and speech styles (our registers) to fit the context we are in. In linguistics, this shift in performance is called code-switching and there is plenty of research that shows that we are all able to do this intuitively and fairly easily.

WHAT MIGHT THIS LOOK LIKE IN THE CLASSROOM?

Consider getting students to switch the 'code' of a text you give them. A really simple introductory task is something like this:

Display on the board: Good morning. I am pleased to meet you.

Ask students: Who would speak like this? What might the situation be? Why?

Students rewrite this greeting for the following speakers and situations:

- Them (the student) greeting friends in the park
- Them (the student) greeting a grandparent, older relative, or respected family friend
- A parent greeting their 5-year-old child when they wake up.

For each of these different scenarios, discuss *how* the language choices have changed and *why*. This is a very simple way to show how register shifts according to context. None of the greetings is inherently better or worse than the others – they are just different.

Students are often fascinated by attitudes to language. One interesting way to explore this would be to collect instances of news reports on attitudes towards language. These could easily be turned into a corpus and analysed using word frequency or keyword searches that we outlined in Section 3. For example in what contexts do phrases like 'bad grammar' and 'incorrect grammar' appear? Another interesting area to explore would be how grammar is framed in schools. The prestige attached to Standard English can be seen in various official education documents (government publications, Ofsted reports, examination board specifications) over many years, and commentators have often been quick to connect so-called bad English with other problems in society. A very famous example of this was the then Conservative Party Chairman, Norman Tebbit, who in a radio interview in 1984 bemoaning the fact that he thought teachers no longer taught accurate punctuation and spelling to their students (it wasn't true, of course), claimed:

> If you allow standards to slip to the stage where good English is no better than bad English, where people turn up filthy . . . at school . . . all those things tend to cause people to have no standards at all, and once you lose standards then there's no imperative to stay out of crime.
>
> In Inglis and Aers (2008: 177)

More recently, there have been a number of stories in the news, some of them attracting a lot of attention, around so-called word bans, effectively when a school decides that some words and phrases are unacceptable for students to use and outlaws them, often in the form of a poster of banned words and/ or a letter home to parents. The banned words are often a combination of non-standard grammatical forms, colloquial words, words and phrases that may have been imported from popular culture or from different varieties of English, and features that are commonly associated with spoken language. Here for example is a recent list from a school in London.

FILLERS

The following words must not be used at the beginning of sentences:

- Ermmm . . .
- Because . . .
- No . . .
- Like . . .
- Say . . .
- You see . . .
- You know . . .
- Basically . . .

SLANG AND IDIOMS

These expressions must not be used:

- He cut his eyes at me
- Oh my days
- Oh my God
- That's a neck
- Wow
- That's long
- Bare
- Cuss

(NOTE: it is critical that students feel that their identity is respected and valued. For students who are multilingual, or who have a cultural heritage which means they use other varieties of English at home, we must avoid making value judgements about language which place one variety above another. Those students must understand how to code-switch where appropriate, but not be told that their way of speaking is somehow wrong or that it has less status.)

These kinds of lists (a quick Google search will reveal others) seem intuitively common sense but are problematic in several ways. First, they conflate different forms of language (e.g. dialect words, words which show speaker support); second, they promote false 'rules' (e.g. spoken language doesn't have sentences as such and there's no reason whatsoever why written sentences should not begin with 'Because' or 'Basically'); third, they wrongly suggest that words should be banned when instead they could be promoting a greater understanding of the idea of register. Finally, they both likely misjudge young people's ability to code-switch and could conceivably affect self-identity particularly if any of the banned words are commonly used in other contexts (e.g. their home language).

So the message is a simple one: help students to understand the idea of register rather than 'wrong' grammar and encourage them to explore attitudes to grammar in an open, critical, and linguistically informed way.

INVESTIGATIONS

In the final section in this chapter, we provide some brief ideas for projects that students might undertake around some of the key ideas in this chapter.

Stylistics: a stylistic analysis can be undertaken with any text. One useful way of encouraging students to engage explicitly with language would be to ask them to rewrite a text (it could be part of a novel, a poem, a news report, etc.) substituting one language feature for another (e.g. replacing all the adjectives with different ones) or else shifting some other aspect (e.g. rewrite a third-person narrative into a first person one, replacing all the pronouns and thinking about what other language features might appear once point of view changes). This kind of textual intervention (see Rob Pope's 1995 book for a detailed over-view) is an excellent way of sharpening students' language awareness. Students could also explore the grammar of particular genres by transforming a poem into prose or into something more radical like a graphic novel. Or they could rewrite a text for a different audience, for example turning a poem into a storybook for young children. Again, in these instances they can explore the explicit language choices they make and how these depend on generic conventions and audience.

Corpus approaches: We think that this kind of work is exciting because corpus tools really do allow for the exploration of larger patterns of text. If you are looking to examine an even bigger set of texts than the poems we have looked at, then you might want to look at the Corpus Linguistics in Context (CLiC) tool that we mentioned, which can be found at https://clic.bham.ac.uk/. You can access a considerable number of corpora of classic novels and novelists. It would be very easy to go to the 'Concordance' tab on the right-hand side, then select either a single text or a larger corpus and enter a word to see all the occurrences of that word in context. Students can then explore the significance of any patterns they see using their knowledge of grammar.

(REMEMBER: we explored the use of Corpus tools on pages 79–84.)

Media representations: Examining agency and metaphor in non-fiction can offer enabling ways of encouraging younger students to explore how texts position readers to accept stories in particular ways. For example analysing who is to blame (and who isn't) in newspaper reporting allows students to understand that there is no such thing as a neutral report. Students could choose a news story where agency/blame is likely to play a role (such as a court case, conflict, dramatic sports event) and then collect as many different versions of the story from different publications, including different genres. How does the grammar work in these representations? Who gets blamed and who doesn't? Could any differences be connected to any ideological/political stance that the text producer has?

(REMEMBER: we looked at examples of language in the media on pages 13–16, and 84–89.)

Accentism: There are plenty of projects that students could undertake to explore attitudes to language. One excellent example would be to explore how accentism (discrimination based on the way someone sounds when they speak) appears in news reports, in politics, in television shows, and so on. Just like the 'banned words' stories in schools, there have been a number of high-profile cases and students could collect examples of these and explore them. What aspects of a person's speech tend to get criticised and what connections are made between speech and, for example competence and intelligence? This kind of work would be a very good way of allowing students to examine the roots of accentism and why it should be rejected just like any other form of discrimination (Edwards 2022).

(NOTE: an example might be this article from 2022: www.independent.co.uk/voices/angela-rayner-tweets-accent-northern-b1992377.html.)

'Standard' English became standard because of the growth of London as the political centre of England. Its prestige happened by **chance**, not because it is 'better' than the other varieties.

Standard English can be spoken in any accent. It has nothing to do with Received Pronunciation (a 'posh' accent)

The different forms of English can be referred to as REGISTERS – avoid saying that some are more 'proper' or more 'correct' than others.

Word bans are a bad idea.

Language use is profoundly personal and tied to identity.

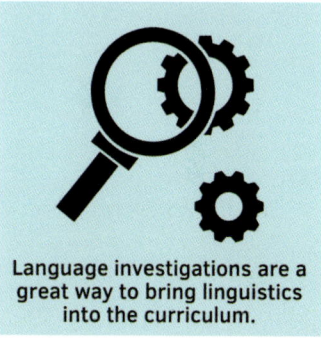

Language investigations are a great way to bring linguistics into the curriculum.

7.1.1

Curriculum and beyond

8   English curriculum

By this point in the book, we hope that we can all accept the following truth: *grammar – language knowledge – is essential to the study of English.*

Grammar is core, and we need highly skilled English teachers working with an expertly designed curriculum for students to become knowledgeable and proficient readers and writers.

But how do we get there?

This chapter will explore the challenges and opportunities of mapping grammar across the English curriculum.

A NOTE ON CURRICULUM

We often use the definite article when talking about curriculum: *the* curriculum. This can be misleading. It can trick us into thinking that curriculum is a definable, solid 'thing' which we create, print, laminate, or publish on our website whereas, in reality, it is a fluid piece of work with no beginning and no end.

Talking about *English* curriculum in isolation is also problematic. The adjective *English* in this case implies that curriculum can be confined to a single subject, when the reality is that, though teachers might just teach one subject all day every day, students actually experience curriculum as a huge interweaved series of lessons in a range of different subjects. We can think about English content and sequencing as subject specialists, but there are so many opportunities to explore cross-discipline links which would enhance learning in all those areas.

It is also important for us to acknowledge that, though grammar is certainly a fundamental part of our subject, it is, of course, not confined to English. Many of the reasons for teaching grammar which we outline in this chapter apply to other subjects, too. Many of the strategies, for example those linked to teaching writing, would work very well in any subject where students have to write (and that's *all* of them).

So, curriculum is a constantly evolving entity which describes *what* we teach and *when* we teach it. We have already explored principles for teaching grammar – the *implementation* of that curriculum in the classroom – threaded with an understanding of how learning happens over time. A great curriculum

DOI: 10.4324/9781003175261-11

is only effective with strong implementation. Throughout this chapter on curriculum, we will continue to refer back to elements of classroom teaching from previous sections of the book so that the relationship between the curriculum theory and the classroom practice is clear.

Curriculum planning means trying to answer these questions:

- What is the **powerful knowledge** which will enable students to succeed, empower them to engage in the world, and inspire them to continue to learn?
- What is the most efficient and effective way to **sequence** the teaching and re-teaching of this content to ensure that learning sticks in the **long term**?
- How can we make explicit links between new and existing knowledge, **build schema**, and enable students to see golden threads developing over time?

(REMEMBER what we said about schema and long-term memory development, referencing Efrat Furst (2018), on page 49.)

- How can we ensure that challenge and complexity **build** in line with student need?
- How can we **deepen and refine** knowledge and skill with every successive re-exposure to content and practice?
- How can we assess how well students learn content and develop skills, and ensure that this **assessment** informs our teaching and curriculum design in the future?
- How can our curriculum be bespoke and be **responsive** to the needs of our cohort?

These questions are open ended. Their answers will change incrementally over time with changes in student populations, societal shifts, and our understanding of how learning happens. Curriculum design, therefore, requires deliberate, intelligent planning and a commitment to keep working on a job which will never be done.

CURRICULUM PRINCIPLES IN ENGLISH

English curriculum is a multifaceted, context-specific, and highly complex beast. Grammar is important, but so are all the other domains of English knowledge and skill which must be given space in a limited time frame. The main issue with many attempts to put grammar into the English curriculum is that it is often an add-on to the main body of work. Schools often plan explicit grammar lessons which sit outside the normal curriculum, or grammar starters or activities which are done alongside the substantive units, but which are not integrated with them.

The most common questions about curriculum and grammar which English teachers ask us are along these lines:

How do we make grammar meaningful and not a bolt-on to the curriculum?
How do we stop grammar from feeling like it's not relevant?
How do we create a successful grammar program?

The problem with all three of these questions is that they originate from the notion that grammar is somehow distinct from 'English.'

Grammar has long been seen as something which is separate and 'other' from the rest of our subject. Perhaps this is a hangover from the historical separation of Language and Literature, or it is a result of people's significant lack of grammar knowledge and subsequent reluctance to teach it, but it has rarely sat comfortably as part of the curriculum. Because of this separation, many English teachers have never prioritised grammar as an area of knowledge they should develop for themselves. There is a dearth of subject specialism in the English profession, which means that we often farm out the planning and sequencing of grammar teaching to those we deem specialists. We buy external grammar resource packages and, as a result, end up delivering English curriculum with added grammar thrown in at strategic intervals. This is nothing close to the complex, deliberate design which we described earlier in this chapter.

We have seen many iterations of this bolt-on approach to grammar during our time in various English departments, such as:

(NOTE: this isn't the fault of English teachers – remember what we said about the history of grammar education in the UK on pages 11–13.)

* Students having one hour per fortnight of one-off grammar teaching which is completely separate from the content they are studying in their main English lessons.
* Students being given 'literacy starters' which are pre-planned ten-minute activities every day during the first lesson of the day in whichever subject they happen to be, delivered by non-specialists under the umbrella of 'literacy across the curriculum.'
* Students being given lists of grammatical terms to learn for regular quizzes, without the use of these terms and features being pulled into the substantive curriculum.

None of these strategies is inherently wrong. As part of a coherent wider plan for grammar, each of these strategies might be perfectly good ideas. The issue is that all of them tick the 'doing grammar' box, but none of them actually fosters a powerful knowledge of grammar which has a meaningful impact on students' ability to write with precision or read with insight.

Why doesn't bolt-on content work?

Based on what we know of cognitive science, the brain's ability to make explicit connections between different pieces of knowledge is incredibly important. As we encounter new information, we connect it to other things we know or have experienced. The connections form structures in the brain called schema. The more connections we make, the bigger and stronger the schema, the more resistant the new information is to forgetting. Every time we learn something new or re-encounter information, the brain modifies or rewires those connections and schema become more complex. How does this relate to teaching grammar? If we teach something as discrete, separate content, students are less able to make those connections in the brain. If, however, we fully integrate grammar into the curriculum, those links are explicit and, therefore, student learning can be more successful. It makes sense that grammar (like any other knowledge) will benefit from being embedded into the main curriculum, frequently revisited, deepened, and refined.

(REMEMBER: we explore these concepts in more detail on pages 49–53.)

The work of Myhill among others has echoed this need for integrated, contextualised grammar teaching. Myhill argued that grammar teaching must be done *in context*, using 'real' texts rather than isolated models created just for grammar instruction. What does this mean in the classroom? Grammar should be one of our curricular threads which is mapped onto the substantive curriculum with everything else.

Grammar: what's the intention?

When we write a curriculum, we must first have a clear sense of what a successful English scholar should understand and be able to do by the end of their course.

We would argue that our aim for students should be threefold:

1. **Writing (and speaking) with precision and possibility**

    Precision means that students have an excellent knowledge of how language structures work so that they can write accurately, but also so that they can make decisions which enable them to say exactly what they intend to say. This does not mean privileging Standard English over other forms of the language, but it does mean enabling students to write with absolute precision in Standard English when the circumstances demand it. This does include the usual 'grammar' things you might already be thinking about: tense, parts of speech, clauses, sentences, punctuation, etc.

    Possibility means that we construct meaning by making language *choices*. Our writing is better if we have more options to choose from. We have more options if we have secure grammar knowledge. The most common obstacle when our own students start writing is that they don't know the range of possibilities which are open to them. It's like they are trying to paint a picture of a sunset but all they have is paint in various shades of blue. By teaching and modelling the use of a range of sentence structures, and explicitly identifying and exploring features of grammar, we can give them access to the whole paint palette.

(REMEMBER, we explore writing in greater detail in Chapter 6.)

2. **Reading texts with a critical eye**

This means that students know how grammar can change meaning and direct pace, tone, and emphasis. Grammatical choices made by writers can be incredibly powerful but can also be subtly manipulative. Students need to understand this, both for academic work and in their own lives in a world full of language in the press, politics, advertising, and social media.

(REMEMBER some of the examples of political and advertising language we have given on pages 13–16, 84–89.)

3. **Grammar as literature (stylistics)**

This means that when students explore literature, their knowledge of grammar is fully integrated into the range of language devices and features which writers employ in their work. There is no separation of grammar from other concepts. Students are able to meaningfully apply their knowledge of grammar to their literary analysis.

(REMEMBER, we go into the value of language awareness for literary analysis in Chapter 5, where there are a number of examples of this in action.)

These *intentions* are clearly aligned with the two central pillars of our subject: reading and writing. Despite this apparent simplicity, building an English curriculum is an incredibly complex undertaking. Our subject covers a wide range of knowledge and skill and, though grammar knowledge is absolutely fundamental, there are other domains within the subject which must also be given space in a limited time frame.

What are the main curriculum challenges for English leaders?

Content: aside from grammar, an English curriculum from Y7 to 11 should cover a wide range of literature from different time periods, genres, and forms; knowledge of subject concepts and terminology (everything from rhetorical devices to metaphysics); knowledge of relevant context, authorial influence, and literary theory; writing in a range of forms and for multiple purposes and audiences; academic analytical writing; skills in oracy; opportunities to build an extensive vocabulary bank; reading, inference, and comprehension skills; and summary, note taking, and synthesis skills. When we consider the fact that KS3 is three years and there are very clear requirements on the National Curriculum, and the GCSE English Language and Literature specifications are very prescriptive, it is easy to see why we struggle for time to fit everything in.

Mapping: the complexity of the subject as detailed earlier also makes any curriculum mapping an incredibly difficult piece of work which requires real vision and expertise, but also significant breadth in subject knowledge.

Perception: in some cases, the perception is that explicit grammar teaching is either unnecessary, too difficult, too boring, or all of the above. Ensuring that teachers have the knowledge, pedagogical expertise, and motivation to teach grammar is critical to successful implementation. That may take some significant change management work within English teams.

HOW DO I MAP GRAMMAR SO THAT IT IS INTEGRATED AND MEANINGFUL?

Getting started with KS2 grammar: building on solid foundations

Good news! We are not starting from scratch when our Y7 students arrive in September each year. Many core grammar concepts have already been covered in some detail by our primary colleagues, and, though these things will certainly need to be revised and returned to regularly, we can build on existing foundations rather than trying to establish knowledge afresh. We would strongly advise that English departments make and sustain good relationships with English leads and KS2 teams in feeder primary schools to understand what incoming students know and what gaps there may be. If possible, try to ascertain:

- Exactly what terminology has been used by primary teachers. Grammar terminology can differ from place to place – many things can be given more than one label. This could cause confusion and misconceptions in students who are still relative novices in this area. Where possible, share practice and ideas with primary colleagues and try to ensure that you are using shared language, or at least addressing differences and unfamiliar terms with students very early on.
- Any key explanations or devices which have been used to teach concepts. Students may be used to certain visual models to explain relationships between clauses, for example. It is also important to understand where these definitions or devices might be limiting in the future. For example if students have been told that a concrete noun is 'something you can touch,' that will lead to significant misconceptions; 'sound' and 'light' are concrete nouns. In cases like this, definitions will need to be unpicked and re-taught.

We would recommend getting a clear sense of what students remember and what they do not very early in Y7, and that the core KS2 grammar content forms part of your retrieval practice content early on so that the grammar gains from primary school are not lost.

English Appendix 2: Vocabulary, grammar, and punctuation

Year 1: Detail of content to be introduced (statutory requirement)

Word	Regular **plural noun suffixes** – *s* or – *es* [for example *dog, dogs; wish, wishes*], including the effects of these suffixes on the meaning of the noun
	Suffixes that can be added to **verbs** where no change is needed in the spelling of root words (e.g. *helping, helped, helper*)
	How the **prefix** *un* – changes the meaning of **verbs** and **adjectives** [negation, for example *unkind*, or *undoing: untie the boat*]
Sentence	How **words** can combine to make **sentences**
	Joining **words** and joining **clauses** using *and*
Text	Sequencing **sentences** to form short narratives
Punctuation	Separation of **words** with spaces
	Introduction to capital letters, full stops, question marks, and exclamation marks to demarcate **sentences**
	Capital letters for names and for the personal **pronoun** *I*
Terminology for pupils	letter, capital letter
	word, singular, plural
	sentence
	punctuation, full stop, question mark, exclamation mark

Year 2: Detail of content to be introduced (statutory requirement)

Word	Formation of **nouns** using **suffixes** such as – *ness*, – *er* and by compounding [for example *whiteboard, superman*]
	Formation of **adjectives** using **suffixes** such as – *ful*, – *less*
	Use of the **suffixes** – *er*, – *est* in **adjectives** and the use of – *ly* in Standard English to turn adjectives into **adverbs**
Sentence	**Subordination** (using *when, if, that, because*) and **coordination** (using *or, and, but*)
	Expanded **noun phrases** for description and specification [for example *the blue butterfly, plain flour, the man on the moon*]
	How the grammatical patterns in a sentence indicate its function as a statement, question, exclamation, or command
Text	Correct choice and consistent use of **present tense** and **past tense** throughout writing
	Use of the **progressive** form of **verbs** in the **present** and **past tense** to mark actions in progress [for example *she is drumming, he was shouting*]

(Continued)

Punctuation	Use of capital letters, full stops, question marks, and exclamation marks to demarcate **sentences**	Table 8.1 (Continued)
	Commas to separate items in a list	
	Apostrophes to mark where letters are missing in spelling and to mark singular possession in nouns [for example *the girl's name*]	
Terminology for pupils	noun, noun phrase	
	statement, question, exclamation, command	
	compound, suffix	
	adjective, adverb, verb	
	tense (past, present)	
	apostrophe, comma	

Year 3: Detail of content to be introduced (statutory requirement)

Word	Formation of **nouns** using a range of **prefixes** [for example *super –* , *anti –* , *auto –*]
	Use of the **forms** *a* or *an* according to whether the next **word** begins with a **consonant** or a **vowel** [for example *a rock*, *an open box*]
	Word families based on common **words**, showing how words are related in form and meaning [for example *solve, solution, solver, dissolve, insoluble*]
Sentence	Expressing time, place, and cause using **conjunctions** [for example *when, before, after, while, so, because*], **adverbs** [for example *then, next, soon, therefore*], or **prepositions** [for example *before, after, during, in, because of*]
Text	Introduction to paragraphs as a way to group related material
	Headings and sub-headings to aid presentation
	Use of the **present perfect** form of **verbs** instead of the simple past [for example *He has gone out to play* contrasted with *He went out to play*]
Punctuation	Introduction to inverted commas to **punctuate** direct speech
Terminology for pupils	preposition, conjunction
	word family, prefix
	clause, subordinate clause
	direct speech
	consonant, consonant letter, vowel, vowel letter
	inverted commas (or 'speech marks')

Year 4: Detail of content to be introduced (statutory requirement)

Word	The grammatical difference between **plural** and **possessive** *– s*
	Standard English forms for **verb inflections** instead of local spoken forms [for example *we were* instead of *we was*, or *I did* instead of *I done*]
Sentence	Noun phrases expanded by the addition of modifying adjectives, nouns, and preposition phrases (e.g. *the teacher* expanded to *the strict math teacher with curly hair*)
	Fronted adverbials [for example *Later that day*, I heard the bad news.]

Text	Use of paragraphs to organise ideas around a theme
	Appropriate choice of **pronoun** or **noun** within and across **sentences** to aid **cohesion** and avoid repetition
Punctuation	Use of inverted commas and other **punctuation** to indicate direct speech [for example a comma after the reporting clause; end punctuation within inverted commas: *The conductor shouted, 'Sit down!'*]
	Apostrophes to mark **plural** possession [for example *the girl's name, the girls' names*]
	Use of commas after **fronted adverbials**
Terminology for pupils	determiner
	pronoun, possessive pronoun
	adverbial

Year 5: Detail of content to be introduced (statutory requirement)

Word	Converting **nouns** or **adjectives** into **verbs** using **suffixes** [for example – *ate;* – *ise;* – *ify*]
	Verb prefixes [for example *dis* – , *de* – , *mis* – , *over* – and *re* –]
Sentence	**Relative clauses** beginning with *who*, *which*, *where*, *when*, *whose*, *that*, or an omitted relative pronoun
	Indicating degrees of possibility using **adverbs** [for example *perhaps, surely*] or **modal verbs** [for example *might, should, will, must*]
Text	Devices to build **cohesion** within a paragraph [for example *then, after that, this, first*]
	Linking ideas across paragraphs using **adverbials** of time [for example *later*], place [for example *nearby*] and number [for example *second*] or tense choices [for example he *had* seen her before]
Punctuation	Brackets, dashes, or commas to indicate parenthesis
	Use of commas to clarify meaning or avoid ambiguity
Terminology for pupils	modal verb, relative pronoun
	relative clause
	parenthesis, bracket, dash
	cohesion, ambiguity

Year 6: Detail of content to be introduced (statutory requirement)

Word	The difference between vocabulary typical of informal speech and vocabulary appropriate for formal speech and writing [for example *find out – discover; ask for – request; go in – enter*]
	How words are related by meaning as synonyms and antonyms [for example *big, large, little*].
Sentence	Use of the **passive** to affect the presentation of information in a **sentence** [for example *I broke the window in the greenhouse* versus *The window in the greenhouse was broken (by me)*].
	The difference between structures typical of informal speech and structures appropriate for formal speech and writing [for example the use of question tags: *He's your friend, isn't he?*, or the use of **subjunctive** forms such as *If I were* or *Were they to come* in some very formal writing and speech]

(Continued)

Table 8.1
(Continued)

Text	Linking ideas across paragraphs using a wider range of **cohesive devices**: repetition of a **word** or phrase, grammatical connections [for example the use of **adverbials** such as *on the other hand*, *in contrast*, or *as a consequence*], and **ellipsis**
	Layout devices [for example headings, sub-headings, columns, bullets, or tables, to structure text]
Punctuation	Use of the semi-colon, colon, and dash to mark the boundary between independent **clauses** [for example *It's raining; I'm fed up*]
	Use of the colon to introduce a list and use of semi-colons within lists
	Punctuation of bullet points to list information
	How hyphens can be used to avoid ambiguity [for example *man eating shark* versus *man-eating shark*, or *recover* versus *re-cover*]
Terminology for pupils	subject, object
	active, passive
	synonym, antonym
	ellipsis, hyphen, colon, semi-colon, bullet points

© Crown Copyright 2013

1. Creating your grammar curriculum: selecting and sequencing

There are a lot of grammar terms and concepts. Many of them are prime for teaching at secondary level. Many of them can wait until A level or beyond. Look at the list of concepts we have outlined in Chapter 3 – this is not exhaustive but is certainly appropriate for a generic secondary curriculum. Make a list of concepts which you feel are essential for students. This will be entirely dependent on your cohort and the specific needs and priorities of your school. You may feel that the entire list, plus some additional content for some groups, would be appropriate. You may, on the other hand, feel that starting with a smaller list would be most effective in your context. We would recommend that you make an initial list of things which are essential, and some things which are desirable but not essential.

Once you have an overview of grammar knowledge which you will teach, and you know what students are likely to bring with them from primary school, you should look at your existing curriculum map. There are many competing priorities which dictate the order of content in a curriculum. We must, for instance consider the complexity and content of texts to ensure that they are age appropriate and offer the right level of challenge at the right time. We also need to think about how units of work build over time and how we reinforce learning in subsequent study; for example we might trace the conventions of gothic literature from a novel in Y7 to creative writing in Y8 and some poetry in Y9. These concepts are clearly sequenced, and student understanding is developed and enhanced every time they are revisited. Much of the English curriculum is determined by this build in maturity level for various text choices, or skill level for writing; I wouldn't ask Y7 to explore non-linear narrative in *The Book Thief*, but this would be absolutely appropriate for Y9 in my setting. We must, therefore, allow that grammar sequencing has to flex to the sequencing needs of other areas of the subject.

We would advise that grammar is taught explicitly alongside units in the curriculum where it is deemed most appropriate, so that it can be taught in context, and examples can be given and studied in the texts which students are studying.

Ask yourself:

1. What is this unit trying to achieve?
2. What texts will students study as part of the unit? What text types are students trying to *write* as part of the unit?
3. What are the interesting language features of those texts?

Once you have identified these language features, these are the ones you can select from to explicitly map into the curriculum at that point.

Here is an example of how that might work for some typical KS3 units:

2. Unit title: rhetoric and speech writing

1. *What is this unit trying to achieve?*
   Students learn to use rhetorical language to write effective speeches.
2. *What texts will students study as part of the unit? What text types are students trying to write as part of the unit?*
   Students will read some famous speeches: Obama (2008), Baldwin (1965)
   They will also compose their own speeches.
3. *What are the interesting language features of those texts?*
   * Imperative and interrogative sentences
   * Emphatic connectives: above all, especially, notably, significantly
   * Modification of nouns and verbs – emotive vocabulary

So in this rhetoric unit, it would make sense to teach the four sentence types (imperative, declarative, interrogative, exclamative) and explore them in the context of the model speeches and in the students' own speeches. It would also make sense to teach various connective words and phrases used to create emphasis in texts (discourse markers), and to look at how verbs and nouns can be modified to provoke emotion in an audience.

This grammar content in this unit makes sense. It is something which will make sense to students because they will see how that knowledge of grammar enhances their writing.

3. Sequencing: grammar alongside literature

To sequence grammar alongside set literature, you must have a strong understanding of the language in those texts. Start by surveying your curriculum alongside the grammar content you would like to teach. Look for opportunities where particular grammatical features are abundant in texts and identify those as places where that content can be explicitly taught. For example teaching sentence types (imperative, declarative, interrogative, exclamative) as part of a study of Shakespeare can be incredibly fruitful. Shakespeare uses grammar as a device for characterisation; for example tracking the changes in Lord Capulet over the course of *Romeo and Juliet* becomes very interesting when you look at his use of violent imperatives in Act 3, Scene 5: 'Starve, die in the streets' 'Hang thee' compared with his mournful exclamatives and asyndetic listing in the next act: 'Despised, distressed, hated, martyr'd, kill'd!' 'O child! O child! My soul, and not my child!' You might plan to teach these grammatical terms as part of the core knowledge for this unit, and then explore those concepts alongside your exploration of Shakespeare's language, using them in models for analytical writing and talking about how they create meaning.

(REMEMBER what we said about sentence types on pages 36–37, and the other models of this in Shakespeare texts on pages 8–9, and 20.)

Another example might be choosing to teach clause sub-types alongside a short story unit. Short stories often provide some of the most beautiful sentence crafting: the form lends itself to even greater precision than longer prose. Look at this sentence from *The Signalman* by Charles Dickens:

(You can read more about clauses on page 34.)

On either side, a dripping-wet wall of jagged stone, excluding all view but a strip of sky; the perspective one way only a crooked prolongation of this great dungeon; the shorter perspective in the other direction terminating in a gloomy red light, and the gloomier entrance to a black tunnel, in whose massive architecture there was a barbarous, depressing, and forbidding air.

If we reduced this sentence to its simplest possible form, we might write:

A train line with high stone walls on either side, going into a tunnel.

This classic Dickensian sentence, with all its complexity and descriptive brilliance, is a prime opportunity to teach students about types of clause, but also about the *reason* why those types might be used and how they create meaning. We might, for instance talk about the third clause, 'excluding all view but a strip of sky.' This subordinate clause is superfluous to the completion or accuracy of the whole but is critical in highlighting the fact that this is an almost completely isolated place where even the sky is mostly obscured. With each subsequent clause, Dickens narrows and darkens the view even more: 'only a crooked prolongation' 'shorter perspective . . . terminating.' The sentence finishes with a trio of adjectives which leave us in no doubt as to the atmosphere Dickens wishes to convey. Compare the potential for this grammatical analysis versus the standard and often vague discussion of foreboding, and I think it is clear which is the more literary and ambitious option.

If we make choices about *where* to teach grammatical concepts based on where they fit best with our texts, we will be able to teach that content in a way which is fully immersed in the subject. Grammar knowledge enhances our reading of these texts, just as the use of these texts contextualises and enhances our teaching of grammar.

In these examples you can see that grammar can be a thread which sits comfortably in the curriculum, whilst also supporting and enriching student knowledge and skill in other areas. Using this approach, teachers don't have to stop in their tracks to teach something which feels disjointed – they are teaching content which genuinely supports students to write better, read more critically, and understand literature at a more profound level. Grammar is always in context – always relevant.

By teaching grammar alongside our reading of literature, we see very quickly that grammatical features are just language features. The uneasy division between 'language' and 'structure' falls apart under scrutiny because all language features, whether grammatical, metaphorical, or otherwise, work in concert with one another to create overall meaning. Some questions we would ask about structure as we read texts might include:

- How do writers create intrigue? Anticipation? Tension?
- How do writers indicate moments of shift or changes in tone?
- How do writers build towards climaxes or create critical junctures in texts?
- How do writers depict the journey of characters or the development and evolution of key ideas over the course of texts?

Any of these questions, answered well, could include a discussion of any and all language features from the micro to the macro. Word choice, syntax, and voice sit comfortably alongside simile, symbolism, and anaphora. In practice, if you provide content overviews or knowledge organisers for students which list 'literary devices,' we'd advocate the inclusion of grammar terms alongside the rest. All devices are literary devices; lending them equal weight in the classroom will encourage more holistic literary thinking in students.

4. Grammar for writing

In Chapter 8, we work through the various ways in which language knowledge is central to teaching writing. Put simply: when we write, we construct meaning by making language choices. Our writing is better if we have more options to choose from. We have more options if we have secure language knowledge.

Our curriculum mapping needs to guide students through a range of written forms and increasingly sophisticated tasks and enable them to write independently with accuracy and precision.

How can this be done?

- **Make time**. Writing is an art. Ensure that your curriculum has significant time allocated to dedicated writing units and that those units aren't activity heavy, but rather that there is space for students to craft, draft, and redraft. For example if a six-week descriptive writing unit tries to get students to create six discrete pieces of writing, there is limited time to really focus on the myriad writing choices which students could make. If the *quantity* of work being produced is lower, more time and effort can go into the *quality* of that work, and there can be space for conscious crafting of language.

- **Focus on skill, not content**. Writing units can often fall into the trap of focusing on *what* students write rather than *how* students write – for example: *students are writing a gothic story, so we spend time ensuring that they have an engaging plot planned and that they can use lots of 'devices' such as metaphors, repetition, and ambitious vocabulary.* This content is important, but a greater focus on the *skill* of crafting language at word, phrase, clause, and sentence level would serve students better in the long run (strategies for doing this in the classroom are outlined later in this chapter).

- **Pre-empt probable errors and weaknesses.** We should sequence grammar concepts across the curriculum but also plan to explicitly teach and re-teach strategies for proofreading, accuracy, and improving expression at word, phrase, clause, and sentence levels. In Chapter 8, we outline the following categories of common grammatical errors and expression weaknesses which students make:
  - Spelling mistake
  - Punctuation error (usually stemming from a misunderstanding of clauses for commas and full stops, or from a misunderstanding of apostrophe rules)
  - Fragmentation (where students accidentally write incomplete sentences)
  - Students accidentally run one sentence into another without using a full stop where it was needed
  - Tense inconsistency (where students accidentally switch tense part way through their writing)
  - Syntax error (where students use words in an order which is wrong or obscures their intended meaning)

These specific categories of error can be tackled by regular proofreading and correction activities. This is less an issue of curriculum and more about the normal course of English teaching. We would argue, however, that if all staff (beyond the English team, ideally) can use the same language when talking to students about written accuracy, students will benefit from clarity and consistency of message.

5. A note on grammar for GCSE English language

The AQA English Language Paper 1 (2015) has a question in the reading section which tests student ability to identify and analyse 'structure' in unseen texts. In 2019, the average mark nationally was three marks out of a possible eight. This is one of the most poorly answered questions on the paper even though, in theory, it is no different in skill to the 'language' question which precedes it. Many students struggle to identify structural features and talk about their impact on the text in any meaningful way. They can all talk about metaphor and vocabulary, but things like sentence structure and voice often present a significant challenge. We would submit that this situation is the result of the systemic and long-term weaknesses in grammar teaching in the years leading up to GCSE.

The English Language papers also require students to write at length in both creative and transactional writing tasks. These tasks combined are worth half of the entire qualification. One of the most common ways in which students lose marks on these questions is technical accuracy – errors like those mentioned earlier: tense, syntax, fragmentation, run-ons, punctuation.

If we sequence our curriculum, not just in KS3, but also throughout KS4, to ensure that we revise grammar content and skills for crafting, accuracy, and fluency, students will make significant gains at GCSE but, more importantly, that language awareness will serve them in their lives as readers and writers beyond the school gates.

8.1.1

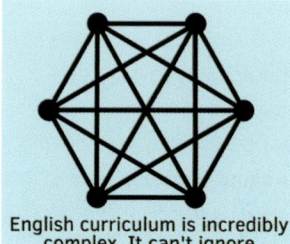

English curriculum is incredibly complex. It can't ignore grammar, but it also cannot revolve around grammar alone.

Grammar has implications for curriculum beyond English.

Grammar can't just be a 'bolt-on' to the substantive curriculum.

GRAMMAR CURRICULUM INTENTIONS

Students can write with PRECISION and a knowledge of the POSSIBILITIES

Students can read texts with a CRITICAL EYE

Students apply their knowledge of grammar to LITERARY ANALYSIS.

MAPPING THE GRAMMAR CURRICULUM...

Map the grammar curriculum onto KS2 foundations.

Sequence grammar content alongside texts where there are examples to see in context.

Teach writing over time with frequent repetition, bringing in new knowledge alongside old, and honing the skill as a craft.

9 For leaders

Language knowledge is powerful, but we must address two elephants in the room:

A significant number of English teachers don't have knowledge or confidence in grammar.

Beyond the English team, teachers in other subject areas often have significant gaps in their language knowledge and sometimes don't see this as something they need to engage with.

NOTE: there ARE many teachers of ALL subjects out there who actually love grammar and language – we don't mean to make crass generalisations, but it is important to acknowledge the real barrier in place for some of our colleagues.

Some common questions we have been asked by teachers and leaders, along with our best attempts at answers, are as follows:

- ***Which bits of grammar are really necessary for me to know? (There is a lot, and I don't know where to start!)***

    We outline the foundational grammar knowledge you need in Chapter 3, but remember two important things:

    1. You don't necessarily need to know terminology by heart. Keep definitions and notes with you and don't panic if you have to look something up in the classroom. Being a great teacher doesn't mean being a walking textbook.

    2. Terminology is secondary – it is just the label we use so that we can talk about things. The most important thing is that you can think and talk about the *meaning* created by different features and uses of language.

- ***As a leader, how can I support my staff with their subject knowledge and teaching of grammar?***

    Staff continuing professional development (CPD) should be sequenced in the same way that you plan the student curriculum – we learn in the same way! Don't try to introduce a grammar-rich curriculum straight away if you know the staff delivering it don't yet have the knowledge they need. Start slower – introduce a unit or two first, teach staff the knowledge they need

DOI: 10.4324/9781003175261-13

(NOTE: the CPD principles outlined in *The CPD Curriculum* by Zoe Enser and Mark Enser (2021) is excellent in terms of planning training for teachers which is meaningful.)

before they teach it, and then let them explore that knowledge through their teaching of it. Once those units have been taught and reflected on, do one or two more. Drip-feeding grammar knowledge works well because it supports the gradual acquisition of confidence. With each successive topic, you can make links with previous ones and build the kind of grammar schema in staff which you are developing in your students.

- *As a leader, how can I begin the conversation with staff about their own weak literacy and improve their skill and confidence without it feeling judgemental or negative?*

    This is a highly sensitive issue in schools. We are centres of education and are meant to uphold high standards in terms of the quality of our communication, but it is common to see inaccuracies in emails, letters, and resources produced by staff. We might also hear things around school in terms of staff oracy which we might want to see change. It is important in these situations that we uphold the following things:

    - Grammatical accuracy has nothing to do with someone's intelligence or value. If someone makes a punctuation or syntax error, that doesn't reflect on them as a person.
    - We are all professionals who believe that young people deserve the best possible education. Sometimes that means we need to learn new things or sharpen our own skills.

    We would recommend that you consider a process like this one to support staff literacy. This is something we would advocate for all staff, whether they are subject teachers or behaviour support, or working in admin.

    1. Talk to all staff about the fact that the majority of adults in the UK were never taught grammar formally in school. Establish the fact that lots of people in the room have gaps in their knowledge and that this is something you can all work on together.

    2. Do a knowledge audit with staff. Before you teach anything, you need to know where your 'students' are. We would recommend a really simple quiz on something like Forms, though you could do this as a paper copy. You might use some of the key content from our definitions of terms in Chapter 3 or look at some of the content from Y6 SATs.

    3. Use this information to identify what you need to teach staff:
        a. all together as a group (for things which everyone is struggling with)
        b. in targeted groups (for a group of staff who are struggling with one specific thing)
        c. in subject teams (for things which are relevant to their discipline)

    4. Use the principles for teaching grammar which we outline in Chapter 4 to teach concepts. Don't try to teach everything at

once – keep it to one or two key things per CPD session and ensure that staff have time to process and practise.

5. Thread this learning into future CPD sessions – give people the opportunity to retrieve prior learning and make links with new things.

- ***Is disciplinary grammar a thing? So would it be different in History or Biology?***

Yes and no! The fundamental framework of how language works is the same in every academic discipline, because it's how meaning is created in the English language. However, there are different conventions and styles across subjects. We have outlined many of the most useful structures for English in Chapter 8, but a number of those would be equally helpful in other subjects – for instance subordinating conjunctions can be used to support fantastic writing in humanities subjects, and we have seen apposition used brilliantly in science to introduce a concept and embed a definition into the sentence. Equally, there are grammar norms in other subjects which don't exist in English – the conventions for writing up the results of an experiment or process in science subjects, or the way in which students should annotate portfolios in art, all pose their own disciplinary questions which are well worth exploring in subject teams.

References

Adams, T. (2020) '*Inside Story* by Martin Amis review – too clever by half', www.theguard-ian.com/books/2020/sep/13/inside-story-by-martin-amis-review-too-clever-by-half

Ahmed, S. (2019) *Human Now*, unpublished.

Anthony, L. (2022) *AntConc* (Version 4.1.4) [Computer Software]. Waseda University, www.laurenceanthony.net/software

Atherton, A. (2021) [Twitter], 2 October, https://twitter.com/__codexterous/status/1444366963531259905

Baldwin, J. (1965) *The American Dream is at the expense of the American Negro*. The Cambridge Union Society.

BBC News (2020) 'Delhi riots: Anger as judge critical of violence removed', www.bbc.co.uk/news/world-asia-india-51644861

Bronte, E. (1847) *Wuthering Heights*. Thomas Cautley Newby.

Brown, P. C., Roediger III, H. L., and McDaniel, M. A. (2014) *Make It Stick: The Science of Successful Learning*. Belknap Press.

Capote, T. (1948) *Other Voices, Other Rooms*. Random House.

Carter, R. (1990) 'The new grammar teaching', in R. Carter (ed.) *Knowledge about Language and the Curriculum: The LINC Reader*. Hodder and Stoughton, pp. 104–21.

Cavdarbasha, D., and Kurczek, J. (2017) 'Connecting the dots: Your brain and creativity', *Frontiers for Young Minds*, https://kids.frontiersin.org/articles/10.3389/frym.2017.00019

Caviglioli, O. (2019) *Dual Coding with Teachers*. John Catt.

Crawford, L. (2022) [Twitter], 17 June, https://twitter.com/think_talk_org/status/1537900460006264834?s=20&t=js6rwg4ZbQBXLRd2WXDQCA

DfE (2013) 'English Appendix 2: Vocabulary, grammar and punctuations', https://assets.publishing.service.gov.uk/government/uploads/system/uploads/attachment_data/file/335190/English_Appendix_2_-_Vocabulary_grammar_and_punctuation.pdf

Dickens, C. (1859) *A Tale of Two Cities*. Chapman & Hall.

Donald, M. (2017) *Origins of the Modern Mind: Three Stages in the Evolution of Culture and Cognition*. Harvard University Press.

Dostoyevsky, F. (1864) *Notes from Underground*, Trans. Wilks, R. (2009). Penguin.

Duff, M. C., Kurczek, J., Rubin, R., Cohen, N. J., and Tranel, D. (2013) 'Hippocampal amnesia disrupts creative thinking', *Hippocampus* 23(12): 1143–9.

Du Maurier, D. (1938) *Rebecca*. Victor Gollancz Ltd.

Edwards, K. (2022) 'People are "accent policing" Angela Rayner – why does this only ever seem to happen to women?', www.independent.co.uk/voices/angela-rayner-tweets-accent-northern-b1992377.html

Engelmann, S., and Carnine, D. (1982) *Theory of Instruction*. Irvington.

Enser, Z., and Enser, M. (2021) *The CPD Curriculum: Creating Conditions for Growth*. Crown House.

■ **References**

Fiorella, L., and Mayer, R. E. (2016) 'Eight ways to promote generative learning', *Educational Psychology Review* 28: 717–41.

Furst, E. (2018) 'Learning in the brain', https://sites.google.com/view/efratfurst/learning-in-the-brain

Giovanelli, M. (2014) *Teaching Grammar, Structure and Meaning*. Routledge.

Halliday, M. (1967) 'Linguistics and the teaching of English', in J. Britton (ed.) *Handbook for English Teachers: 2 Talking and Writing*. Methuen, pp. 80–90.

Hancock, C. (2005) *Meaning-Centered Grammar: An Introductory Text*. Equinox.

Hellier, J. (1961) *Catch-22*. Simon & Schuster.

Herbert, F. (1965) *Dune*. Chilton Books.

Hosseini, K. (2013) *And the Mountains Echoed*. Bloomsbury.

Hurston, Z. N. (1937) *Their Eyes Were Watching God*. J. B. Lippincott.

Inglis, F., and Aers, L. (2008) *Key Concepts in Education*. Sage.

Jones, K. (2019) *Retrieval Practice: Research and Resources for Every Classroom*. John Catt.

Kaufman, S. B. (2019) 'The Neuroscience of Creativity: A Q&A with Anna Abraham', https://blogs.scientificamerican.com/beautiful-minds/the-neuroscience-of-creativity-a-q-a-with-anna-abraham/

Kolln, M., and Gray, L. (2016) *Rhetorical Grammar: Grammatical Choices, Rhetorical Effects*, 8th ed. Pearson.

Lakoff, G., and Johnson, M. (1980) *Metaphors We Live By*. University of Chicago Press.

Lee, H. (1960) *To Kill a Mockingbird*. J. B. Lippincott & Co.

Lemov, D. (2017) 'Foreword', in J. Hochman and N. Wexler (eds.) *The Writing Revolution*. Jossey-Bass, pp. xi–xviii.

Loewus, L. (2017) 'Q&A: "The writing revolution" encourages focus on crafting good sentences', www.edweek.org/teaching-learning/q-a-the-writing-revolution-encourages-focus-on-crafting-good-sentences/2017/06

Mahlberg, M., Stockwell, P., Wiegand, V., and Lentin, J. (2020) 'CLiC 2.1. Corpus linguistics in context', clic.bham.ac.uk

Mannion, J. (2022) [Twitter], 16 June, https://twitter.com/RethinkingJames/status/1537502271751217152?s=20&t=lTNcnHmvT7bwLSe_fBTrig

Márquez, G. G. (1967) *One Hundred Years of Solitude*. Jonathan Cape.

Márquez, G. G. (1968) *A Very Old Man with Enormous Wings*. Casa de las Americas.

McCarthy, C. (2006) *The Road*. Alfred A. Knopf.

Melville, H. (1851) *Moby Dick*. Harper & Brothers.

Morrison, T. (1977) *Song of Solomon*. Alfred Knopf, Inc.

Obama, B. (2008) *Yes we can!* Chicago

Orwell, G. (1949) *1984*. Seckler & Warburg.

Plath, S. (1963) *The Bell Jar*. Heinemann.

Pope, R. (1995) *Textual Intervention: Critical and Creative Strategies for Literary Studies*. Routledge.

Quigley, A., Mujis, D., and Stringer, E. (2018) *Metacognition and Self-Regulated Learning: Guidance Report*. Education Endowment Foundation.

Rosen, M. (2021) 'Dear Gavin Williamson, could you tell parents what a fronted adverbial is?', www.theguardian.com/education/2021/jan/23/dear-gavin-williamson-could-you-tell-parents-what-a-fronted-adverbial-is

Ross, J. (2020) 'Write like a short story writer', in J. Webb (ed.) *Teach Like a Writer*. John Catt, pp. 97–118.

Saha, S. (2020) 'No full stops', www.telegraphindia.com/my-kolkata/people/no-full-stops-in-booker-prize-winner-bernardine-evaristos-life/cid/1790380

Sassoon, S. (1983) *Diaries 1915–1918* (edited by R. Hart-Davis). Faber and Faber.

Simpson, P. (2014) *Stylistics: A Resource Book for Students*, 2nd edition. Routledge.

Solzhenitsyn, A. (1962) *One Day in the Life of Ivan Denisovich*, Trans. Willetts, H. T. (1991). Noonday/Farrar Straus Giroux.

Tolkien, J. R. R. (1954) *The Fellowship of the Ring*. George Allen & Unwin.

Tolstoy, L. (1878) *Anna Karenina*, Trans. Volokhonsky, L. (2003). Penguin.

Wilde, O. (1890) *The Picture of Dorian Grey*. Lippincott's Monthly Magazine.

Willingham, D. T. (2008) 'What will improve a student's memory?', *American Educator*, Winter 2008–2009: 17–44.

Index